Singing to
the Goldfish

www.BretwaldaBooks.com
@Bretwaldabooks
bretwaldabooks.blogspot.co.uk/
Bretwalda Books on Facebook

First Published 2013
Text and Photos Copyright © Bev Pettifar 2013
Bev Pettifar asserts her moral rights to be regarded as the author of this book.
Bretwalda Books
Unit 8, Fir Tree Close, Epsom,
Surrey KT17 3LD
info@BretwaldaBooks.com
www.BretwaldaBooks.com
ISBN 978-1-909698-35-2

Printed and bound in Great Britain by
Marston Book Services Limited, Oxfordshire

Singing to the Goldfish

Bev Pettifar

With love to my family, my husband, and Jeanne; my reader-in-chief, without whose constant advice and encouragement this small memoir would never have been

Chapter One

'HELLO DEAR. Over here'.

The voice came from the far side of a dim, cluttered room. At a small table sat a middle-aged woman who, pointing to a chair, murmured "I'm Mrs Potter. Make yourself comfy. What's it to be dear, Crystal or cards?"

I hesitated for a second. "Cards please."

Nodding, she moved the crystal globe to one side and after covering it with a black cloth, picked up a worn pack of playing cards. These were shuffled and then passed across to me.

"Cut please, dear. Three times."

The crystal had sounded quite appealing, but with Mrs P. resembling more the wife of our local greengrocer than the Gypsy Rose Lee I'd anticipated, my faith in the exotic faded.

The cards were laid in five, neat vertical lines, then "Right dear. Ready are we?" We were off And how. So accurately were people, places and events from my past assembled and described that she might have been reading from an information sheet. For a mad moment it crossed my mind that a potted history of my life had been passed on by the friends who not only had talked me into the "consultation" but had also booked it and delivered me here.

"Now" she said, more to herself than to me, "What's this?"Carefully placing the remainder of the pack on the appropriate columns, she began slowly to forecast my future. At the phrase "There's a man in uniform here" the jaw dropped steeply - mine, not hers - and "You want to marry him but..." her lips pursed as she positioned the Queen of Spades. "There's big opposition. Big opposition...From an older woman." Amazed at her succinct summary of my predicament, I began to fiddle with my engagement ring, scarcely two weeks old, secreted deep inside a pocket. The voice continued "But you'll get your way... I see you in an old building, very old... greyish. A sort of castle. There will be lots of travel...In a year or two's time you'll be living in a country where people's skins are darker than your own." Pause. "Three? No... two children. You'll never have great wealth but you'll

Yours truly

never be poor. "And you'll always land on your feet...He's a good man...Bit older than you. But that's all right."

For the first time since I'd joined her at the table, she looked up. "Right dear. That's all for now... Come and see me again. Good luck."

Less than an hour after entering the room, I emerged, in today's vernacular, totally gobsmacked: my three and sixpenny future -

eighteen whole pence - mapped out before me. Later, the two friends responsible for my 'reading' and I, sat huddled in a grey shelter on Folkestone seafront, oblivious to the howling gale outside. Well used to what passed for an English summer's afternoon, we puffed away serenely, shrouded in smoke from our Kensitas tipped, analysing every last word and sentence of Mrs Potter's predictions for the future. Having first been through all the "You have to be kiddings" and "How on earth could she possibly know that?" we ended by dredging the final 'What if's' and 'Supposing you - or he...' from the lengthy postmortem. Two pairs of blue eyes stared glumly back into mine. "So what are you going to do? What about your mother..." Wouldn't want to be in your shoes" said Sally. Mine's difficult... But yours..."

Ah yes. Mother.

A true enigma. Beautiful and charismatic; of average height and slightly built. The bluest of blue eyes, pale Irish skin and thick, wavy shoulder-length hair, once the shade of deep mahogany and later, pure white. In her twenties she might have doubled for Vivien Leigh, and later, Zsa Zsa Gabor. Clever, quick-witted, restless, colourful, funny - a gifted mimic - surprisingly practical, fearless, curious, mercurial, generous and a total law unto herself; and in a phrase borrowed from a friend 'reliably unreliable'.

In the early years, she'd sometimes pop up at school to whisk me off for "A weekend home" (seldom ours; every trip an adventure). Summoned to the pale-green and cream parlour, the convent's receiving room, I'd wait for a second or two before offering my cheek, stiff with pride as the nuns, dazzled both by her appearance and her smile, stood by nodding happily, quite unlike their usual selves, as if presented with a rare and unexpected gift. (Years later, whilst considering whether or not my very first appearance in Mother's world might have perhaps produced a similar reaction to that of the nuns, the conclusion reached was that a three-weeks-premature, and probably jaundiced, four-pounder, would not have been quite what she'd envisaged).

Then there was Father. Tall, dark, good-looking and older than Mother by almost twenty years. He was also difficult, quick-tempered and insanely jealous, with a disconcerting habit of accosting any male he might spot casting an admiring glance at his 'property', with a raised eyebrow and a measured 'You know my wife?' During one of their more tricky periods he forbade her any contact with her three brothers; a directive which, as with virtually all his instructions, she totally ignored. For whatever reasons, times spent with my father were brief. The Daddies of that era, as well as the children (due partly to the War) were also seldom seen nor heard. Sometime after my third birthday, however, his visits, usually in uniform, became less frequent, though memorable. Who could forget such a vision of shining perfection - toecaps gleaming and Service Dress belt shimmering like patent leather across an immaculate uniform - he epitomised the complete English army-officer. Quietly spoken - but with S's that whistled - he was sporty, clever and possessed of a fine light-baritone singing voice. We were never close, but now and again I'd be hauled onto his knee and jiggled up and down to rousing versions of Camptown Races or Polly Wolly Doodle, of which there seemed to be endless verses.

Later however, post-war, very occasionally and without warning, he'd appear on a Sunday afternoon in the convent parlour, sometimes clasping a new jigsaw or a box of Terry's Spartan chocolates (yum: all dark-chocolate-covered hard-centres) ready to take me off for tea. It might be a smart hotel (too quiet) or - my favourite Lyons Corner House - always warm and buzzy. There, riveted by either bouncy "Ena Baga at the Organ" - small, round and smiley, deep crimson lips gleaming against perfect white teeth - or "Falkman and his Apache Band:" three ageing violinists fiddling at a frantic pace, headed by an accordionist (welded to his instrument) all clad in ruffled satin shirts and red bandanas - I'd demolish a poached egg on toast, followed by a small "iced fancy" or a Knickerbocker Glory. Wow. This tall glass of heaven bore three scoops of different ice-creams, layered with brilliantly-coloured fruit and jelly, crowned with a swirl of mock cream and a shiny cherry. Eaten with a very long spoon and made to last as long as possible, I always invited Father, who seldom bothered with more than a pot of coffee "a taste" which was inevitably refused with a very polite "Not today, thank you".

Father's reactions to my unexpectedly early arrival have never been discussed, but like most males of his generation, he was probably delighted to have missed it all. That particular morning, Mother's trip to North London where her sister and brother-in-law owned a restaurant, would have been better abandoned, but lacking any sensible information regarding her "condition" (this being the '30s) she'd simply treated a bout of post-breakfast nausea with a hefty dose of peppermint oil and hot water and set off for either bus stop or cab-rank. As someone for whom the word "determined" might have been invented - the letters distributed evenly through her being as the word "Brighton" through a stick of seaside rock - nothing short of either flood or earthquake would have kept her at home. No doubt the journey was partly responsible for what happened next, as half-way through lunch, serious launch movements began and a doctor was called.

The brief examination, prompting a swift "Hmm. More appropriate surroundings, I think," put Mother, by then installed in the staff flat above, immediately into reverse. With no intention of entering either clinic or nursing-home, she announced her symptoms had flown and settled down with a cigarette and a newspaper. Apparently, having summoned a midwife, the doctor did the same and just before dawn, after a period of stop-start activity, I finally emerged.

And there we stayed for the next two weeks, in the care of two nurses, who, as well as protecting my thin skin by bathing me in olive-oil, filled me regularly with a creamy formula called Ostermilk, the high-fat content of which would probably put it on one of today's banned lists. After six weeks I bloomed, my frequent guzzling soon earning me the title 'Baby Dumpling'.

My interest in food (which must surely be linked to having started life above a restaurant - sheer greed having nothing to do with it) has continued to thrive and undoubtedly, stems from the maternal genes. Mother was a great, as well as an inventive, cook and no-one produces fantastic food in less time than our daughter; our son has cooked well from his university days and my sister's offerings are never less than seriously delicious: a true queen of the casserole who also delivers the very best of all traditional Christmas meals. And me?..My culinary skills would be put to the severest test of all when, at the tender age of seventeen, having left school barely a year earlier, I accepted a proposal of marriage. More of that, later.

Mother's admirers ranged from bus conductors and taxi drivers ("You're the best looker/loveliest lady I've had in my bus/cab all year"); no problem with PC in those days, to members of the aristocracy - one of whom she almost married. Impossible to keep up with, she darted in and out of my life like quicksilver.

During the early years - mother's life being in constant motion - I was cared for and treated as her own, by Emma, a kind, patient woman, then in her mid-sixties, who produced non-stop tender care and few cross words. Tall, with a slight stoop, a long, pale face, kind eyes and bobbed, faded brown hair, she smelt deliciously of toilet soap and violet cachous - tiny perfumed sweets - two or three of which she would often leave, as a treat, on my bedside table when I stayed with her. Semi-retired, she lived in a warm, welcoming flat on two floors of a terraced house, in North London. I loved being with her, even when the familiar wail of the siren and the dreaded "thump" of Germany's prime weapon - the dreaded V1 (better known as the Doodlebug) sent us off to the cellar, clutching our candles, to wait for the all-clear. Huddled together under an old, solid table, Emma was probably scared witless but never once gave the slightest indication that such "little interruptions" were anything other than a small inconvenience. As efforts to flatten London increased, we'd sometimes escape to stay, for a few days, with her son and his family at their farm, near Romford. The journey began with us being driven to Liverpool Street station - always in the early morning - by a black-cab driver who lived nearby. Once there, Emma, having queued for the tickets and handed over to a porter our one suitcase and a bag containing books and lunch, would grasp my hand tightly as we made our way along the platform. Such excitement: I'd skip along beside her, brown Clarks sandals gleaming from her regular attacks with the Cherry Blossom, until we reached the engine. Simply unforgettable, the wonder of that beautiful monster; huge, shiny and breathtaking. After greeting the driver and his mate, busy shovelling coal into the furnace, we'd trot on, find a carriage and settle ourselves in. Ecstasy. A lifetime of travelling the world has found nothing to compare with the sheer joy of those very first, delicious, steam-train rides to Little Warley, where there was so much to look forward to: the farm animals, Emma's grandchildren to run wild with each day and great food. There, I recall my very first taste of stuffed roast chicken, blackberry pudding with thick custard, and delicious, fragrant rabbit pies.

Before long however, Emma succumbed to a combination of age, war and the responsibility of a young child, and was advised to take life more easily. I returned to live with Mother but, after what seemed a very short time, found myself, aged just four and a half, installed as a boarder at a small convent school in Barnet. Within weeks, the startling change of environ- ment, combined with the shock of being sent away, manifested in an attack of such desperate homesickness that I developed pneumonia, whooping-cough and measles, ending up in an oxygen tent at the local hospital. And so passed the next five or six months. Today, one can but speculate whether, without the advantages of modern medication, such a recovery would be possible.

With the war over, the landscape which had been London, lay pitted with deep craters. Somehow, the family had remained intact, despite a bomb totally demolishing the restaurant over which I'd been born. Unbelievably, Mother's sister, husband and children, as well as the restaurant staff, bar one, had all escaped unhurt and soon, her three brothers, one of which had helped build the dreaded Burma railway, were demobbed from the Forces and returned to their homes.

It was a memorable time for everyone and as my childish ears flapped constantly, I noticed that virtually every adult conversation contained the word "food". By the middle of '46, a few "Before-the-War" flavours (previously little known delights for me) began to emerge. First, it was ice-cream: a twopenny bar of frozen creamy bliss wrapped in a square of greaseproof paper, or a carefully tailored scoop on a small cornet. Oh joy. Then came the banana which, when available from the local greengrocer, was strictly limited to one per child and then only on production of a green ration book. The first bite was disappointing and, pulling a face, I complained at the lack of juice. But the taste of the first cherries made up for it; deep red and sweet and juicy. Best of all, though, were Smiths Crisps, complete with a tiny screw of salt in blue paper: a small, waxed bag of crunchy delight. Then, one day, Mother appeared with three (so delicious) corn-on-the-cob and a tin of peaches. Each week, it seemed there was a new and exciting "something" to try. Grocers began stocking unbroken biscuits, a novelty; eight ounces only per customer all weighed out carefully from square silver tins into brown paper bags. Soon, foods previously available only on the under-the-counter Black-market, such as tinned red salmon, tinned meats and fruits as well as "special" boxes of chocolates, were, though still rationed and in short supply, at last on sale to all, provided the necessary coupons, or points were produced. As supplies increased, if news spread that the butcher might have something extra, nothing less than an invitation for lunch with Royalty would have taken precedence. Meat was rationed until about '54 but the population as a whole, having grown used to restrictions and presented with a few odd choices along the way (whale-meat sausages and every conceivable form of offal) could generally be relied upon to try anything. One December afternoon, in the late '40s, I particularly remember a visit, with Mother, to our local butcher, after a phone call from friends whom she'd rashly invited to Sunday lunch.

We arrived just before the metal shutters went down.

"Sorry, Nick." said Reggie "Nothing till the next delivery. Monday."

Mother produced "The Smile" full beam. It usually worked.

"Reggie. There must be something... I'm desperate." Reggie's head shook sadly, then. "Ang on a sec. Come in..." and, before disappearing, he touched his nose murmuring, "Q.T. O.K?"

Seconds later he was back, bearing a sizeable lump of meat which he slapped on the counter with a thump. Aged almost ten, I was well-schooled regarding cuts of meat, but this? Reggie's voice gave nothing away. "It's er... It's 'alf a badger, Nicky".

Mother closed her eyes and I, snorting loudly began to giggle.

The eyes opened. "Reggie... Is it edible?"

"Now you know I wouldn't sell you nuffin' you couldn't eat... Cook it like pork: lots of stuffin'...Bit of apple sauce. We 'ad the other 'arf last Sunday. Lovely it was. Bit pricey though."

'Pricey' was ten shillings and sixpence, just over today's fifty two pence but then, almost double the equivalent of an entire week's meat ration for a family of four. Mother looked speculatively at me and pointed to her mouth.

"Keep it buttoned. Understand? Not a word. If asked, you don't know..." And delicious it certainly was, but despite all the compliments, on that particular day Mother was vegetarian.

Shortly after Christmas, in '46, I returned to stay with Emma for a week or two before starting a new school, this time, a small convent in Highbury. Viewing the prospect of boarding again with a mixture of anxiety and resignation, all the "You'll love it Darling," from Mother, did little to reduce my misery - but as usual, when choice barely featured, hope sprang eternal. No fuss was expected - bar an anxious glance toward Emma whenever the subject was raised - and none would be made. Meanwhile, we contentedly resumed our routine. Shopping - joining any queue that looked hopeful, visiting the library

- Ethel M. Dell (and surprisingly) Zane Grey's tales of the Wild West, for Em. and Hans Andersen and Grimms Fairy tales for me. Then, in fine weather, an hour at the local park, where the equipment was still intact and in working order, having, unlike Em's front railings, escaped the munitions factory. Once at home, there would be high-tea in the cosy, gas-lit kitchen warmed by the gleaming, black range. Together we'd sit at a large (was it, I wonder?.. .to the child most things looked large) mahogany table, its length of scarlet American oiled cloth covered by an immaculate tablecloth. With the majority of foods still rationed, faddiness was neither encouraged nor tolerated and, as expected, my plate would be cleared. Emma tried to produce favourites; offal, liver and onions or stuffed lambs' hearts, or very occasionally, a lambs' kidney. Or there might be fish:crisply fried Sprats or creamy soft Herring roes, on toast, or maybe "A nice piece of smoked haddock" (years later christened yellow fish by our children) or, when ration points permitted, some baked beans. Cheese, when available, might mean a dish of Macaroni cheese or even Welsh Rarebit, always enhanced with a squirt of Worcester Sauce, a teaspoon of mustard and a splash of milk. But a real treat was a (not quite) fresh, lightly boiled egg, served with thinly-sliced white bread and "best butter". Scrambled eggs made with dried egg powder went down well too, as did toast, cooked close to the bars of the range at the end of a long, brass toasting-fork. This would be spread with butter and a little jam or occasionally, Golden Syrup. Puddings were usually plain; rice, semolina, tapioca, macaroni or bread and butter, with possibly a scant sprinkling of currants or sultanas, or, depending on the season, stewed fruit - apples, pears or plums, or now and then (not being a favourite) prunes, all served with custard. On a Sunday, a pink blancmange might appear, in the shape of a rabbit, or a junket (still obtainable but seldom served) which is a very slightly curdled mixture of warmed milk, flavouring, rennet and sugar: the "Curds and Whey" of Little Miss Muffet.

When we'd eaten, I'd do a jigsaw or read until bedtime and at seven, having been washed from top to toe, baths being restricted to one a week, would be tucked up under flannelette sheets, thick white blankets and a puffy, paisley-printed eiderdown. Above the bed hung a jolly print of "The Three Graces" - all smiles, flowers in their hair and gleaming, naked, Rubenesque curves. There I'd doze off, lulled to sleep by the hum of the trolleybuses, whirring and clicking their way rhythmically along the wide, main road towards Holloway.

The new school, staffed by an order of mainly French nuns and housed in two late-Georgian buildings, half-way along a private road facing Highbury Fields - happily - turned out to be just a short bus ride from Emma's flat, a comforting realisation that made everything bearable. Although for some weekends and occasional holidays, I would be at home with Mother, who, having moved from our house facing Clapham Common, had settled in a sizeable flat, also near the common.

Feeling a little like Alice Through the Looking Glass, I dipped in and out of the world known as 'home' with a certain detachment, always in best behaviour mode, Mother's mood being unpredictable. But it can't have been an easy time for her. However, with each visit an unknown quantity, I viewed it all with a tingle of excitement and more than a little trepidation. But dull it wasn't, as life day-to-day (that is, life lived by the majority) held little appeal for someone fuelled by a fierce energy and a constant need of variety.

Our days together, uninterrupted by the simplicity of trips to the park or library, varied widely from those spent with Emma, and I never once recall us joining a queue - except for the cinema: 'the flicks' which I loved. Once breakfast was over, Mother's comprising just coffee and cigarettes, I'd watch intently as, before dressing, she'd make up her face; a process which never failed to fascinate. First, the early morning application of Nivea was removed with a home-made mixture of Rosewater and Glycerine, then, seconds later, the Leichner foundation (diluted with a dab of white cream) would be carefully smoothed over her face and neck. Next, a small smudge of shadow was blended onto her eyelids and followed by face powder from a cut-glass bowl, pressed on firmly with a smooth puff before a final dusting off with a fluffy one. After this, two coats of Max Factor's "Brownish Black" (mixed sparingly with saliva) would be stroked expertly over her thick lashes until finally, smiling at her reflection 'So I can see where the rouge should go' she'd blend a little over her cheeks before a coat of matte, scarlet lipstick completed the image. She'd then disappear to dress, emerging ready to dazzle, invariably squinting over her shoulder - unless wearing 'slacks' as trousers were then called - to inquire "Are my seams straight?"

Her work commitments were mixed. There might be "something in the theatre" - chorus, or cabaret work, she certainly had talent; maybe some filming: an occasional, minor part - or the odd modelling job, mainly shampoos or toothpaste (the maternal teeth being white, beautifully shaped and perfectly even.) And then hats became her thing: with such bone-structure even a flowerpot would have looked stylish.

In between she'd serve as secretary to a wealthy food-importer, in premises situated somewhere along Walworth Road, where, if allowed to accompany her, I'd spend time clacking away on an old typewriter for which there seemed to be endless reams of paper. When an audition cropped up and my desperate "Please, please, can I come" was taken seriously, I'd sit silent and still, totally starstruck, keen to spot a famous face, carefully scrutinising - and probably thoroughly unnerving - all other assembled hopefuls. When sometimes left alone in the flat (plus telephone) trusted but unsupervised, time passed smoothly enough with a radio, books, paints and packs of cards for building card houses and playing Patience - by the age of eight I might have qualified as World Champion - although if a new Saturday Evening Post magazine had arrived, via a friend in the States, the hours fairly melted. With its wonderfully detailed Norman Rockwell cover and a fat, pull-out section of cartoon strips, there was nothing in England at the time to compare. Eating arrangements varied but sometimes involved lunch in a nearby restaurant, where Mother's earlier briefing to the staff found me seated alone, instructed to speak only to the waitress or another woman, never a man. Food was selected carefully, either fish or offal, and the words 'Rissole' or 'Vienna Steak' ignored (Mama's knowledge of catering lumped all such delights together as 'Everyone's leftovers put through the mincer'). At that time I'd have been aged somewhere between six and a half and eight and I suspect that by today's standards, a young child eating alone in a restaurant would be considered 'inappropriate ' by vigilant Social Workers, possibly even involving a Care Order.

As time passed, I became aware that the occasional few days spent with mother differed considerably from the home lives of my friends. Her combination of looks, energy, charisma and glamour (on a good day she oozed the lot) together with a brilliant imagination and the ability to squeeze the last scrap of humour from virtually any situation, attracted a string of interesting and diverse characters. Some of these - famous as well as infamous - had lived lives which have since filled books of their own, and apart from one or two, fell into the category of 'entertainer', some more loosely than others.

Who, for instance, could forget Babs, christened 'Babs the Exotic' by Mother. A slight figure with slanting black eyes and olive skin, whose cabaret act in a west-end club featured Lionel, her constant companion, a length of dozy python which usually hung from her neck. 'Are you sure he's still alive?' I'd inquire politely; though looking back, it's possible that his inactivity might well have been due to excessive smoke inhalation, Babs seldom spotted without a cigarette. Or perhaps he was overfed - or maybe even drugged. Her spasmodic appearances always merited my full attention as, having treated me to no more than a brief nod of acknowledgment on arrival at the flat, she might later suggest that I join 'Us' for "A little walk" - no more than a hundred yards or so - Babs's triple-wedge, ankle-strap trotters not being quite up to a hike. The consternation of passers-by on realising that her muffler might well be more than had appeared at first glance, was, to an impressionable child, worth at least three Laurel and Hardy films.

Now and then there might be a lunch 'in town' to meet friends at a smart restaurant (which might, or might not, include food for the adults.) Though often ignored - being the only child present - I was never bored and occasionally someone might take the trouble to chat. However, trained never to either interrupt or (sin of sins) repeat any adult conversation, or to fidget, I'd sit quietly with a book, both ears flapping, digesting, along with my food, every sentence. Whilst working wonders for my vocabulary, my intense curiosity regarding the (to a child) often rather odd behaviour of grown-ups, worked overtime and had I understood even half the gossip, or the innuendo, or indeed, been a blabbermouth, one or two lives might well have drastically changed course.

These lengthy lunches might extend to a mesmerising evening - for me, anyway - of 'Variety' at either the Empress, in Brixton, or Collins Music Hall, on Islington Green, or maybe there'd be a trip to 'the flicks'. At that time, the life of the music-hall was limited, with some already closed, but the programme of those remaining usually included a singer, a magician, a ventriloquist or fire-eater and maybe a troupe of 'specialist acrobats' - with a 'C or D' list stand-up comedian; or a double act, topping the bill. Whilst not exactly the tops, I enjoyed them all, clapping each enthusiastically, with the exception of, dare I say, the xylophonist: there always seemed to be one. Afterwards we'd go backstage 'Just to say hello' (without doubt, the longest hello's in living memory). Not that I ever complained. As the youngest groupie in the business and always spellbound amidst any form of entertainment, the advantages of having a mother who seemed to know everyone meant that by the age of nine, I'd met a few stars as well as many has-beens and never-would-be's.

If 'lunch' finished with a trip to the cinema, Technicolour musicals being favourite, we'd be found in the rear stalls, almost invisible through dense clouds of cigarette smoke, then an integral part of every cinema interior in the land. In those days of the double feature, a few unmusical and often very un-childlike offerings were included. Memories of Peter Lorre in 'The Beast With Five Fingers' stayed with me for years, as did scenes from the brilliant though disturbing film, 'The Red Shoes.' Those, plus a few evenings at the Everyman, in Hampstead (where I must have been sneaked in, it then being a members-only cinema-club, specialising in foreign films) provided me with glimpses of humanity that I might well have been better off without. While unable to recall seeing anything overtly sexual, the sheer misery and despair of Emile Jannings' memorable portrayal of the hapless professor in 'The Blue Angel' left me with deep feelings of unhappiness as well as a long-standing (and quite unfair) loathing of Marlene Dietrich. One of Mother's best impressions was of Marlene's gravelly-voiced rendering of 'Falling in Love Again' (featured in the film) which, whenever she performed, caused me to leave the room; although she never really understood why, accusing me of 'Doing a Sarah Bernhardt again, are we...'

On reflection, one cannot help but believe that despite the grim, terrible miseries and privations of war, youngsters weren't in some ways at less risk then than the present day. Now, an excess of everything sees previously undreamed of diversions readily available at the press of a button, resulting in different and far less easily resolved sets of problems. Once, the now ridiculed norm. meant being expected to stick to the rules, behave responsibly and to keep out of trouble - or to 'Just use your common sense' - a phrase I recall as invariably delivered in a tone of total exasperation. One simply didn't dare argue. Well-drilled from birth, we learned to 'Get on with it' sometimes almost choking on our resentments which were, one discovered much later, actually considered perfectly natural by the adults - provided such feelings were never voiced.

Emma, so much part of my life until she retired to Essex, was the exception. I never once recall her showing anger or raising her voice. Instead, her demeanor was one of calm, orderly gentleness and tolerance, accompanied by lots of cuddles. Shortly after she'd moved, we heard from her son that she'd sadly died; but it was a while before I was told. My sister and I, having inherited a fair share of mother's genes, survived our unusual upbringing, eventually landing in the adult world with the phrases 'Because I say so' 'Please don't ask' and 'I'll think about it' reverberating throughout our beings. Motherhood would never have been a first choice on the list of careers for our particular matriarch, but beautiful people are often different: the rest of us just learn to fit in. Until we realise there might be choices.

Devilled Kidneys (for 4)
2 tabsp. oil of choice
2 lamb's kidneys per person – skinned then cut each half into 6 pieces
50grm. Butter
1 small onion: finely chopped and softened in a little oil
40grm plain flour
Level teasp. English mustard
1 tab.sp. Sherry
1 tab.sp Worcester sauce.
Just under 300ml milk
3 tabsp. double cream
Soften onions in oil in small pan and remove; add butter & melt: add kidneys, season and stir over med heat 3-4 mins. Add flour and cooked onions – stir for about 2mins.

Slowly add milk and stir well as mixture thickens. Add mustard, sherry and W. Sauce. If mixture a little thin, sprinkle over 1 or 2 teasp. flour, stir well and cook for 2 mins. Finally add cream and serve on toast.

Chapter Two

UNTIL THE MID-50s, with many non-luxury foods still limited, producing an interesting meal required patience and imagination and occasionally, even courage (hence the badger.) By the age of twelve, both my interest on the food-front as well as my ability in the kitchen, had increased considerably. Domestic-Science at school had been well taught but it wasn't until after leaving - having been accepted by a nearby Art School - that my culinary talents moved on. With no specific plans for the remainder of the summer (the words "gap-year" had yet to surface) I became part of Mother's new project, a Victorian country pub and restaurant - or 'Grill-Room' - in Kent. With extra help always needed and catering staff having long been a transient lot, there was no shortage of work, but as our chef's attachment to the bottle had finally overtaken his attachment to the job, after a spell of waiting on table, I was slotted in.

   This probably sounds more difficult than it was, but a grill-room, by its very definition, meant a simple menu. Starters were seasonal and uncomplicated - usually soup, melon or grapefruit, complete with - yes - the glace cherry; or a small plate of assorted hors d'eouvre - followed by a steak: rump or fillet, or two large chump chops, or a mixed grill. This most popular dish comprised a lamb chop, lamb's kidney, a sausage, a rasher of bacon and a 'minute' steak - its size meant it cooked in just a minute - all garnished with a sprig of parsley, a grilled tomato and a mushroom - and served with chips or new potatoes and a green vegetable (side-salads being seldom requested in the '50s). There would then be a choice of (three) cold desserts, cheese and coffee.

   'Speed' I decided - hmm - as opposed to haute cuisine, would see me through. After several crash-courses taken throughout my working life, this first, from Mother, soon had me producing edible rare, medium, and (trickiest of all) well-done, but still palatable, steaks : and proper soups, involving, in those blenderless days, a good stock-pot and a selection of sieves and wooden spoons. Soon, following a formula of preparation, organisation and synchronisation; plus deep sinkfuls of hot, soapy water and the help of 'Carrie at number two' (the pub came with three cottages) a workable pattern of sorts began to emerge - except on Saturday nights when, heavily booked, I simply floundered my way through, incapable of even recognizing the word 'organized'.

By today's catering standards we were pathetically under-equipped, although the kitchen housed two cookers: a normal-sized domestic gas cooker and a temperamental solid-fuel Rayburn, which sulked when the wind didn't suit (virtually every other day). A massive double-doored catering 'fridge took care of hygiene and into this - terrified of killing our customers that first sticky summer - I would cram just about anything remotely classifiable as perishable. On top of this machine stood, alongside a caged, blue Budgie - much beloved of my sister - a large china bowl, into which Mother, when she remembered, would toss bills and receipts.

Before long, the contents of this usually overflowing container, requiring from time to time the attention of 'Lovely Gerald' our-oh-so-patient accountant, would redistribute itself throughout the works at the back of the machine, as well as across the surface of the floor beneath. When summoned, Gerald, one of |Mother's oldest and most devoted friends (and would-be lover, though never encouraged) would appear and with little more than a resigned sigh and a nod, murmur 'Time to move, Bev.' Together we would heave, from side to side, the big, white monster, rocking it back and fore until every scrap of paper had been safely harvested into brown paper carriers.

For a while, with my evenings mostly committed, via a steady stream of bookings, the phrase 'social life' barely featured. Matters only improved after some of the younger locals - many of whom worked and flat-shared in London - began appearing at weekends; our beer and food (so we heard) being the draw. A friendly lot, they soon invited me to join the local Jazz club: 'Don't you dare accept any drugs...' If they were there, none were ever offered, although we all smoked tobacco. Mother's warnings were enough. 'You'll end up like the Dean Paul woman' - a socialite with problems who often featured in the tabloids. Not that we felt deprived. The atmosphere was enough, particularly one Summer evening in maybe, mid '55, when someone by the name of Lonnie Donegan and group, complete with broom-handle and string "Double bass," as well as a washboard, appeared for a thirty-minute slot. Immediately, the raw energy of this streak of talent, scarcely heart-throb kit but later to top the charts as 'King of Skiffle,' on that particular night, just looked in serious need of a good meal. But his effect on the crowd was riveting and with the room exploding as never before, he was obviously heading for a big future.

Then there was the Yacht Club, which in Mummyspeak meant Much Nicer People : (richer). Yacht Clubs always win over Jazz Clubs with mummies. In fact, the reality meant that the combination of more cash equalled higher booze consumption, which along with the availability of a few spare rooms, produced opportunities for furthering a teenager's education way above and beyond anything the humble Jazz Club had to offer. Whilst backward, I was beginning to see how it all worked.

Lacking any real interest in booze meant that life in an alcohol-fuelled environment had its drawbacks, usually involving over-friendly males. These - mostly middle-aged and heavily-married acquaintances - would appear in the kitchen and, finding me alone, refuse to leave without a 'little kiss,' as if their patronage included some form of watered down "Droit de Seigneur". It took a while, but having found the effects of an excess of alcohol on some of the nicest people (when sober) unnerving, my puny stock of put-downs soon swelled until I was able to cope (almost) with just about any given situation.

However, some months before I left school, there had been a brief spell when an older boyfriend, quite unaware of my age, had introduced me to the sweet and pungent "Rum and Black." At the start of a no-plans-for-the-Easter-holidays, we'd met by chance, in a local shop, where he and the proprietor had stood discussing the merits of Walls Ice Cream. Suddenly, this vision of loveliness turned to me and having explained his position - Manager of the local Walls Depot - said 'Why don't we ask this young lady for her views'. The fact that such a tall, blonde, sophisticate - exquisitely turned out and obviously some years my senior - (later discovered to be twenty-eight and named Henry) might be remotely interested in anything I had to say, rendered me virtually mute. But not for long, as soon - having accepted his unexpected invitation - Miss Cautious with a capital C could be found well away from Mother's airwaves, sipping 'frothy coffee' in a nearby cafe. We got on well, he was charming and funny and after a long chat, we'd settled on the possibility of a date.

Whilst a late Easter meant the evenings were lengthening, mine would remain exactly the same, outings being restricted solely to the exercising of our large, black Labrador, Bongo. There was nothing for it but to invent a virtual anthology featuring my 'Terribly strict parents...' (necessity being the mother of invention, teenagers swiftly become remarkably skilled liars, although I'm said to be one of the worst: but better on the phone).

Soon, we'd planned the strategy of our first - and as it turned out - every subsequent, date. In the early evening, Bongo and I would race off to the depot, just a half-mile away, from which, with dog promptly stowed into one of the many ice-cream vans at H's disposal (no 'Elf and Safety then) we'd chug off to a country pub. With my dog-walk period timed at around an hour and a half to two hours, we'd sit and chat, fitting in just two or three drinks - in my case, Rum and Blackcurrant. Throughout the drive home, to mask any fumes, I'd unromantically crunch my way through a half dozen of the strongest (always available due to my weak chest) cough sweets. Not once in the short time we were together (before my return to 'college' - more lies) did that potent and pungent spirit produce the merest blip of inebriation. The slightest sniff of those outings would have seen me incarcerated for the rest of the holidays, apart from which, Mother's tongue was not for the faint-hearted: life at home being all about trying to maintain a balance. But Bongo, my one excuse for getting out, was heaped with treats, mainly Smiths Crisps, then his newest favourite, promoting quizzical statements from Mama 'That dog"s putting on weight, are you sure he's getting enough exercise'?.. The words 'Dumb animal' were never more appreciated. No wonder my drinking legs never really developed. Even now am in no way a proper drinker, having developed an intolerance to, amongst other things, alcohol.

Move on now to early Summer, at home, when, having popped into one of the bars, I found myself being chatted up by a soldier whose regiment had recently taken over a nearby barracks. The next morning he - George - rang to ask me out and I suggested a walk - usually a good way of getting to know someone. It must be said our first date promised anything but a future. At the age of twenty seven (to my sixteen) and used to giving orders and having them obeyed, my new walker was a bit pompous and bossy, but even worse, distinctly unkeen on my dog. However, to be fair, his wit and humour held my interest and whilst shorter than I'd have liked, he wasn't at all bad looking.

And so we continued to see each other until, unexpectedly, within a few months he was posted to the Regimental Headquarters, in the Tower of London. Meanwhile, in between the occasional weekend together, my evenings off were divided, more or less, between the Jazz and the Sailing clubs.

Ours was a sparky relationship but after less than a year, quite unexpectedly, one Saturday, he proposed. Equally unexpectedly, I accepted. Optimistically ignoring details concerning age - mine - and the eleven year gap, plus the need for parents' permission, we agreed that as there was no hurry it might be wise to first seek approval to become engaged. Mother's reaction was understandable, considering my age, although to me, at the time, simply appeared unreasonable. 'Are you pregnant? If not, just what - exactly - do you think you're doing? You have no right to say you'll marry anyone: certainly not at your age'. Etc. for weeks. How totally daft I must have been to have anticipated anything else. Predictably, it was all grim and by week five or so, furious with Mother for denying she'd ever promised me the coming weekend off (to attend a parade in London at which the regiment would be receiving new Colours) I laid my chequebook on the kitchen table and with a sniffy 'I want nothing from you. Ever' flounced upstairs to pack a bag. With a whole £6:10:0 (today's £6:50) in my purse on which to survive until a job was found, I was determined to manage somehow.

Artichoke Soup. (for 4)

500grm Jerusalem Artichokes - scraped and par boiled

2 med. sized leeks - cleaned, chopped and sauteed in mix of oil and butter (2 tabsp. oil,/20grm butter.

1 med. aubergine sliced and cooked in oil & butter (20grm butter 2 tab.sp oil)   .

5-6 med. sized mushrooms -chopped

Seasoning

900mls good chicken stock.

Place all veg together (incl. cooked veg) in baking tin and cook in mod.oven 15/20 mins.

Cool and liquidise with stock.

Add scant 300ml full-cream milk.

Season to taste.

Enjoy!

Chapter Three

MY NEW LIFE COULDN'T HAVE VARIED MORE from the old had I taken up lion-taming. Having been housed by my bemused future mother-in-law, I'd swiftly scoured the Evening Standard jobs section and within days, had joined William Hill, the large betting company in the City, which then, as now, paid out on sports winnings. On day one as Pools Clerk, my new title, I was met and escorted to a large room full of tables and chairs to become the eighth woman alongside seven others. The work was bafflingly non-skilled and having been told that speed was essential, particularly when the 'payout' was large, I soon caught on. Briefly, it comprised of opening and sorting piles of post from piles of mailbags, each envelope containing a pools coupon and one or more postal orders, the value of which covered the number of 'lines' submitted. Having stamped and checked the coupons - retaining all winners to be paid out later - we'd sit speculating on how to spend their cash (in those days a £75,000 win was the maximum). It seemed unbelievable that such hassle-free work warranted a wage-packet. Full of chat, fuelled by gossip and smoke (almost everyone did) we worked fast and within weeks I knew what seemed like every engrossing detail of my co-workers existence, each day bringing forth yet more riveting information.

At that time, the girls were all native-born Londoners, bar two; beautiful, blonde, Birgitte, from a small town in Germany - the fastest, neatest worker on the floor - and Thelma, a quick-witted Mancunian, renown not only for her truly phenomenal consumption of chips but also for being first with the filthiest of jokes, the delivery of which could, as a stand-up, have kept her in luxury for life. Soon, having realised that my initial quiet demeanor was down to shyness, as opposed to 'We thought you was stuck-up' they began quizzing me about my former life with a daily 'Any news from home then?' As the baby of the group, I was well looked after and at lunchtimes, hauled off to Fred's Cafe, in City Road, for 'Egg and double chips, two slices and a tea, please' before moving on to Doreen's.

What a shop. Always friendly and packed with the latest fashions; a small deposit secured any garment. 'Quality" barely featured on a weekly wage of £6:00 (overtime paid extra but cropped up only two or three times a month) but who cared? Any overtime was useful as G. and I were saving hard - a new experience for us both - and trying to spend wisely. Ignoring the constant echo of Mother's voice and the phrase 'Cheap tat' wasn't easy.

A few weeks after joining W.H. I arrived one Monday morning to find larger than usual stacks of mailbags piled everywhere, unopened. Two or three of the older women were circuiting each table in turn, instructing everyone to 'Leave the bags. We're on strike.' A strike; a real strike. I felt like a character in a film as everyone sat around smoking and chatting, debating if and when there would be a settlement, murmuring 'Let the buggers sweat. You wait, they'll have to come round in the end.' The problem was overtime rates, not exactly generous at £1:50 for a Saturday, 9:00-5:30 and, £2:50 for the same hours on a Sunday - although it would never have occurred to me to have made such a stand. Throughout the morning, management appeared briefly and intermittently with a cajoling 'Now come along girls, back to work, if you please' to no effect whatsoever. By 2pm. they were back, looking seriously worried and stationed at the top end of the room, pleaded with us 'Please, girls. Please get back to work'. After two hours when no one had moved, negotiations went up a rung or two and by 5pm it was all over; although a few stalwarts stayed on to move the backlog. Such excitement. A totally new world and I loved it.

But outside of work, life was moving on. Soon after the Suez crisis began, sometime in late summer, the regiment was warned for standby. Should either sickness or welfare problems affect any of the senior N.C.O's - Non-Commisioned-Officers - thus keeping them behind, G. would be called forward as a replacement: selfishly, we kept all fingers and toes tightly crossed - although the possibility of us ever actually getting to either Registry Office or altar was becoming increasingly unlikely.

Then G. was told that shortly, a two-bed, centrally-heated (in 1956!) fully-furnished quarter, in the Tower of London could be ours, provided we were spliced. And rules were rules. We decided that once again, I should seek permission; or lose the flat. Following several brief, frosty phone calls, Mama and I met up at a London restaurant where, that particular evening, words, as well as food consumption, were limited and after a scant glance at the consent form and a -'I've no intention of signing that so you may as well put it away. I"11 have you made a Ward of Court first' - we parted. Miserably, I caught the bus and sat alone, on top, quietly grizzling my way through the journey home.

Later, after talking things through we decided to present our case at the Magistrates Court: a difficult and reluctant decision but Mother and I shared the same stubborn streak. However, needing advice, the following morning I rang a family friend - Mother's solicitor - an elegant, urbane Welshman who immediately invited us to his home for supper. There, having first calmly and 'Sorry darling' questioned me at length, he smiled at my 'No, I'm truly not pregnant, not even a teeny bit' before turning to George. Somewhere around eleven, we left, feeling grateful and even a little hopeful.

Some two months later, all was resolved - out of court - and with the form signed, we settled for 10am, Monday, 5th November (negating all future cries of 'Sorry I forgot our wedding anniversary') at St Pancras Town Hall, before going off to celebrate with a Spag. Bol. at the Bamboo Bar, in Goodge St.: renamed, but amazingly,still there. Deciding to keep things simple, my-never-to-be-described-as-frivolous wedding outfit, consisted of a grey suit and gloves, gunmetal stilettos and clutch bag, and a fuschia hat. The friend who'd promised to bring a camera forgot, so we have absolutely no record of the happy event. My battle-weary Mother - complete with equally dazed-looking friend, along with my younger sister, had - against all odds - appeared for our brief ceremony, doubtless wishing they hadn't, as to Mother's horror, the wedding break-fast amounted to six cups of coffee in a nearby ABC Tearooms. Weakly, she'd announced that 'I really could have done with a large brandy' (seldom can the desire for the soothing qualities of alcohol have been exceeded) so we suggested they share our cab to Paddington and the joys of the station buffet. Once there and suitably fortified, they waved us off to Penzance, where, thanks to G. having signed on for further military service, a gesture which earned him a bounty of £100:00, we were to spend a week's honeymoon. I was now an army wife.

Chapter Four

AT THE TIME IT NEVER OCCURRED TO EITHER OF US that part of G's bonus
might have bought a decent dinner service or some rugs, or bed linen.
We simply took advantage of the fact that everything was 'issued' from
floor-cloths upwards, and were prepared to survive on it all for a while.
However, our quiet nuptials, attended by just a handful of family and
one good friend (the regiment being otherwise engaged in Egypt)
meant few gifts; although the girls at work had sweetly clubbed
together and presented me with a green-faced, wooden clock which
ticked away noisily for years. Not that any of it mattered and the small
cheque, rather reluctantly handed over with a sigh, by Mother, and
which I (ungraciously) almost refused, still sat untouched in our
account. Having enjoyed a seven day honeymoon at a small hotel we
simply considered ourselves lucky, especially when Mother-in-law
kindly donated a lovely silver tea-caddy, as well as an antique china
tea-service, both of which had once belonged to G's paternal
grandmother.

With so few possessions, our No.1 move was uneventful, but
wishing to get it over with, G. hired a car. As our allocated quarter in
the Tower was being re-decorated (another bonus), for a few weeks
we'd be renting a "Hiring" in, amazingly, Clapham Common. This
small furnished flat, one of several privately-owned properties rented
by the Military to offset a shortage of army housing, consisted of three
rooms in the top of a private house, plus bath. There, our shared hot
tubs took on pantomime proportions as we peered at each other
through the moist clouds of hot fog belching from the ancient gas
geyser. Both guardian angels must have been on extra-special duty as
we finally managed to exit without the wretched thing actually
exploding. For years I expected to come across the headline 'Vintage
Geyser Wrecks London Flat.' Not that anything really mattered. We
loved it, and for the first week or so I rose with my bemused husband
at six, presenting him with a cooked breakfast, until one morning he
said 'Please go back to bed, I'm fine with toast'. Oh joy.

Time passed uneventfully. Having first cleaned through (happily polishing the kitchen floor on my hands and knees to which Mother's answer was 'You quite obviously need a psychiatrist') I'd take off, with a friend, to the launderette or to Brixton Market, where, feeling very grown up, we'd root around for hours. It was then back to the kitchen for supper preparations and (yes!) Mrs Dale's Diary.

One of G's supper favourites (then) was a bacon and onion pudding - a mix of bacon, sliced onions and tomatoes, encased in a suet roll and boiled/steamed for about two hours; a recipe from his Mother and described by mine as 'That bacon house-brick thing.' I soon learned to jazz it up with extra everything, plus a few herbs and lighter pastry, but it didn't appear on our menu often, although I was fast becoming an expert on thrifty meals.

Evenings, those first freezing weeks, might be spent either at the Majestic cinema in the high street, or round a big fire with a good book and background music courtesy of Radio Luxembourg... All those great, gooey '50s hits. Al Martino - an Italian-American with a great voice and dark, hunky looks whose powerful 'Here in my Heart' made as all swoon, as did Johnny Ray, sobbing his way through 'Cry' and

S on the bridge of HM Submarine Grampus in Nov 67 off Gibraltar

Frankie Laine belting out 'I Believe'.

Separately, they'd topped the bill at the London Palladium, leaving the mainly female, teenage audiences in states of hysteria often associated with mental illness. Soon, baffled parents, clueless as to how to cope with their unrecognisable young, sought advice from each other. Little did they know that this was just the beginning. Two Palladium cleaning ladies, when interviewed by a tabloid journalist, summed it all up in one word. 'Sex' they said 'Just sex...'

Meanwhile, the music scene gathered momentum. Tommy Steele and Cliff Richard 'Singin' the Blues' and Nancy Whiskey and Chas.McDevitt's 'Freight Train,' along with the frantic skiffle of Lonnie Donegan, increasingly filled pubs and newly-formed folk clubs. But the biggest change of all was the advent of Bill Haley - surely the most unlikely heart-throb ever: slightly chubby, with a trademark kiss-curl and in age, probably closer to thirty than twenty. With his 'Comets' he'd slammed into the hit parade like a rocket, changing forever the lives of an entire generation. As 'Rock Around the Clock' throbbed its way round the world, parents, formerly the swooning fans of '40s Glen Miller, viewed the uninhibited new dance style called Rock and Roll through jaundiced eyes, conveniently forgetting their own jitterbugging years. The Teenager had arrived.

And then it was Christmas; unfortunately, spent apart, due to my having sprouted a couple of problems which needed surgery. Early one mid-December morning I was hauled off in severe pain to the South London Hospital for Women and Children (now a branch of Tesco) and taken to a ward where a young nurse on learning my age, had grunted disapprovingly 'Huh, I'll have to go down to the Childrens' ward for a form, we don't keep kids ones up here... Your husband will have to sign it. I suppose he's over twenty-one?' I felt, and probably looked, about ten years old. But my stay was fine and uneventful. The food was, well, hospital food and I looked forward to enjoying a piece of the large goose which G, having scooped first prize in the Sergeants' Mess Christmas Draw, had passed to his mother to cook. On Boxing Day he rushed in and, nestled in with a bag of tangerines, was my Christmas dinner. One can only be thankful that the poor creature had actually died before meeting the flames. Always an impatient cook, Mother-in-law had managed to stop just short of actual cremation and, whilst possessed of good, strong teeth there wasn't a chance of my

Jan 1968: G is on 6 month unaccompanied - children and I join him for Christmas - he borrowed the '4 of an RAF couple who were returning to UK flat for 3 weeks.
George with Domini.

finding the merest morsel of anything remotely edible on the charred drumstick (scarcely surprising, its fate having been firmly sealed in a household where as a matter of course the offer of 'A Rennie'? rounded off every meal. No Choccy mints for us.)

On the morning of New Years Eve, I was home, having spurned the hospital's offer of a 'Week's convalescence in the country.' Whilst good to be back, I despaired at the chaos in which men can usually be relied upon to live, and set about restoring order. That evening, we made plans to return to Cornwall for another week's stay, this time in St.

Ives, with Mother's oldest friend, the lovely 'Aunty Loffie'.

Soon after returning from Cornwall we moved to the flat. Having added little to our possessions, bar some table linen and a piece or two of Cornish pottery, packing was swift and G's instructions for the 'March Out' dutifully followed ...'Everything will be inspected by the BIA man and all must be left as if no one has ever lived here. I'll deal with the Inventory'. More trumpeting disbelief from Mother, who, now living nearby, visited often. But she was right. Tight-lipped and unquestioning, I scoured and polished our already pristine flat as the logic of the military - not for the first time and certainly not the last - totally escaped me. Soon it was time to go and with everything crammed into a cab we closed the door, thanked our landlady and handed over the keys.

Next stop, HM Tower of London.. .What had Mrs. Potter said 'I see you in an old building. Very old, greyish - a sort of castle....'

Stuffed Lamb's Hearts (for 4)
4 lamb's hearts - depending on size: hearty eaters need 2 - washed and trimmed of ducts
  75grm. Chopped onion
  125 grm chopped mushrooms
  125grm chopped streaky bacon
  50grm butter
  Half teasp.chopped sage or thyme (or dried)
  225grms. Fresh breadcrumbs
  Grated zest of I lemon
  1 beaten egg
  4 lev, tabsp plain flour
  300ml stock plus 3 tablsp.sherry
  2 tabsp. Oil

Use half the butter and lightly brown onions, mushrooms and bacon, stir in herbs, bread - crumbs, rind and season:bind with egg. Fill hearts with stuffing and skewer together (or sew if you like and have time...)Toss hearts in flour, place in heatproof casserole and brown in remaining butter and oil. Pour over stock & sherry and bring to boil. Cover and cook at 150c for about 2 hrs or until tender (test). Slice hearts, pour over juices and serve.

Chapter Five

MY OWN FEELINGS ON MOVING to the famous Tower of London, had first amounted to disbelief followed by delight, although never having been a chicken-counter, I'd secretly doubted it would ever happen. But here we were. My pragmatic husband, of course, took it all for granted and just wanted to get settled as soon as possible. Standing on the cobbles facing Old Hospital Block, with our collection of suitcases and cartons, I waited whilst he went off to find a couple of soldiers to help transfer everything up to number seven, on the third floor, the very top. Whatever the future held, we'd certainly be fit.

The early-Victorian building, modern, in comparison to those surrounding it, had indeed once been a hospital but was converted when extra homes were required for the Tower staff. Although it's unlikely that what appears to the public to be two four-storey Queen Anne houses, opposite the White Tower, is in fact a block of eight flats. Neither is it apparent that the Tower environs houses, as well as the majority of the Yeoman Warders working there (commonly known as Beefeaters) and their families, several other members of staff who, in their various roles, keep the place together. It is almost a village in its own right with over a hundred dwellings, two chapels and a social club. Tower Green, home of the Resident Governor and several of the other more senior officials, is the most attractive spot to live with some of the finest Tudor architecture in the country, some of which are said, naturally, to come complete with ghost.

Regimental associations with the Tower date back to 1685 when the new regiment was raised there: The Royal Fusiliers, City of London Regiment. The title of Fusilier originates from the "Fusil" which at the time was a type of rifle issued to the soldiers. In 1967 however, we became The Royal Regiment of Fusiliers, having amalgamated with three other regiments - the Lancashire Fusiliers, the Warwickshire Fusiliers and the Northumberland Fusiliers. When G.

and I moved to Old Hospital Block, shortly before the ending of National Service (the most famous N.S.Fusiliers being Michael Caine and the Kray twins) the buildings housing the Crown Jewels, one or two gift shops and various other offices, were, for a couple of centuries, a small barracks. However, government cuts and re-shufflings equals change and before long, the Regiment, though still lucky enough to retain a toe-hold in the form of a London Headquarters, wonders if its time there may be limited. As our grandchildren have all been christened there, in the lovely chapel of St. Peter Ad Vincula (marriage as well as christenings in the chapel being available to members of the regiment) it is hard to imagine the place free of regimental privilege.

Our accommodation at number seven was similar, though larger, than the Clapham flat. No open fire but we're now mid-way through January in the '50s and had real central heating. I felt like putting up a sign. Furniture was, well - basic - and carpets came there none: military floor coverings for ORs (Other Ranks) being rugs or rugs; a choice of either embossed sludgy brown or heavily-patterned multi-coloured, commercial-hotel style c.1900: three in the sitting/dining room and one in each bedroom. Our hall floor gleamed. A solid runway of bottle-green lino, a colour which appeared regularly throughout G's army career - and in this case the result of someone's seriously hard work. It soon dawned - my original first flush of wifely polishing zeal having faded with our move from the Clapham flat - that any future gleaming was down to me; although that particular problem was soon solved by my introduction to the delights of the bumper - virtually a square, maybe twelve by ten (inches, of course) of tightly compressed bristles, about four inches in depth, from the centre of which sprouted a long, wooden pole.

It resembled nothing I'd ever seen before or since. G however, all heart, kindly explained. 'Spread the polish evenly! across whichever surface requires attention and wait until it dries"... This solid lump of bristle was then to be heaved fore and aft until the required depth of shine appeared. Within a month I was not only mistress of the art, but had also sprouted a new set of bulging muscles and an entirely new vocabulary.

It was about then that G., having casually asked whether or not we'd be sticking with the two armchairs already in situ, or swapping them for a sofa, received my puzzled reply 'Both actually, may we not have both?' Oh, dear me, no. There were rules.

After deciding that the most economical way of solving the (lack of) sofa problem was to buy a single divan and have loose covers made for that and the armchairs, the following Saturday was spent chasing fabric. I'd already earmarked a carpet locally, a pale-green Belgian 'carved' cotton square which we reckoned would virtually cover the sitting-room floor, at just under ten pounds.

By comparison, fabrics were expensive but, conscious of our budget - though doubtful of my choice - G. finally agreed on the most inexpensive and strongest, a black sateen blackout material at two shillings (a whole 10p) a yard... Within a month, the newly covered divan and chairs, complete with piping, and a selection of green and orange cushions (covers hand-sewn, by me) sat in splendour on the new carpet. The small tiled fire-place, invisible under a white-painted sheet of perforated hardboard hung with striped Tradescantha and trailing Ivy plants, had taken on a thriving horticultural life of its own, whilst above the divan hung shelves, complete with a set of white porcelain Chinese horses and more trailing ivy. All very contemporary - the phrase of the time - and certainly different. The issued curtains - greenish and heavily patterned - sort of blended in with the walls (through narrowed eyes) but were better than nothing. Then came the china. A Sunday morning in Petticoat Lane yielded a six place-setting breakfast set - and six dinner plates, polka-dotted in black and white, plus three black dishes for vegetables. No other couple in the entire history of the world could have been more delighted with their lot. Days later, Marie, an older, lovely new friend who lived immediately below, popped up for 'A coffee and a look.' Gazing at the black divan and swallowing hard, she said quietly "Well.." Not exactly short of nerve, are you... But I don't think Bob would have let me go for the black."

So there we were, snug, happy and with the nearest shops over the bridge, in Bermondsey, increasingly well-exercised. Getting to the bus-stop on a fine Summer's day meant negotiating streams of incoming tourists and soon I'd perfected a nifty sideways glide which, as a Cancerian, appeared to come naturally. Bermondsey was friendly, scruffy and full of bargains and it was obvious that the NAAFI - until then our weekly grocery supplier - just couldn't compete. Without a 'fridge, but not intending to shop daily, I'd need to revise our diet and whilst fresh meat would keep maybe 48 hrs. in winter, summer suppers would include more egg, pasta and vegetable based dishes. So much for a carnivore husband.

In '50s England, apart from a handful of Italian restaurants in Soho, pasta was seldom, if ever, seen on any menu except as Macaroni Cheese, or as a pudding, baked with milk and sugar. The pasta and pizza offerings of today had yet to arrive from the U.S. and Elizabeth David's informative bible had scarcely reached us. Luckily, thanks to Mama, I could produce both a decent Spag. Bol. and Spag. Neapolitan - although with Parmesen and garlic not only scarce but expensive, a compromise was reached with extra onions and the strongest available cheddar. We all had degrees in recipe-juggling then.

Due to G's love of meat, real vegetarian options, such as a nut and lentil roast or baked stuffed onions, were out. Instead, I'd produce a substantial omelette filled with chopped, bacon offcuts, sauteed with potato, onions and tomatoes or when available from a market stall, mushroom stalks (five pence or one old shilling a half pound). Hard-boiled eggs in a curry sauce, with chutney and rice, was another option. A hash, made from tinned corned-beef, lots of onions, baked beans and tomatoes, all topped with mashed potato soon became a favourite, as well as Unox, a pork luncheon-meat Spam substitute from which I'd make fritters and a unique casserole (probably best forgotten). When cheese became off-ration, as well as omelettes, we'd have cheese souffles, macaroni cheese or cauliflower cheese topped with either sausages or crisp streaky bacon, or a home-made sausagemeat 'rissole'. The versatile sausagemeat also went into a Toad-in the-Hole with sliced onions and tomatoes, or a sausage pie. Savoury pancakes were another option, filled with just about anything edible and available, and if we'd had a small joint on a Sunday, the metal mincer, screwed to the kitchen table and fed with leftover meat, onions and carrots soon became either Cottage or Shepherds pie. Fish was also a good deal, although only kippers could safely be kept uncooked overnight in summer. In Winter, G. - having swiftly given up on herrings - 'Too many bones' - finally succumbed to crisply fried Sprats after the initial "You mean you eat it ALL", and soon took to soft herring roes on toast. We enjoyed smoked haddock - alone or made into Kedgeree - and fish-cakes made from delicious fresh cod which, apart from Coley, was almost the cheapest fish on the slab. I also devised an alternative fish-cake, using tinned tuna - handy if I hadn't shopped, although on a Friday, an early visit to the fishmonger might produce a large, fresh crab. As a skilled picker (due to Mother's firm belief in child-labour) meant it usually took me less than an hour.

Not that we lacked fresh meat. Meat and bacon rationing had stopped in '54 and having discovered an obliging butcher, the choice improved daily: pigs liver and kidney, lambs kidney, sheep's heart, shin of beef for unctuous stews, oxtail, ox-cheek, hand of pork and boned and rolled breasts of lamb, as well as the king of what remains one of the the finest cuts of all - best end neck of lamb: delicious with some chopped kidney in a Hot Pot. Oddly, Belly of Pork - unlike today- simply never appeared in the shop, possibly serving as the basis for Harry-the-butcher's sausages; tasty but fatty. Roasts were saved for a mid-week supper, G's philosophy being 'Why succumb to the tyranny of the Sunday lunch, any day will do' - forward-thinking for a '50s male. You may have noticed the absence of chicken on this list, but then still considered a luxury, supplies were short and pricey - although we found a shop in Brixton which occasionally sold "Boilers". At two shillings each - a whole ten pence - which after a lengthy session in the pot would become fricassee (more mushroom stalks) or chicken pie, with the stock used for soup. During the war, rabbit, masquerading on many restaurant menus as chicken, had been extremely popular but was swiftly wiped from the shopping lists following outbreaks of Myxamatosis. There was also mince, but having been constantly warned against 'Shop Mince' (which Mother swore contained 'Everything they want to get rid of, plus a good handful of sawdust') I'd sometimes choose a piece or two of so-called 'Frying Steak', usually Chuck or Flank, and provided business was quiet, persuade Harry to pop it through the mincer. At home, with the addition of an egg yolk, pepper, some minced onion and a pinch of dried mixed herbs (then a kitchen staple) this mixture became 'Hamburgers' much beloved by Husband when served with fried onions, tomatoes and creamy mashed potato.

Something of a problem, G. v vegetables. In fact, he'd probably prefer to do without altogether - barring sprouts and tinned garden peas. Fried onions and grilled tomatoes are acceptable but carrots have to be grated before being 'disappeared' into casseroles - whilst Spring greens and cabbage - finely sliced and cooked in a minimum of boiling water before being tossed in butter, pepper and a pinch of sugar - are just about tolerated: but not often. As for salad...Some thirty years later (as you'll read if you stay the course) having baffled the medical profession by recovering from a massive Subarachnoid Brain haemorrhage, G. very carefully explained to everyone that the cause had been 'Too much salad. We eat it almost every day, you know...' Now, he'll tolerate Ratatouille (home-made) and broccoli and marrow under sufferance, although preferably under cheese sauce. Pumpkin, squash, mange-tout, courgettes, kale, artichokes and undisguised peppers, are ignored whilst swede, mashed with butter, pepper, onion and a little carrot are acceptable occasionally, as is sweetcorn. Turnips - no matter how young and fresh - just forget the turnips, but the humble parsnip, well. Family folklore tells of his drooling delight - not to mention disbelief - following a first taste of Mother's chunky slices of baked wonderfulness, which, having been placed around a large Sunday joint - usually ribs of beef - were eased from the pan, coated in dark sticky juices.

With G's salary accounted for, apart from family gatherings or meals with friends, we ate out seldom, preferring an evening at the theatre: always up in 'The Gods' never paying more than 20p (four old shillings) each, often less. That year, 1957, West End theatres offered an amazingly diverse selection of drama, dance and musicals and we probably saw them all, from a company of African dancers to 'The Pyjama Game' and the controversial 'Look Back in Anger,' to a memorable play about Australian cane-cutters called 'The Summer of the Seventeenth Doll.' We loved our London life and probably took in something of everything the city had to offer, from trials at the Bailey to hiring the odd motor boat for sunny Saturdays on the Thames. A balmy evening might be spent wandering through Wapping High St. (then full of pungent spice warehouses, now converted to luxury des. res.) to the famous 'Prospect of Whitby' pub, on the river, for a couple of halves of bitter and a shared packet of crisps. On then to Commercial Road (and fish and chips from the paper) just about the time the local working girls were dispatched - probably by their pimps - from sleek, black cars. Culture, we decided, could wait, although having discovered Gilbert and Sullivan at school - not exactly heavy stuff but a step up from our usual - I dragged a reluctant G. to a couple of excellent productions in obscure locations. To his amazement he became hooked, remaining so to this day.

But back to early April, and with the flat finally organized, it was time to look for a job. Thanks to a friend, I soon found myself being interviewed and subsequently engaged as 'Grill Chef' in a branch of an old established wine-bar, near the Strand. Mr. D. my prospective employer, a beetle-browed Dracula lookalike (Bela Lugosi, early Hollywood) turned out to be a man of remarkably few words. Odd for someone whose job required a certain sociability. Following the first

Mummy July 69 W super Mare

brief questions he suddenly stood up and said "Right" before grabbing my elbow and briskly, steering me toward what would be, perhaps, my working space - the end of a long, mahogany bar, complete with six high stools. Carefully, I listened, as in filtered sentences my duties were listed. With his voice gathering momentum, the dark meet-in-the-middle eyebrows took on a life of their own, the longest hairs thrusting upwards like a set of curious antennae. Transfixed, I stared shamelessly until somewhere a phone rang and he dashed away, leaving me to check out the equipment. Someone, it seemed, had thought of everything. Behind the counter sat a decent-sized stainless steel sink and drainer, beneath which was a small 'fridge, where a quick peek revealed eggs, bacon, 'burgers,' sausages and four packs of Stork margarine. To the left, against the centre wall, sat a large, solid electric hotplate, with a tall metal 'hot' cupboard, just about wide enough to take a stack of plates and some bread rolls. Opposite, the remaining space held shelves containing napkins, cutlery, sauces and sets of salts and peppers. With some good scissors and a sharp knife, we'd be about ready to go.

'Trade varies' Mr. D. had said. Indeed. 'We open at ten thirty but you're here by nine. Prompt. Sausages take longest, so get them on first...You stop serving at two, we close at three. You finish at three thirty... Everything to be left shipshape. Right? And no dirty dishes. You'll be responsible for all food ordering. Right? And in case you wanted to know, it's six pounds a week, Monday to Friday - plus tips...Not that you'll get much out of this lot.' He then gestured towards the hotplate. 'Bit of a bugger that... Stuff sticks.. .You'll see..."The entire delivery of this speech must have lasted at least ten seconds but ever the optimist, I decided he'd probably improve with knowing.

The following Monday, having arrived early, intending to 'prove' the hotplate prior to cooking, I switched it on, smeared the surface with olive oil and after sprinkling over the salt, left it all to heat through. Available only from a chemist, the oil had been expensive, but anything to avoid the possibility of losing custom or struggling with sticking, mangled food on day one. Totally absorbed, attacking my target with a thick pad of greaseproof paper, I jumped, turning as Mr. D, thumbs in his braces, stood muttering quizzically 'Ere. What you 'doin?' Swiftly, I explained the usual cure for a rogue metal cooking surface but, this being Monday morning, within seconds he'd simply shaken his head, muttered a disbelieving "Gettaway" and rushed off to check a delivery.

By 2pm our stools had accommodated a steady stream of middle-aged men, many of whom might have qualified as models for 'Tailor and Cutter,' each bearing either a copy of The Times or Telegraph (can never once recall serving a woman during my almost six months of working there). Swiftly, papers folded to the appropriate pages, my neat lines of males had sat steadily chomping their way through rapidly dispensed permutations of egg, bacon, sausage or 'burger, nestled deep inside either a Stork 'buttered' soft, white roll or uniform slices of equally soft, white bread - courtesy of our daily deliverer, Mr. Wonderloaf, '50s Britain's favourite baker. Grateful that the first lunchtime session had - so far - produced neither disaster nor death, I set to, clearing the debris before inspecting the saucer - put out by Mr. D. - for tips. It looked hopeful and having carefully emptied the coins onto a paper napkin, I totted up the spoils. Amazing. Just under ten shillings, almost fifty pence. Not bad for day one considering my weekly wage was only six pounds. From nowhere, Mr. D. appeared. "Well girlie" he said ('Girlie..') "Ow much you got in that saucer then"? I actually told him the truth, but decided immediately that with this man, honesty was probably not the best policy. My tips were my business.

That evening, the Beloved, anxious to hear the day's news, delightedly decided that my weekly wage could perhaps be almost doubled with a few more customers, but agreed that tips were my department alone and nothing to do with Dracula: 'You earn them, you keep them and if he asks, just halve it.' He was, of course, right but as the summer became hotter and both tourists and trade increased, so did the tips. Having become familiar with the regulars - in the main, a pleasant and generous bunch - I enjoyed the job and being naturally curious, would have loved more time to chat, but with the volume of trade, our exchanges were limited to little more than a few quips and inquiries about the new cheeseboard.

The weeks flew past. September steamed its way into October and an Indian Summer and with business still remarkably brisk, Dracula even smiled occasionally - though usually in the direction of the tips saucer. Finally, one Friday afternoon, having just handed over my brown envelope, he made an announcement which went something like "Right, girlie. I think it's time we sorted out your tips"... Patting nose with forefinger, he continued 'I also reckon, having kept an eye on things, that you've probably doubled your wages ...Well, I don't think we can have that, can we? In future, as the manager, it's half to me... OK. Understand?" It wasn't and I understood perfectly. Then, Mother's voice echoed. 'Dreadful man...Tell him you're not there to be exploited and that he may keep his job. Just walk out with dignity'. O.K. Briefly, with limited confidence and pounding heart, I said my piece, finally adding one or two well-spaced remarks regarding the treatment of staff, and swiftly left the premises. Oh, for a camera. Never before, anywhere, had I witnessed on anyone's face such total disbelief.

Stomping indignantly down Villiers Street towards the Tube (though unsure that my speedy departure had been the right move) I thought ruefully of the customers, hoping my replacement would look after them. But there could be no turning back: although Husband, being something of a negotiator, might well disagree. As it happened, whilst discussing the day over supper, he agreed my reasons for leaving were right, but that walking out had been wrong.

'You've left him in the lurch' he said. 'Unfair'. Maybe. But it was too late now. Feeling unreasonably resentful but not yet willing to admit he might have a point; childlike, I sulked my way to bed.

The following week was news week. G. announced that in January, we'd be rejoining the Battalion, then based in Dover, for just three months, before sailing ("In a real ship?"... "No, a canoe") to either Africa or the Persian Gulf. Apparently, two thirds of the regiment was destined for Kenya and the remainder for Bahrain. I fancied the latter and G. had no preference but knowing it would be either, we realized that life was about to change with a capital "C".

Indeed. With Christmas - split between Clapham and the Tower - safely over, we had our first real discussion regarding the forthcoming move. This led on to "The Boxes": large, wooden, containers, provided by Uncle Army, the number required to be assessed by me, which once packed, went on to G., who fitted and screwed down the lids before they were taken off to a military workshop somewhere and banded with metal. Whilst totally unqualified for such things, I took a guess and decided that three would be about right. Having in the past watched various removal men pack china (amongst other things

Mother was a great mover) in tea chests, G, happily met my requests for cartons and newspapers (our one real extravagance being two dailies and six Sundays, tabloid to broadsheet, plus weekly editions of The Spectator and The New Statesman).

And so it came to pass that surrounded by our assorted breakables, the first real packing of my new life began. All before the big clean-up. Oh joy. Never once did I think at the time that twenty-five years or so later, I'd still be at it.

Economical Fish Pie (for 4)

400 grm. fresh white fish, coley cod or haddock +200grm undyed smoked haddock, poach together in 300ml milk (10 mins) reserve liquid - or, large tin of tuna in brine or tinned pink salmon, drained. Flake chosen fish into heatproof dish. Add 50grm frozen prawns.

5 largish potatoes, cooked and mashed with pepper, butter and a little milk. Mix in one med. onion, chopped and softened in butter or oil

Make sauce from cooking liquid + 1flat tabsp, plain flour +25 grm butter - add 1 tabsp. Anchovy sauce + 1 tabsp. mayonnaise. No extra salt needed. If too thick add little extra milk

100grm strong cheddar, grated.

Cover fish with sauce and top with mashed potato. Rough-up with fork and sprinkle over grated cheese. Cook in oven heated to 180c for 25mins. Serve with spinach.

Chapter Six

G. HAD BEEN FAIRLY QUIET regarding our new home, apart from 'It's due for renovation... Sub-standard actually...We won't be paying the full rent... But it'll be for less than four months... And you'll sort it out, I'm sure'. Somewhere in the distance was a faint peal of bells: alarm type bells.

Sometime in mid-January, the bitterly cold train from Charing-Cross slid slowly into the unprepossessing and even icier delights of Dover Priory Station; the Beloved having travelled down in a three-ton military vehicle with 'My men'. Tightly grasping my lifeline, a carrier bag containing - unbelievably - paper twists and a bundle of wood ('You'll need to light a fire as soon as you arrive - the coal I ordered was delivered last week, so don't worry') I skidded along the empty platform and out of the station in search of a cab.

The one thing in the house's favour, perhaps the only thing, was its proximity to the local NAAFI shop, less than a hundred yards away. Numb with cold, I was, initially, luckily, for just a short time - totally incapable of appreciating the reality and awfulness of it all. First stop had been the kitchen where every surface was covered with - in strict alphabetical order as per the inventory - piles of ancient cooking kit, some very large, others very rusty, some both large and rusty. But it was the brick walls that really resurrected the alarm bells. Mm-mm. A combination of thick, pitted and peeling bottle-green and mustard paint (Plaster. ..Dear me, no) complete with rivulets of running water (Leak? Damp? Condensation?) Cooker came there none. Instead, a derelict-looking black(ish) kitchen range would be providing our meals for the next few months. "How are the mighty fallen". Indeed. At that particular moment, the thought of flushing the now Very unBeloved, followed briskly by a gallon of bleach, down the nearest loo, was strangely comforting. Next, came the tiny, damp sitting-room complete with two damp rugs and two damp armchairs. Taking a deep breath before mounting the stairs to inspect the one bedroom, I reached the top and opened the door: all equally damp; complete with broken bed and piles of sodden blankets and linen, clean but wet. Furiously, I thundered down to the kitchen and having grabbed a container, made my way to the garden in search of a coal bunker. Heat, that's what was needed... 'But when she got there...' Jumping, I quickly gazed upwards as a broad Lancashire voice shouted down from a neighbouring window 'Yer coal's bin pinched. All coal round 'ere's pinched. I'm Joyce. I'll lend yer a booket if yer like.' Dear Joyce. She did, plus a pot of tea, some toast, and many kind words of commiseration, plus a few choice phrases featuring 'The bloody army'.

Husband's first evening in his new home is best overlooked. Enough to say that, the following day I began to scour and dry out the house and after a few furniture replacements, life improved - and at least our black range turned out to be a boon, keeping the kitchen snug and cooking our many pies and casseroles beautifully. Not once did it let us down, proving far more reliable than the sulky Rayburn of my previous life. But no matter how almost reasonable we felt the house to be, one thing was certain, Mama must not be allowed within spitting distance. Having shut off the sitting-room and moved the armchairs into the kitchen (where we lived until we left) Mummy-entertaining wasn't an option and we kept in touch via the red 'phone box, nearby. Her disapproval of everything - justified or not - would have created angst beyond belief so we simply battened down the hatches, joined the mobile library, listened to the radio and teamed up with friends for the occasional meal. Luckily, with the Arctic winter lasting almost into April, Mother was in no rush to visit dreary old Dover.

And G had been right; time was passing swiftly and with the new posting just seven weeks away, he returned home one evening with instructions to 'Think about packing for Bahrain', our first choice. Riveted by early bible-stories (resulting in several childhood searches for my very own Moses) as well as believing 'Tales from the Arabian Nights' to be more fact than fiction, the thought of becoming part of it all made me tingle: the reality of the world moving on a few hundred years or so seeming totally irrelevant.

But so far, as a fairly new army wife, I'd had little to do with 'the system' and barely considered its meaning, until one morning, two or three weeks before we were due to leave, I answered the door to an attractive young woman who introduced herself as the wife of a senior officer, G's immediate boss. Briefly, over coffee, she explained that

Charlottenburg schloss in Berlin, summer 1970 G B Don & friend

we would shortly be visiting the young wife of a Corporal who 'Has problems ... particularly on overseas postings when she is inclined to become over-friendly with the local males. She has a propensity for turning out in sheer nylon blouses... And her husband is such a nice man.' Puzzled, I asked 'But what on earth is that to do with us, surely it's hardly our business?' Mrs. C gazed at me pityingly as if I'd suddenly announced that water was wet. 'Any bad behaviour reflects poorly on the regiment. There were problems in Germany, then later in Khartoum, and with Bahrain also being an Islamic country we have to ensure that she realises the meaning of the word 'decorum'.

Desperate for a glimpse of the regimental Jezebel, my expectations promptly dissolved when fifteen minutes or so later we were shown into the gleaming sitting-room of a small house, by a thirty-ish, dumpy woman with glasses and mousy over-permed hair. Carefully, over more coffee, Mrs. C. breezily announced that we'd 'Just come along to chat about the new posting and were there any queries' before gently but eloquently, moving on to the problems of dress, behaviour and status of women in Muslim countries, ending with a matey 'And of course, we always have to consider our husband's promotion..' A true lesson in diplomacy. Neither a patronising word nor a blatant warning. I was full of admiration. (Although the entire conversation resurfaced some fifteen months later when, assembled on the quayside at Sitra, bidding farewell to our Bahrain friends before boarding the ship for our next posting, Malta, one couldn't help but witness the touching tableau nearby as Mrs D said a sad and lengthy adieu to a dark, strikingly handsome male who must have been a very good friend indeed, judging from the copious stream of tears. Stoically, just yards away, her spouse had stood, staring firmly in the opposite direction, eyes fixed upon his boys.)

And so packing for our first 'deep sea' move began, One of the compensations of living close to the NAAFI meant an endless supply of cardboard cartons, before G went in search of' dead 'pillows. Working on the assumption that all breakables had to be wrapped tightly in newspaper, so that nothing moved, and the base of each box then lined with pillows, as well as extra between the cartons and on the top, we needed lots - ensuring that once the lid was screwed down, the entire container would be rigid...Finished at last. With the boxes stowed safely in the barracks we discussed the big clean-up 'So unnecessary' I groaned 'The builders will be moving in virtually as we move out.' True. But rules were rules.

Economical Savoury Pancakes (for 4)

Make pancake batter from 125grm plain flour, 1 beaten egg, pinch salt, 300 mls half milk, half water. I tabsp. Oil. Blend all together (in liquidiser if poss). Leave to stand in or out of fridge for an hour or so.

Filling:

I med. onion, finely chopped and softened in oil then add half a red pepper, thinly sliced - cook until soft.

Any chopped leftovers of ham, chicken, corned beef, bacon or pork.

3 or 4 chopped mushrooms - cooked in oil or butter for a moment or two.

Make sauce from 15 grm. butter, 1 flat tabsp. plain flour and scant 300mls either stock or creamy milk (melt butter, stir in flour, gradually add liquid and cook for 2 mins. Stir in chosen filling and season).

25grms, grated strong cheddar

As each pancake cooks, spoon in filling and roll pancake up - place in lightly greased ovenproof dish.

When all mixtures used, sprinkle cheese over pancakes and heat through in hot oven for 10 or so mins. (175/180c).

Welsh Rarebit. (More than cheese on toast)

Mixture - covered - will not spoil if left in fridge for a day or two. I slice bread p.person - toasted on one side only.

Mix together 175grms strong cheddar cheese, one small beaten egg, teaspn. made mustard, one egg-cup beer or stout & dess. sp. chutney-optional.

Spread on uncooked side of toast and place under hot grill until brown (ish).

Chapter Seven

Two weeks later, with all upheaval of moving forgotten, we stood in the early afternoon sun at Southampton Docks, waiting to board Her Majesty's Troopship, the white and gleaming Dunera. The first glance of a large passenger ship can be overwhelming and I was uncharacteristically silent. 'Impressed?' G. had said grinning, as we joined the queue for cabin allocation. I nodded, and as the paperwork was checked and waved through, he murmured 'Right, follow me' and off we trekked, along what felt like a mile of rabbit warrens. Then 'That's us, on the left.' Mmm. Compact, immaculately clean with double bunks - 'Bags I the top' - and a porthole. As we unpacked, G explained that only Warrant Officers and above were allocated 'Accompanied' cabins, whilst wives of lower ranks shared with each other.

Horrified, I remarked sharply that the only good thing about such an unfair system was the fact that we wouldn't have the daily embarrassment of facing his sister-in-law and brother (a Sergeant in the regiment and travelling alone, his wife to be called forward at a later date) knowing they'd slept apart. The whole principle struck me as totally wrong, particularly as it inevitably created a great deal of bad feeling.

The scene at Southampton later that afternoon reminded me of an old newsreel I'd seen, featuring evacuees. As the ship took its slow and stately leave of the docks, the Regimental band boomed out from the top deck, whilst the cheering crowds waved flags toward friends and relatives watching from the quay. All rather moving, particularly as we'd not long completed our own family goodbyes.

The following three weeks was virtually one long jolly, with the men working only part-time and wifely chores limited solely to laundry. We ate: often and well. Cooked breakfasts, three-course lunches, tea - the real thing, sandwiches and cakes - and four-course dinners, plus extra alcohol. Such was our gluttony, maintained not only by a lack of bathroom scales but also the delusion that our leisurely trots around the decks might actually reduce our bulging waistlines.

The first shore-leave was a morning in Gibraltar, which, with its red telephone boxes and red pillar boxes, left us with the impression of having pitched up on a distant and previously unexplored part of Surrey - complete with palm trees, colourful Bougainvillea, and open-fronted shops. English seemed to be spoken everywhere and the majority of windows appeared to be curtained with large Union Jack flags. After shopping for souvenirs and coffee in the English tearooms, it was time to visit the apes, which turned out to be more tactile than expected and quite scary. Something to do with all those sets of sharp, yellow teeth.

As we moved into the Bay of Biscay, G .a desperately poor sailor, tottered down from the swiftly emptying dining area, to our cabin, where he quietly groaned his way through the next 48hours. I, having inherited Mother's addiction to vertiginous fairground rides, found it exciting and with a remarkable lack of imagination, despite the violent switchback heaving of the ship, never once considered the possibility of disaster. It wasn't until day three, when extra-choppy seas found us anchored far from the harbour, that the appearance of a large launch to take off the Cyprus-bound passengers alerted me as to how rough our ride had actually been.

A day or two later, after a leisurely journey through the, now problem-free, Suez Canal, bordered, as my six-year-old self recalled from bible-story illustrations, by sand, date-palms and the odd small, flat-roofed house, we set-down closer to the coast and haggled for local giftware with the Egyptian 'Bum-boat' owners. Next, came the 'Gully-Gully' men, practiced entertainers, who came on board to show-off their skilled and zippy magic routines. With no previous experience of Egyptians I found them chatty, full of fun - especially when entertaining children - and with a sense of humour similar to our own. 'Just remember' said Husband, 'It's your money they're after'. True. But one barely noticed, so skilled were they at extracting it. And anyway, it was all too exciting to matter.'Just a day or two more ' G. had said that morning, 'And we'll be there.'

Corned Beef Hash (for 4) Children love it.

One and a half tins corned beef – crumble into heatproof dish and mix with 2 large (ish) chopped onions, first softened in oil for about 10 mins over low heat.

Add 1 large tin baked beans

Sprinkle with brown, tomato or Worcester sauce and fork together.

Cook 5 largish potatoes and mash well with butter, pepper and milk. Fork over top and add sprinkle of grated cheese. Cook in hot oven 185c – for about 30 mins.

'Fresh Cream' (a good substitute for real cream).

260ml fresh creamy milk - but UHT works well too

225grm Unsalted butter - OR de-salt salted butter by adding 225ml water to 225 salted butter - bring slowly to boil - remove from heat and place pan in 'fridge until butter solid. Remove and throw away salted water. Replace butter in pan with milk and heat - do not boil. Pour half into blender and whizz for about 2mins. Pour into jug and repeat with other half. Stir and leave in 'fridge pref. overnight but about 2 hrs. is fine. Will whip.

Chapter Eight

AT LAST. BAHRAIN, where a third of us disembarked, leaving the others to cruise on to Kenya. Once settled in a rather elderly bus, we bounced along the rutted road, chatting with the two other families destined for 'Our patch' before being dropped off on a narrow track by a clearing of dark-green, pebble dashed, flat-roofed bungalows. Ours was No 1, and sitting on the steps leading up to our front door, was a dark, bearded man wearing an immaculate white djellaba. Waving a file he called out to us 'Hello, hello, welcome to my country, welcome. I am Yusef, your agent'.

Leaving our luggage in the wide hall, we followed 'our agent' into an L-shaped sitting/dining room, complete with six fly-proofed windows, off-white tiled floors and magnolia-painted walls. Furniture was brown and '40s style, comprising an uncut-brown moquette three piece suite, and a coffee table; at the dining-end stood a brown varnished table, six chairs, a sideboard and a tea-trolley. Next came the bedrooms, both doubles and both, almost-but-not-quite, en-suite, with furniture similar in style to the rest. Each bedroom had an air-conditioner slotted into the wall and every room, so far, had a fitted ceiling-fan. We couldn't believe our luck - all this lovely space, and two bathrooms - in 1958. For just us. There had to be a hitch. 'And now the kitchen' said Yusef, throwing open a door. It was a reasonable size, if a little dark, but the furniture seemed okay; a pale, wooden kitchen table, four chairs, three glass-fronted cupboards, a stainless-steel sink and drainer and a sizeable 'fridge...But there seemed to be something missing. Ah yes. Against a wall on the right-hand side of the room, stood a four-legged, metal-framed 'thing': maybe two thirds of a metre in length, waist high and a third of a metre across. Hanging upside-down, on the left, was a metal-lidded squat, glass bottle containing, maybe, just over half a litre or so of pale-pink liquid, and further along were three burners, similar to those found in old oil-lamps (recognised from part of my childhood spent in a beautiful - but electricity-free - Welsh country house). In front of each burner was a small brass screw. On. And Off. Surely it wasn't? Couldn't be? Was it? It was - the hitch: the cooker. Our former kitchen range instantly became highly desirable. G, having not yet caught on, glanced around and said brightly to Yusef 'There's no cooker '. Yusef's smile would have lit the darkest room. 'Here', he announced jubilantly, pointing to the object. 'Oil cooker'. I tried to look suitably impressed before murmuring weakly 'Oven. Is there an oven?' Looking as if he'd just been offered a free trip to Mecca, Yusef reached down and triumphantly pulled up a black, square, metal box which he then placed proudly over two of the burners 'See? He beamed. 'Oven. Good, Yes?' Oh yes. Excellent.

Forty eight hours later, with the fridge filled and the cooker sussed (sort of) we unpacked the boxes. Just a handful of minor breakages. Then, having thoroughly examined the furniture and discussed finances, it became apparent that the Families Officer could have landed a far better deal on the furnishing front. The monthly rental for such poor quality goods seemed excessive. 'Sorry' said G. 'I've no time to sort it out... All I know is it's a family business and you'll need to deal with Ibrahim. OK?'

Ibrahim turned out to operate from a cool, modern, pristine office, at the top end of Manama, the capital. Twentyish, and very good-looking, he sat facing me, immaculate in a light, exquisitely-tailored suit, listening politely, without interrupting, as slowly, I explained our problem. In excellent English, he replied 'I understand perfectly We shall go to the warehouse and you may choose from the selection of furniture there. Come.' After a swift trip in a red and black Cadillac, air-conditioned of course, we pulled up outside a one-storey building where I was given the run of what felt like Aladdin's Cave. Within the hour, I'd virtually re-furnished the house but followed Ibrahim's advice to retain 'the oil cooker' which at least worked, rather than replace it with a modern electric one, our power cuts, apparently, being long and frequent.

Once back at the office, having first presented me with an iced coca-cola, Ibrahim sat scribbling on a pad before announcing 'The new charges will be' and quoted a whopping figure. Whatever made me imagine we could probably just do a straight swap. Oh... Tentatively, my (very small) voice said 'But I thought we might do a straight swap?'

'But your new choices are of a higher quality' he replied calmly. 'But that's why I chose them'.

He seemed to find this amusing and masking a smile said kindly 'I think you need a larger air-conditioner in your sitting-room. I will change the one you have and with all the new furniture, your bill will be just twenty-one rupees extra a month.' Such tact. He seemed happy and I certainly was: no wonder he became a good friend.

Bahrain turned out to be everything this novice traveller had imagined. Super exotic, hot, and initially, before the humidity set-in, dry. Shopping was fascinating. It was all fascinating, particularly the gold market with its dazzling window displays; never top of my personal list of wants, but a revelation nontheless. Happily, we'd wander the fruit and veg. markets, haggling for produce, before moving on to Moon Stores, a small supermarket selling groceries, frozen meat, and smoked rashers of streaky bacon from the U.S, all rolled in greaseproof paper and sold in tins. Apart from several open-fronted shops, offering everything from enamel jugs and basins to nail polish, there was Ashraf, a small but well stocked department store. Everywhere, staff were helpful, courteous and always trusting. A small example of this was, when having bought a record-player shortly after arriving, we were shopping a few months later and spotted by the store owner. Beckoning us inside, he rushed toward the till, opened it and handing G a twenty rupee note, said excitedly 'You pay more. Yes?' Having caught on instantly (not I) my astonished husband replied 'You mean I pay too much?' Yes' replied our Bahraini gent, smiling broadly. 'Too much, too much.' Such honesty.

Now more or less settled, we rated our existence as idyllic, barring the heat and the wild-life: spiders and roaches - both being ugly and king-sized - plus hordes of flying ants. We'd made several new friends, discovered the joys of Zellaq beach - all white sand and crystal water - joined the camp library and bought a car... The master of instant decisions had arrived home driving a large, solid 'two-tone' (black and real rust) vehicle:a two-door American Ford, similar to that once much-beloved of Al Capone. It had cost an entire £35 but 'At that price, a real bargain...Goes like a rocket'. Each Saturday morning, armed with a large can of shiny, black spray-paint, G would painstakingly cover the rust patches, although due to the climate, the periods of enhancement were short. For our entire stay, that car was soon the butt of a stream of jokey remarks from the young boys manning the local car park who delighted in showing off their grasp of the vernacular with 'Oh Sir. Very smart car, Sir. I wash your new car, sir? Car very posh, Sir...' (Prior to leaving, we sold it for ten pounds over the original purchase price - freshly sprayed of course - and G. hoped the buyer would continue to use the same parking place, if only for the boys amusement).

Sometime after my nineteenth birthday, celebrated with a party on our flat roof, we reasoned that the apparent sickness bug from which I'd been suffering might actually have another cause. Whilst hazy on the calculating front, the clue might just have been the time spent on my knees worshipping the porcelain. Next stop: Maternity department

G in Alberta 73

of the Bahrain Government Womens' Hospital. 'No doubt here' said my new consultant, Dr. Doeg, a jolly, dry-humoured Scottish woman, before forecasting D. Day as 'Somewhere around 22 February' (it was then August). 'I'll see you again in a month.' Stacked with iron, vitamin pills and 'Something for the nausea' I couldn't wait to get home. Thrilled and thankful, and so far problem-free, we began to eagerly look forward to February. Unfortunately, due to the effect of the pungent pongs of kitchen kerosene on my newly-delicate digestive system, cooking had become a chore. Local eateries - bar small cafes - hadn't looked too promising, but one evening, I blanched as G announced what to expect at a meal we'd been invited to share, with a new friend, at a local hotel.

His first sentence was fine 'It'll probably be some sort of spiced lamb and rice. Mould it into small balls, using only your right hand' then 'But if you're offered the sheep's eye - really, a great honour - I'm afraid you'll have to swallow it'. Mmm. With luck, I might die first. A few days later, we followed our host across a dimly-lit, hotel dining-room, to a white-clothed table, complete with immaculate starched napkins. 'I order very special meal for you. Yes?' Smiling, we thanked him. Perhaps as the male guest of honour, G, (please) might be first on the big-treat list, which, he'd kindly explained, usually came at the end of the main course. With a broad grin the waiter then handed each of us a hand-written menu. The spelling was interesting but it all translated as 'Brown Windsor Soup, Roast Beef and Yorkshire Pudding, Prunes and custard and coffee.' Oh these lovely people - to have gone to so much trouble on our behalf. Thank you Lord. As enthusiastically as possible, we tucked in. The sheep's eye could wait.

Just before Christmas '58, due to a delicate situation further along the Gulf, the remainder of the battalion, until then based in Kenya, suddenly appeared in Bahrain, minus their wives. 'We must invite a few people for lunch. You know. Christmas ' said G. taking pity on them. Rapidly, the list grew to a cosy twelve around a table designed for eight, maximum. We discussed a menu - not exactly haute cuisine but choice was limited and kind friends opposite offered their electric oven. The turkey cooked beautifully, but rushing between the houses, I tripped, staring helplessly as our glistening, brown bird flew straight up into the air, landing neck first, in a heap of sand. Deep-breathing time. Later however, our gritty offering, rinsed and patted dry, was carved and served with - fried - stuffing, tinned, creamed sweet corn and frozen vegetables plus (vaguely) roast potatoes. But the gremlins were still out. As our guests finished their NAAFI Christmas pud - served with evaporated milk - I stood in the kitchen, still blushing at my round of 'Applause for the cook' whilst carefully pouring boiling water into a large pyrex jug. Almost immediately, and with a loud crack, the jug shattered as flying glass and scalding coffee grounds rapidly distributed themselves over my seven month old bump. Few deep breaths of restraint this time.

Come January, shortly before G took off to the Sharjah desert on a training exercise, Ibrahim joined us for supper. The two men got along well and prior to leaving, Ibrahim, on hearing I'd be alone for six weeks, asked G's permission to 'Take Beverley to the cinema,' in Awali, the oil town, a few miles away - or 'Out to dinner. You know I'll look after her.' G agreed, but later it occurred to me that as an unaccompanied Christian, married, pregnant European female, I might well be considered by the family of a Muslim male to be the epitomy of unsuitable company for their unattached son. 'Just explain that to him.' said G. later that evening. 'He'll understand'.

G was right. A couple of weeks later, Ibrahim, having listened carefully to my explanation as to why I was refusing his offer of an evening out, simply nodded and said 'I understand, but please don't worry. I'll pick you up at seven'. Which is how I ended up being driven across a starlit desert to spend the evening in a distant cinema with five young Bahraini men, watching 'The Sun Also Rises,' not a word of which four of my handsome chaperones were able to understand.

It was an interesting six weeks. A storm, the force of which had never before been experienced by the Bahrainis, featured golf-ball sized hailstones. Judged to be not only rare, but precious, these previously unseen offerings were promptly scooped up and placed into pockets along with any other handy container. A day or two later it was locusts. Very biblical. The disposal of these poor creatures, dead from crashing overnight in their hundreds against our closed windows, left, instead of Ali, our recently recruited houseboy (apparently enjoying an awayday) just me, to reluctantly and tearfully sweep into piles the pale-green transparent bodies, all resembling giant grasshoppers. Next came floods - three in all. The villagers nearby suffered badly, being housed in Barastis - flimsy, self-built huts - but we also managed to acquire a waterlogged house, due to a small, outstanding repair featuring a drainage pipe overhanging the porch. Whilst gardeners, sent by agent Yusef, swept out the water, I moved in with Tess, a lovely Irish friend, who lived opposite. But by day four, fearing another flood and with the house still sodden and the pipe still leaking, I stopped the monthly rent cheque - previously always handed over on the due date - following several promises to 'Repair pipe.' The result of my high-handed, but desperate action, was the instant appearance of three workmen whose speedy solution reduced me to choking giggles by its sheer simplicity: a length of slightly wider piping, pushed onto the end of the original to extend it - all secured by a metre or so of strong, thick string.

Staying with Tess, always full of tales from her nursing days, seemed an ideal time for a detailed session of ' Enquire Within' regarding the actual birth process. Needing to seriously update five years of school biology, it seemed reasonable to hope that a qualified midwife and mother would willingly enlighten her dopey friend, whose ignorance had led to increasingly lengthy and uncomfortable periods of speculation, complete with magnifying mirror, whilst closeted in the bathroom. Even the book 'Becoming a Mother', purchased just after our news was confirmed, skirted coyly over the pain aspect, and any photos featuring second and third stage labour simply sent me scurrying back to the bathroom. All I needed were a few straight answers. Instead, my tactful questioning produced the oddest responses, as if the release of any useful information equalled treason. It was 'You'll find out soon enough' accompanied by knowing nods, even from Tess, who'd added 'Well, in my experience, no two births are the same. But don't worry. You'll be fine.'

Shortly afterwards, two weeks before the exercise was due to finish, G appeared late one evening, quite unexpectedly. Following a lack of mail (we wrote daily) and desperate for news, he'd accepted a lift on an overnight military flight, but was due back in Sharjah early the following morning. Faced with the appearance of a deeply tanned, long-haired - by military standards - red-mustachio'd (red?) stranger, who, complete with Arab head-dress, seemed to have replaced my short-back-and-sided, clean-shaven husband, our new minder, a large, beige, boney refugee from a pack of scavenging pi-dogs, went into full, protective mode. Grateful for his presence, we stood at the door watching as growling softly, he slowly circled my bemused, but totally immobile husband. "Pleased to see you're being well looked after' he said and after kissing both Tess and I consulted his watch murmuring' Sorry I couldn't warn you, but as I'm being picked up at 5am, may we go home, please.'

Feb. 22 came and went. Time our little lodger found a new home. Half-way through March, with my ability to count constantly in doubt, I watched anxiously and enviously, patting my bump, as friends packed for Malta, our next posting. Finally, it was 'Right. In you come. We'll start things off. But on day four when all viable medication had failed 'The baby hasn't engaged... 'I was allowed home, daily, between the hours of ten am to ten pm.

At last. On 23rd March, naturally and without a hitch, our gorgeous, eight and a half pound son arrived. We named him Simon. We were the proudest parents of the most beautiful baby ever born.. Of course. Recovery was swift. But as visions of filling our boxes overtook all previously imagined spells of quiet leisure spent in baby talk, baby-gazing and lullabies, it was 'Please, I do need to get home...' Really? Away from my comfortable room, where the press of a bell produced not only piles of clean nappies but also delicious meals plus tea and coffee served from silver pots, with fresh cows milk sent up from the one experimental farm, along the coast.. But why not? Our little 'hoover' was sleeping and feeding well. Dr.D. appeared puzzled. 'We've cut it down from fourteen days to ten and now you want to leave in less than a week. Surely your husband can see to the packing...' (Today's new mums, out in 24hrs.would question the fuss). Day seven and the three of us were home, complete with a mountain of instructions, a bottle of scarlet Mecurachrome, for the still-attached cord, and a hundred or so pills. How strange everything felt.

Just a month later to the day, with the house packed up, scoured and 'Marched Out,' we stood on the quayside at Sitra, once more waiting to board the Dunera. Our furniture, viewed by the incoming occupant and deemed 'Too pricey', had been removed early, due to a mix-up between delivery times, so with nowhere to feed our babe, bar the loo, I went ahead and took advantage of the seat. Our initially sleepy bundle of loveliness however, no doubt due to my anxiety of trying to fit in real life around the packing, had, shortly after arriving home, become a victim of (according to Dr. Spock's Baby and Child

Care manual, our new bible) 'Six pm colic'. Regularly, for the previous two weeks, at 6:45pm, I'd sat anxiously in the back of the car, patting Simon's back, whilst G drove us round and round until our exhausted babe finally dropped off. With luck the motion of the ship would have the same effect. Dr. D. had granted me leave to travel purely on the understanding that I continued to breastfeed saying 'Ship's water is no good for young babies. I don't care how long it's boiled for'.

Abracadabra. A week into the voyage and he was comatose from six till six. At last, with time to plan, we considered the possibility of a shipboard baptism and following a chat with the priest, arranged it for the following Sunday, after the morning Service. With the ship's bell utilised as a font, Simon - who gave not a squeak throughout - was christened on the high seas, with G's best friends as Godparents. Unlike our wedding, we actually have the photos.

Lamb Pilaff (for 4)

800 grm. Lean, cubed lamb

10 dried apricots

One large finely chopped onion, and 3 cloves garlic fried gently in oil for about 10 mins. (do not brown)

300gr. Long grain rice

Mix of oil and butter for browning lamb (about 50grm butter + 2 tabsp. oil of choice)

3 teasp. coriander seeds, 3 teasp. cumin seeds, teasp. ground cinnamon, 2 tabsp. Flaked almonds. Ground black pepper and salt to taste.

Generous 900mls. thin stock

Half bunch finely chopped coriander.

Heat oil with butter and brown lamb in batches on stove in heatproof casserole dish. Remove and add rice to pan and stir continuously until all rice coated in oil. Turn rice into a bowl and reserve. Grind spices with mortar and pestle and stir them into the onion.. Pour on hot stock and bring to boil. Add meat, and apricots season well. Cover with lid and cook in oven at 160c for 1hr. Remove from oven to top of stove and add rice to dish; return to simmer, stirring well. Cover and return to oven (now at 175c) for 25 mins or so until rice is tender and majority of liquid has been absorbed. Stir well and check seasoning.Toast almonds and strew with coriander over top before serving.

Chapter Nine

STEEPED IN HISTORY AND WITH AN ATTRACTIVE CLIMATE, Malta, in May, still green from the Winter rain, appeared an exciting place in which to spend the next two years, particularly as for the first six weeks, we along with other families, were to be housed in an hotel. Full of optimism after an interesting drive from the docks, we were dropped off in time for lunch at a pleasant building on the seafront, in the town of Sliema. Whilst lunch was fine, our accommodation was grim, squalid, in fact, lacking several basics, and our request for a cot ignored. Mr. Unavailable, the manager, finally tracked down on day three, was shamed into action. Within hours our room had been thoroughly cleaned, the hand basin unblocked, a new cot supplied for our rapidly expanding infant, along with new twin divans and rugs, working bedside lamps, with shades - a pile of fresh towels - and the curtains re-hung on new fittings. At G's inquiry as to what actually produced such a prompt reaction I suggested that maybe it had something to do with my restrained but cutting delivery rounded off with a 'We'd expected rather more of Maltese hospitality.'

Soon, with Simon in a new pushchair we explored the town, usually accompanied by the dreamy tones of Dean Martin's 'Volare' or 'Mambo Italiano, pulsing out from the bars. The Maltese, mostly fluent English speakers (their seldom-mastered-by-outsiders native tongue being a mix of Arabic and Phoenicean) appeared gregarious, helpful and friendly, peering cheerfully into Simon's shaded pushchair with a complimentary remark. We braved the local buses (king-sized dodgems) all owner-driver and each equipped with its own tiny shrine, watching closely as everyone paid their fare with one hand whilst crossing themselves with the other. Acknowledging the Almighty before travelling soon struck us as a very good move indeed.

Before long, G, by then restless and disenchanted with hotel life, decided - with no quarter in sight - to accept the offer of a hiring, situated in the desirable area of Balzan. As our stay there - just about three months - would be too long to live out of suitcases, it would mean unpacking the boxes.

Our new home, owned by two elderly sisters, was the top floor of an old, c1800, honey-coloured house, situated near the lovely San Anton Gardens. Once installed, most evenings after Simon's supper and bath, we'd pop him in his pushchair and head for the Gardens to spend an hour or so ambling through the shade of the lush, vibrantly coloured avenues of tall Bougainvillea. (I believe, the powerful and influential Archbishop Gonzi had a home there, political reports of the time consisting mainly of the ongoing loggerhead situation between Gonzi and Dom Mintoff, the Maltese anti-British Prime Minister, caused by Mintoff's overtures towards an alliance with Libya to which the Archbishop was vehemently opposed.) But, Balzan being far from the barracks, we'd need a car. This time it was a second (third? fourth?) hand, tiny, shiny beige Austin: two doors but four seats. As I recall, it never once let us down despite Husband's propensity for attempting to explore every track and inaccessible inch of the island.

With good regimental friends, also waiting for a quarter, living nearby, we enjoyed the civilian environment, along with the house. We had no garden, though ample roof-space, and as summer hotted-up the thick old walls kept the interior - a large bedroom, sitting-room and kitchen, plus an ancient bathroom complete with equally ancient plumbing - really quite cool. We were even lucky enough to find a young girl willing, for a reasonable rate, to help out with baby-sitting and ironing. Cheerful and energetic, Frances, the eldest of nine, turned out to be not only super-efficient on the baby front, but on every other front too, and stayed with us until we left for home.

Too soon it was moving-time again.'We've been allocated a house just outside the barracks. Sorry' said G. 'More packing But it means I can walk to work and after driving lessons you can have the car'. Immediately I pictured myself at the wheel of our tiny chariot, negotiating - dodgem style - the Sliema-Valetta main road.

Our new home, a renovated, turn of the century and rather cramped, two bed. semi-detached army quarter, one of several close to the camp, lacked all the charm of the old. But at least it was clean. Sad to leave Balzan, I tried to adjust, but found our semi. impossible to love, perhaps sensing what lay ahead. But as was fast becoming a pattern, we settled in and soon, it became home.

Scarcely a week later, my sister, Celeste, now taller, chattier and with short hair, and Mother - impossibly a grandmother and looking wonderfully youthful and glamorous - landed at Luqa airport; plus a friend (something of an instant decision, this holiday.) As plans to settle them into a nearby flat melted ('Too far away') a quick reshuffle saw us all in together, at home. Cosy, but it worked and with temperatures similar to those of an English July, the island was at its best. My sister loved her new nephew and Mother loved it all, though disapproved strongly of her grandson's pre-bedtime quickie at the breast. 'Should have been off all that months ago. Not to mention all those teeth.' I recall giving a wry nod. Six months equalled - unusually - six teeth.

Exercise time again.'Six weeks in Libya' said G. 'And I might even be back for our anniversary'. Having passed the driving test, plus a thumbs up from G., I was now available for shopping trips; interesting little sorties to outlying villages where small, friendly shops produced delicious fresh fruit and veg, rabbits, fish and local tomato paste at 500grm for six old pence, and bring-your-own-bottle-just-about-drinkable wines for one old shilling - with the production company's name of S. Crechi and Sons, it was promptly christened 'Screetch' by the soldiers.

Before the men flew off we'd surprisingly been issued with a free delivery of coal. The days were mostly still warm and it was hard to imagine needing a real fire, but later, in the dank November/December drizzle, we relished the extra heat.With husbands absent, Service wives become closer, relying heavily on each other for company, baby-sitting and general help. Indeed, despite the differences between '50's women and those of today, the friendships formed then will probably last for life, although Mrs 2012, often with either a job or a career to consider,

D~~ad~~ in Berlin
Aged 13
Summer 76

will have less time to spare for organised Wives' Clubs or coffee mornings.

After our first Christmas as a threesome, a trip to the M.O. confirmed that, come September, we'd be four. With just eighteen months between our siblings, life would certainly be focused, with perhaps more chance of them becoming good friends. Happily we looked forward, dripping our way through a broiling Summer, although the island climate usually produced a breeze somewhere. Great for Husband who, as the Sailing Club's newest and most fervent recruit, had taken to disappearing at weekends.

Nicola, our first daughter, was born on 6 September, 1960, and died, three months later, in the British Military hospital, in Malta, of Cystic Fibrosis. Our exquisite baby, with dark, soft curls, deep blue eyes and the palest of skin, had, at 7lbs 14 oz, appeared healthy. To everyone but me. From my first glimpse at the very moment of her birth - just the two of us - the neglectful staff being otherwise engaged, the usual emotions, delight, excitement and joy, were strangely absent. Instead, I was swamped by a surge of inexplicable, intense sadness, along with a fear that following her swift entry into the world, the cool air pulsing from the frantically whirling ceiling-fan would leave her severely chilled. On day nine, whilst still eight ounces short of her birth weight but having gained just one ounce (discovered when I suggested she be test-weighed before and after each feed) Nicola and I were discharged: despite the fact that from day three, she'd suffered severe diarrohea. I was told 'She might have to go on the bottle: your milk is probably upsetting her.' After almost two weeks at home, Nicola's symptoms, which by now included a cough, worsened, and we battled desperately between surgery, baby clinics and a Consultant Peadiatrician, who appeared unconcerned that at four weeks of age she had only just regained her birth weight. Meanwhile, the handful of symptoms describing Cystic Fibrosis, then known as Pancreatic Fibrosis, in our copy of 'Dr Spock's Baby and Child Care' (an American publication) fitted her totally. Fretting and pleading constantly for tests, I begged for a hearing, but was loudly shouted down and then ignored. Finally, after thirty minutes with a new consultant - who not only listened quietly but had actually experienced C. F. at first hand - Nicola was admitted to hospital. Two weeks later, the bleak diagnosis confirmed, she died.

So extreme was her condition that maybe, even with today's expertise, she may have survived little more than a month or two longer. However, whilst professional lack of knowledge and experience can sometimes be acceptable, arrogance and rudeness, combined with a total lack of kindness or understanding are surely inexcusable. Suffice to say that the expertise and caring attitude of the majority of today's medical profession, to which it is vital to stress here, my husband and I both most gratefully owe our lives, once included among its ranks, those who had difficulty accepting a patient's ability to walk, talk and perhaps even think at the same time. Over the past fifty years this has improved beyond recognition.

By February we were once again surrounded by packing cases and bound for Colchester. The bad news was that Simon and I were to travel home on H.M.Troopship, Dilwara 'Unaccompanied' whilst G, as usual part of the Advance Party, flew on ahead. With our two best friends already in England, it was not a good time to be making the trip without him.

Chapter Ten

THE MONTHS FOLLOWING NICOLA'S DEATH passed in a fog, suppressed grief leaving me, for once, with fewer detailed memories than usual.

G's early arrival meant he'd already taken over and moved into the house and bought a car - I believe, a Ford Anglia. He'd also rented a television - our first. Situated on the corner of a noisy main road, the small army quarter, a red-brick semi, resembling part of everyman's Council Estate, eventually began to feel like home. Colchester is an ancient attractive town, near the coast, but my enthusiasm for virtually everything, including exploration, had vanished. Weeks passed and we celebrated Simon's second birthday. Tall, and well advanced, he was a naturally curious toddler who chatted fluently to us, whilst inclined to be shy with others, he was also inclined to pick up any stray bug: no doubt the result of my over-anxious surveillance. We longed for another baby but I was unable to totally dismiss the possibility of CF recurring in a second child, although we'd been told before leaving Malta 'It's like Mongolism, Mrs Pettifar' (the term 'Downs Syndrome' not then, apparently, in common usage) 'We have no idea why it happens. Go away and have a dozen babies...' But the feeling persisted and when G. left, in July, for Kenya, on an open-ended emergency tour, we were no further ahead.

Somehow, the next four months passed, due, in part to our large, corner garden, combined with the fact that our particular part of Essex held all the prizes for strong, profuse bindweed. Come September, my persistence with the hoe yielded piles of healthy potatoes, carrots, onions, beans, lettuce, tomatoes and strawberries as earlier, during April, anxious to use the space, G. had planted them all..

That Summer, as well as vegetables, I'd collected several new acquaintances, including members of the nearby Jehovah's Witness church, Kingdom Hall. Finding a captive audience, they were only too happy to chat and I, at the time severely at odds with my lapsed R.C. Faith, was equally happy to listen, finding them, Peter, and his shy, Indian wife Jaya, interesting and gentle, if not very credible. As the days shortened, their visits, by now quite regular, included their joining Simon and me in the kitchen, for the odd coffee or lunchtime snack.

Meanwhile, irregular letters arrived from G, who for several weeks had been stuck in Aden, lacking the transport to proceed further (in the shape of an abundance of planes minus seats, several of which having arrived without, were consequently sent back). 'We are' he wrote ' V. cheesed-off and doubtful as to whether we'll be home for Christmas...' It was then early October and they'd left on 4 July. 'Independence Day' I'd thought sourly. At one time a passing senior officer had knocked on the front door and rather hesitantly, asked if I knew the actual 'Whereabouts of the advance party' (G. being a member). 'Stuck in Aden, waiting for a plane with seats' had been my polite, but somewhat acid reply, adding that I'd begun addressing my mail to 'The Forgotten Army.' Then, after four months absence, which had included less than a month's stay in Kenya, on 5 November - our anniversary - totally unexpectedly, the warrior returned. His face, on learning that supper, that first evening home would include our new friends, Peter and Jaya, had been a picture.

Before the month was out G had not only received a posting order, to Bury, in Lancashire, but had also been promoted to the rank of Regimental Sergeant Major. He'd be the new R.S.M. of the Territorial section of the Lancashire Fusiliers, based directly in the town, at the old Castle Armouries. 'And we'll be moving before Christmas...' Heigh ho.

Once more began the familiar pattern of 'Pack, scour and march out' this time included a very sad farewell to good friends who had eased me through the summer.

Toad -in-the-Hole for 4 (Family Favourite).

First make batter from 2 eggs, 300mls milk and water (half & half), 125grms sieved plain flour, good pinch salt. Whizz all together in blender for 3-5 mins. Reserve.

10 or 12 good pork sausages – quarter cook and reserve.

Slice 1 large onion thinly and soften in oil, halve 4 tomatoes. Place all, with sausages, in a metal, not non-stick, baking tin and add 25 grm. lard or 2 tablesp. olive oil. Heat oven to 210c, add baking tin for 2-3 mins until lard,or oil, is hot. Stir batter and pour batter over sausages etc., Cook for 25/30 mins. until batter well risen.

Baked Stuffed Apples (for 4)

4 evenly sized cooking apples – cored..

Mix just over half jar of sweet mincement with nuts of choice and fill cored apples.

Place in heatproof dish with cup of water or apple juice. Sprinkle with Demerara sugar and place in oven 200c for about 25 mins. or until soft (depends on size of apples).

Chapter Eleven

LEAVING COLCHESTER WAS HARDLY A WRENCH but having never before lived North of Watford, we looked forward to the change. 'Bloody cold' a friend had said 'But lovely people'. She was right on both counts. So-o cold: even dreary Dover ran a close second. But the locals turned out to be kind, helpful, friendly and always first with a dry quip. Our introduction to the members of the Sergeants' Mess and their wives produced the warmest of welcomes, complete with vast helpings of Lancashire's favourite dish (bar the delicious and famous Bury Black Pudding) a home-made Meat and Potato Pie. That first evening was to be the first of many 'Socials,' full of local gossip, laughter and always questions. 'How did you two get together? What's the age difference, then? You're really young to be an RSM's wife (I was 21). Bit of 'ard bugger, your man... but fair; likes things doon reet...Like that at home, is ee?' No punches were ever pulled and somewhat startled, I'd reply as honestly as I could. But their candour took some getting used to.

The house, one of four owned by the M.O.D. in a civilian area, was a three bedroomed semi, and a considerable improvement on the last; but as for heating...The sitting-room fire, in the usual inadequate, small, tiled fireplace, housed a back boiler which, despite the services of a local sweep, stubbornly refused to function. G; working each weekend - such are the joys the T.A. Posting - but with Wednesdays off!- produced a selection of oil heaters, which, dotted throughout, kept the room temperatures just above freezing (daylight hours only) but soon, getting up each morning to ice-covered bedroom windows, complete with decoratively rusty small, square steel frames, became the norm. How spoiled we'd been that first perfect year in our cosy Tower of London flat.

The Christmas of '61, one of the coldest on record, was spent with mother, in Surrey. It was to be our first visit to her lovely beamed cottage, and after a five or so hour's drive from Lancashire (the then infant MI covering barely more than forty or so miles) we arrived, looking forward to a huge log fire and a cosy kitchen. Lavishly decorated with branches of holly, gilded ivy and fir cones, the house oozed season's greetings but being somewhat out on a limb, had yet to receive the benefits of either mains gas or electricity. That year, the generator, housed in a garage, kept us all guessing, functioning as it did on a maybe or maybe-not basis, whilst the container of calor-gas, essential to feed the cooker, had frozen solid in the sub-zero temperatures. This left the quixotic kitchen Rayburn. Also, the sitting-room inglenook chimney had recently cast its cowl and, depending on wind direction, sometimes enabled us watch TV and, due to either quality or quantity of the day's smoke, sometimes not. But we bumbled along - G. acting as intrepid chief shopper when ten days of extra guests (we'd intended leaving after five but heeded the AA warnings) produced a shortage of supplies. Finally, despite the adverse conditions, come Twelfth Night, we packed the car and, joined by my sister, set off for home. Several hours later, the journey North increasingly resembling a wiped-out wasteland, we pulled up outside the house, praying hard 'No burst pipes. Please...' During the eleven-plus hours it had taken us to drive from Surrey, we'd passed less than thirty moving vehicles.

By the end of March, my third pregnancy was confirmed. Our new GP proved no stranger to Cystic Fibrosis, due to some close friends, both medical, having lost two children with it.

Two...He explained the accepted odds were one in four. Shocked, but not really surprised, I begged him to be totally frank, and promising not to panic, stressed the difficulty of dealing with a situation when minus the full facts. A day or so later (for maybe a whole two minutes) we considered his offer of a termination, by which time G had also read an informative article from the B.M.J., produced by a concerned medical friend. We decided to go ahead. From now on it would be hope and prayer.

Domini, our beloved daughter arrived safely - and late - weighing in at nine and a half pounds, on 25 September, 1962 at Fairfield Hospital, Bury. Born shortly before midnight, I remember the midwife later summoning two of the incoming day staff with a 'Just coom and look at this little lass; 'ow about that for a loovely little bum.' The staff of Fairfield Hospital were among the most kind and efficient anywhere and despite my angst, there was no shortage of humour. One memorable trainee nurse, a young redhead, with glowing skin, would skip down the ward with the breakfast trolley, barely stopping as she tossed us each a boiled egg with a cheery 'C'mon. Wake oop - Catch!' On day two, my tentative request for an eggcup was met with a broad grin and a 'What do you want one 'o them for? It's not posh in 'ere, y' know.' I also remember a very weary mum who, having just produced her tenth, announced loudly to us all 'Well, that's that. Ten's enoof fer any booger an ah've warned 'im - coom near me with yer bright ideas an' ah'll bloody coot it off.'

Three days before Dom and I were due to be discharged, having learned more of CF over the previous months, I confessed my fears to one of the ward-sisters. Aware that the (then) definitive test wouldn't be possible for some time, due to the fact that as well as lung problems, an enzyme, vital for a fully-functioning digestive system, Trypsin, is often not formed for the first months of life. In other words, we were in for what felt like a long wait. The result of this conversation was that a Consultant Paediatrician, Dr. Basil Wolman, one of the kindest and most empathetic of men, as well as one of the most skilled in his field, was called in from Bury General Hospital and immediately agreed to take Dom into his care. How very lucky we felt when he included his home telephone number 'Just in case' on the back of his card. Happily, we never needed to use it. We saw him three times, at monthly intervals, and just before Christmas he decided to test for Trypsin, fully explaining the possibility of it being a long shot - the usual age for testing being six months. Dom was so obviously thriving and 'I'd so love to give you good news for Christmas'... Alas, the result was negative but such was the faith he inspired, we'd have been churlish to have lost heart. We also had tremendous support from our GP: an understanding gem of a man and father of three girls under five who, soon after Dom and I arrived home, took to popping in for a quick morning coffee and 'A look. Just to see how she's doing.' No visits have ever been more appreciated. We 'd got to know him quite well, some weeks earlier, when he'd seen me through a bout of pneumonia and pleurisy, our Summer holiday (G's idea, bless him) having included three nights in a tent in a very damp field in Somerset. 'I think Simon's old enough to enjoy camping now...'

Soon, we were faced with another problem. Simon, by then almost four, often sprouted high temperatures, sore throats and bouts of sickness. Whilst usually treated with antibiotics, a firm diagnosis remained elusive, being put down to either 'Tonsils' or 'A virus', but on hearing from Dr. W, that a young CF patient aged six had recently died, I haltingly asked if it were possible that Simon might also be affected - until then believing CF to be a purely infantile illness. Quietly, he suggested that he would take both children in for testing. As our gorgeous smiley girl, who seldom cried unless hungry, became a happy seven-month-old, both children were admitted to the care of Bury General Hospital. Simon, under the impression he was there purely as company for his sister, accepted the situation with equanimity but soon began to complain that 'I know I'm only here to look after Dom, but why do they do everything to me that they do to her...' Each day, we would leave our empty house and after dropping me at the hospital, G. would go on to the Drill Hall before appearing again around 5pm. In those early days, parents, though permitted to spend the days in the ward with their children, were not accommodated at night, so once we'd done baths and bedtime stories, off we'd go, bereft, to our quiet house. The entire scenario felt unreal and when day ten 'Going-home day' arrived, before visiting the ward, we first shakily presented ourselves at Sister's office for the verdict. The poor woman looked shattered. 'I'm so very sorry. Dr. Wolman is in the States for two weeks, lecturing, and he's the only person qualified to read the results for you. I thought you'd been told.'

Just two weeks later, Dr. W opened his office door and patting both our shoulders said quickly, with a broad smile 'It's all right. Don't worry: You have two healthy children. Congratulations'. We could scarcely believe our luck and I recall thinking how there really, really had to be a God. Some ten years or so ago, whilst reading Dr. Wolman's obituary in The Telegraph I just felt so enormously grateful that we, and so many others, had been so very fortunate to have had our lives changed by his knowledge, skill and care.

And so life in Bury, now unbelievably minus the threatening shadow of C.F., began slowly to fall into place. Whilst attachment to the TA for a regular soldier has its moments, it is seldom considered Mrs.Average-Army-Wife's favourite posting, due to the husband's working life requiring two or three regular evenings a week 'at work' as well as weekends. TA soldiers, being employed on a part-time basis, all have civilian jobs, which leaves only the weekends and evenings for Exercises and Training.

Bury was then and doubtless still is, a busy town, full of humour. I remember the street markets; heaps of bargains, as well as the thriving, covered market, all surrounded by beautiful, wild countryside. There, just a mile out of town, we celebrated our good news at a then, fairly new French Restaurant, 'La Normandie' - spiffy occasions only - started by a wonderful chef, Yves Champeau, which is now, we recently learned, owned by his son. The weather was seldom lovely (very seldom) but friends made up for any disadvantages and we certainly laughed a lot. One couple, close neighbours, with similar-aged children, introduced us to the Roulette tables and Alma Cogan in cabaret - all froth and bounce, and the tiniest waist - at the Manchester Whisky A Gogo nightclub, and it was Betty, a slender, stunning, blue-eyed Strawberry-blonde, who, one day in M&S told me 'Ooh Bev, we don't buy white undies oop 'ere; you'll find all the lace 'ems of yer slips black by the end of day. The air's really moocky.' They were such fun; down to earth, kind, and exceptionally generous, and we stayed in touch for years. We also got to know a couple of the original cast of Coronation St, now long gone, who, as honorary members of the Sgts' Mess, turned up at several Saturday evening parties. Interestingly, they looked and sounded exactly as they appeared on screen. And it was on a typical rainy Manchester night we saw our first James Bond film, 'Goldfinger,' as well as braving the local Chinese restaurant (I say 'braving' due to speculative reports in the local press regarding the final whereabouts of a few absent moggies). Our outings, all then being down to Mother who, with us for a couple of weeks, had kindly stepped in as babysitter. Unimpressed by her surroundings her succinct summing-up of 'The North' had been a simple 'Hmm. Rains a lot here.'

And then we were off. Sutton Coldfield this time -'The Midlands' ('Oh God. The Midlands' said Mama) a new experience for us both.

Mother's Hotpot. (for 4)

8 good-sized pieces of trimmed best end of neck of lamb - or 1200grms. trimmed lamb chops

4 lambs kidneys: skinned, core removed and quartered + 120 grms sliced mushrooms, 2 large chopped onions + (optional) 2 cloves garlic crushed, all softened for 5 mins in oil. Good sprig fresh thyme.4./5 thickly sliced potatoes, all brushed with melted butter or oil.

3 medium carrots,peeled and sliced. Chop 4 anchovies (drained) and mix with 500mls.stock and splash of wine.

Flour and fry kidneys briefly. Then chop 4 drained anchovies and add to stock. Butter base of a large casserole and season -add layer of potatoes. Layer all ingredients in casserole, finishing with potatoes. Shake over salt, pepper Worcester sauce and stock to almost cover potatoes.

Cover and cook in middle of oven - 160c about 3 hrs then uncover and brush potatoes with butter. Return to oven for abt.a half hr.and turn up heat to brown potatoes

Chapter Twelve

OUR MOVE, IN THE SUMMER OF '62, had gone smoothly, following a great send-off from members of the Bury Sergeants' Mess. We'd shed few tears on vacating our Lancastrian ice-house with its boggy garden and, while there's usually a downside to moving, by now it was becoming a habit and we seldom lost touch with good mates. G. was also happy with the new job - RSM of the Regimental Depot, in St George's Barracks - and delighted to be back with the Regular Army. On a warm August day, just prior to Dom's first birthday, in a suburb a few miles short of Birmingham, we took over our three bedroomed quarter - the only M.O.D. property at the end of a quiet, civilian road. The garden was small and our immediate neighbours friendly and hospitable. Within walking distance was a primary school, for now-almost-five Simon, plus a reasonable parade of shops. And the house

Brunei '78 April Good Friday. A trip up river Bev dragging a prau

sparkled - oh joy. The unpacking seemed to take less time than usual (maybe I could join Pickfords) and with decor the usual green and cream, our only surprise was the provision of a sofa AND two armchairs. Progress indeed.

Soon, Simon, articulate and tall for his age, was happily settled into school, whereas Dom preferred to point to her needs rather than to vocalise them. Having uttered scarcely a word until a month or so before her second birthday, to everyone's astonishment, she began chatting away in complete sentences, virtually non-stop, to anyone and everyone. Both our young showed signs of possessing a good sense of humour and we never stopped considering how very lucky we were to be the parents of two normal children. We discovered, that first freezing Winter, that the town had been aptly named due to the lack of high ground between it and the Ural Mountains in Russia. But a bonus, even in the winter, was Sutton Park, much of which, resembling open country, was great for young families. Shortly, we'd also found a reliable babysitter. Pat, a lovely girl, the eldest of a family of four and in her final year at school, turned out to be a real asset. Capable, tall and slim, her thick curtain of dark hair and fringe often almost obscuring her face, she was, following a quiet start, soon full of teenage chat, mostly about Twiggy and The Beatles, particularly Paul, her idol, with George a close second, dreams of both occupying most of her waking moments. Years later, imagining her with a growing brood of her own, we heard that instead, childless by design, she and her husband had settled for a dynasty of miniature Yorkshire Terriers.

Our social life revolved mainly around the Sgts. Mess and as wife of the RSM, I had more to do with Wives' Club evenings than previously. These monthly meetings gave people the chance to air their grievances, often proving invaluable for getting to the root of a particular bit of unkind gossip or welfare problem. When we weren't playing Bingo or just chatting, there would be trips to nearby places of interest, an occasional demonstration with a Tupperware agent, or an Avon make-up consultant; or simply a meal out. Not a male stripper in sight.

At the end of that first year in Sutton, Major Frank Daly, the Quartermaster, suffered a severe stroke, which saw him invalided out of the Army. Frank, and Vicki, his wife, had been a popular couple and would be much-missed. However, with the gap needing to be filled, within the month, G. was offered and accepted a Commission, appearing for lunch one day minus the leather wrist band on which had previously sat a brass Royal coat-of-arms. Instead, his shoulder epaulettes boasted gleaming Lieutenant's pips but sadly, I noticed nothing and, grimacing, he was forced to point them out. A couple of weeks later he was promoted to Captain.

A commission meant another move but this time, less than a mile away, up to 'The Patch' (all groups of officers' homes are known as patches.) This one lay just off a main road, close to the barracks and was one of a dozen houses-with-garage some of which - ours included - were detached. We had our usual three beds. but elevation had its advantages, superior furniture being just one. A mahogany desk and nest of tables, a tea-trolley! and a 'fridge - as well as thicker curtains and a larger sofa and chairs, complete with linen loose covers. China and kitchen gear was a notch up the scale too, and we had carpets: not fitted, but who was complaining. In the kitchen, always warm in winter, thanks to the boiler, I was to make bread, until our strained seams - all that extra butter - sent me scuttling back to the local baker. Our new neighbours were kind and exceptionally welcoming and despite the muttered warnings that 'It'll never work, moving up there; you'll find it really snotty' our transition to patch life couldn't have been easier. Forty seven years later, we still have treasured friends from those first two years

Initially, life as an officer meant funding several extras, mainly in the wardrobe department. Scraping the barrel to finance extra suits and shirts, G was delighted and grateful when a reasonably priced second-hand Mess- Kit and British-Warm overcoat materialised from someone of similar shape (who was exchanging his commission for Holy Orders). I needed smartening up too - though jeans for daytime were still mostly fine - if not quite as fine as they are now. And Mother turned up trumps on the hat scene; having once modelled them, she had stacks, and usually the best, bar the odd 'find' somewhere: such perfect bone-structure turned even a flower-pot into a Treacy.

Swiftly, kitchen creativity came into its own, despite my belief that just about every thrifty permutation had been fully explored. It was interesting to discover that we were all pretty well on the same budget when it came to food, with joined-up meat reserved mainly for dinner-parties. Casual patch suppers produced interesting variations of vegetable stews, meat loaf, sausage and kidney casserole, Spag. Bol., (very) economical fish pies, and a selection of 'whatever' with rice - and one bottle of wine - though more at a dinner-party (but not much). As No 1 on everyone's agenda was school fees - we were all either saving like mad or actually paying them - cash was at a premium. The civilian belief that the government issued all three Services with free accommodation, free utilities, free coal and free public-schooling, was for many years, rife, but true neither then nor now. In an effort to provide our young with continuity of education (though there were always families who chose to keep their children at home) we were able to claim one third toward boarding- fees, be the choice Eton or a BFES (British Forces Educational Services) school and the allowance was not scaled according to fees. There was a small subsidy on furnished housing (rents were never considered 'economical') and for gas, electricity, fuel and water, the rules applied as for any other civilian household - we coughed up. The only 'freebies' I recall was the startling one hundredweight of free coal issued to help see us through the Winter, in Malta, and much later, free housing and utilities, financed by the Sultan of Brunei, to whose army G. was attached for almost three years towards the end of his service. There were always a few fortunate souls whose families produced fees either from a Trust or who just chose to help, but on the whole, we'd have a grouse with our friends about the stingy salaries, the army, sometimes our husbands for being part of it, the government (though strangely pay rises were usually more generous under Labour than Tory) and then of course, got on with it all. As Infantry regiments sometimes find themselves on a regular 'Tour Roster', with each tour averaging four and a half months in the case of Northern Ireland, where the regiment completed six in just under four years (plus the usual overseas training exercises) it is easy to understand the resulting number of complaints and welfare problems. But, we'd chosen our lives and in comparison with today's situation, one cannot help but feel that while the ultimate price has been paid by many, there were others, ourselves included, who had very little to complain about.

As the children grew, wives took jobs: now the norm. then, less so. In my own case, being neither nurse, teacher nor secretary - usually the first to find themselves employable, I began looking for something part-time that would fit in with school hours and those of our cleaner, a jolly, reliable, middle-aged woman who came for three hours a week as a 'Batwoman' (phased out by the next set of Government cuts) who said she'd be delighted to combine some extra work with 'Keeping an eye on your scrumptious Dom.'

But life is full of surprises. Just a day or so later, Husband, looking very pleased with himself, arrived home one mid-morning, carrying a gorgeous, squidgy baby boy, who I guessed to be about a year old. From a lightly tanned face, surrounded by blonde, wavy curls, large brown eyes stared unblinkingly across the kitchen at me in that disconcerting mind-reading baby way - the one in which all babies seem to specialise. What a cherub. 'Present for you' said G. 'His name's Ricky and he's ten months old.' Then, handing him over he looked at his watch and said 'Must dash... He needs looking after for a bit... Problems at home.' Grinning at Ricky he said 'This is Bev. She'll look after you. You'll like her.' (Maybe not the exact words but it all went something like that). Then 'Fill you in later. OK? Oh - a cot and playpen will be delivered in about an hour.' (Such are the powers of the Quartermaster) 'Er. Clothes?' I said 'Nappies. Bottle?''There's a grip some-where, with some kit. I'll send someone over with it. You'll have to improvise till then. Bye.' No-one has ever once accused my husband of wasting words.

Obviously well-used to strangers, Ricky turned out to be a little treasure. Placid and smiley never once during his entire six weeks stay did he refuse a meal or produce a real tantrum. He ate and slept well, played with his toys, seemed happy when popped into the spacious playpen, and grinned at everyone. I wasn't wild about returning to the nappy front - all by hand then, Dom being eleven before we ran to a washing machine - but it was Summer and we could always rely on a strong drying wind, straight from the Urals. And with Ricky insufficiently mobile to interfere with their kit, the children found our new situation something of a novelty.

Meanwhile, G. worked on finding Ricky's parents a house. The father, a young soldier whose wife lived with her parents in a cramped East London flat, had, following a disastrous weekend's visit, simply thrown a few things into a bag, scooped up his son, and brought him back to barracks, where after a tip-off, he'd been found by G. The soldier, given leave to sort out his problems, was, before long, reconciled and settled in a two bedroomed quarter, with his family.

So it was back to the Sits. Vac. page. Choice was limited but before long, having replied to a large ad. I found myself about to join the fascinating, frustrating, and often hysterically funny, ranks of the Market Researcher.

Oxtail Casserole (for 4)

3 large onions + 3 garlic cloves, thinly sliced +1 large red pepper, thinly sliced and de-seeded.

2 tabsp. Olive oil

Heat oil and add 1kilo oxtail - brown all over - remove; then add onions, garlic and pepper to oil - cook until soft and browned. Transfer to casserole dish. Then stir in the following and season :

Juice and grated rind of an orange

120g pitted prunes – halved

3 bay leaves

260mls dry cider

Teasp. Juniper berries

I tin chopped tomatoes.

Heat oven to 230c. Put covered casserole on shelf and cook for about 20 mins, till liquid just bubbling. Then turn down heat to 135c and continue cooking for 2 and a half hrs, or longer if oxtail tough. Test with a fork.

Chapter Thirteen

'LADIES, EARN CASH IN YOUR SPARE TIME' the ad. had said 'Fit in with your children's school day. Market Researchers, with clean driving licences are required to carry out interesting work. Good rates of pay and expenses. Full training given.' Well...Having completed the necessary paperwork, I accepted an invitation to join the three-day training course; turning up, plus the other thirty-nine applicants, a week or so later, at a nearby country hotel. The two company recruiters possessed the ability to make carrying out surveys on just about everything from loo paper to politics, sound as fascinating a pastime as being an invisible member of the royal household. Though maybe not quite fascinating enough. By day three, our number had dwindled to fifteen, of which I was one. Having explained the basics of the job, along with 'Good interviewing techniques' we then learned about 'Quotas' and how to find and slot the required members of the public into the correct boxes. Quotas were structured by profession, beginning at the top with the A's and B's, usually located in either large, single, detached houses or smart estates, down to 'Retired, Unemployed and/or 'Registered Unemployed' normally found on council property. The As and Bs, usually the easiest to slot in, were tackled first and then it was a question of working through the remainder. In the early days, needing to complete my quota but lacking experience, I found myself hunting a single, unemployed female, aged between fifty and sixty-five, resident in a C 1 household where the 'Head of the Household' was male and in full employment. Thanks to a local G.P., my probably one - and - only was finally tracked down, 'done' and ticked off.

Looking back, it seems extraordinary that the general public were, by and large, happy to reply honestly to the mass of intrusive questions: Age? Married/Single? Employed/Unemployed? Income-bracket? Number/Ages of children? Tenant/Owner? Number of bedrooms? In fact almost everything bar the colour of their underwear. Incidentally, the majority of interviews were carried out in respondent's homes so one had to either hope to be invited in or complete the interview on the doorstep. No wonder the entire scenario has changed. When asked 'How long will this take' the answer was always 'Just a few minutes, depending on your replies...' And one learned never to linger in case they changed their minds half way through. After training, and accompanied by a supervisor for the first two or three surveys, we'd be 'in the field' and if then considered sufficiently competent, would be sent out alone, armed with a stack of pens, a sandwich and an up-to-date map of the area. Luckily, I began in the summer and quite enjoyed it all, but winter could be grim. We worked to a deadline, selecting our hours to suit, and if unable to work; no problem. And rates of pay? The completion of an average length survey, 6/7 pages, requiring 30/50 interviews, would yield, in 1965, perhaps £14, plus six old pence per mile, for petrol. Wealth indeed.

Cheating was rife. One woman, who, having filled her quota (proving the respondents actually existed) then had her husband complete the questionnaires at home. Company checks, we were warned, were frequent, but she was never once caught out and despite admiring her nerve, I wasn't brave enough to follow suit (although later, was known to finish-off the odd form when told 'That's enough...Too many questions').

It was an interesting two years. My first summer turned up a farmer, solidly belted (with rope) and booted, who, finally convinced I really wasn't part of the 'Min. of Ag'(riculture) breezed through it all, swiftly answering every query before asking 'Interested in paintings?' I was then hauled off to his drawing-room to view two exquisite Gainsborough?? paintings, each maybe six feet in height. 'Copies?' he said, at my gentle inquiry 'Course them's not bloody copies. Got them in the War. Some bugger owed me money...Them's real. And worth a pretty penny.'When asked had they been registered, his reply had been a blank stare.

Then there was the time when advised by a neighbour not to call on ' The loonies at number twelve'. I did. At the open door, having shown my card and explained my mission to the seemingly pleasant woman facing me, I was invited in and left with husband. Less than five minutes later the woman suddenly reappeared, waving a long carving knife and screaming 'Get out 'a my 'ouse: leave my 'usband alone. Load a muck, load a muck...' I fled, almost knocking flat the worried-looking resident from next-door-but-one who'd advised me earlier against calling there. 'You had a lucky escape' she said. 'Maybe I should have told you more about them; but it seemed wrong. She's been 'In' you know. For treatment. And he goes on the cider...' Later, my first street survey involved two two-hour stints outside a local Co-op. the subject being favourite brands of loo paper. By the end of the day, I knew both the lavatorial habits and medical histories of just about every Co-op user in the vicinity: amazing how willing people are to spill out reams of totally unsolicited - and in this case seriously unattractive - information to a total stranger. A few weeks on, I agreed to take on a tedious 'Baked Bean' survey, involving four visits per house, spread over the month. The day's final participant involved Mr Pukka himself, who, sitting opposite and clad in a smart, silk dressing gown 'So sorry. Just out of the bath' sat languidly pondering the question 'Would you rate last week's bean samples as too large, too small or normal-sized ?' Awaiting his reply, I watched as his legs slowly uncrossed and the robe parted, exposing a full set of crown jewels, unencumbered by nothing so boring as Boxers or Y-Fronts. I doubt it was intentional, but unwilling to take the time to find out, fiery-faced, I looked him straight in the eye and brought the interview to a swift conclusion with a breathless 'Thank you. Please don't move. I'll see myself out.'

The realisation that we were almost on cue to leave the chilly Midlands, came suddenly, with a posting order to Watchet, a small coastal town in North Somerset. Apart from the weather, we'd enjoyed the past three years, made many good friends and once again, moving would be a case of mixed blessings. Dom was almost ready to start school and Simon, at nearly eight had become a voracious and fluent reader, thanks largely to the help of Miss Evans, a teacher who'd spurred him on with the Narnia series. He had now spent almost three years at Falcon Lodge Junior; but it was time to seriously start thinking of prep schools. We'd discussed it as a family and so far, Simon had raised no objections and as a child of the Services, appeared to accept that it was the only real way of receiving an almost uninterrupted education. However, whilst times had changed, my own unhappy experiences still loomed large and the thought of him experiencing a similar degree of misery was deeply unsettling. Unfortunately, when asked much later, as adults, how they'd felt about boarding, both Simon and Dom remarked that whilst they'd had no real objections at the time, it was unlikely they'd have owned up to them anyway as 'Children usually tell parents what they want to hear'. How we do fool ourselves.

Finally, after discussions with friends Weave and Trevor Phillips, we took their advice and decided to view Trevor's old prep school, St. Dunstan's, at Burnham-on-Sea, where Andrew, his eldest son, was about to begin his last term. Also, along with the Headmaster remaining a firm friend of Trevor's since their schooldays, there were other considerations, such as the mere 30 miles between school and our new home, plus the close proximity of 'Granny P, Trevor's mother - well-known to Simon from her regular visits to Sutton - and who, living so close to the school, was used to Andrew and his friends drifting in and out of her flat.

Our first sight of St.D's, situated just yards from the beach, was favourable and soon, the Headmaster's attitude and manner, along with the school's homely atmosphere and cheerful-looking boys, left us agreeing that provided Simon gave the thumbs-up, we'd enroll him. By the end of the following weekend, he'd approved it all and would be starting his new life in early April. I remember, driving in the drizzle to Burnham for the start of the Summer term, having stopped in Bristol for lunch and a trip to the Zoo, keeping up the flow of bright chat reserved for such times and which fools nobody; certainly not a child. Dom, who had been left with the Phillips for the night, had kissed her brother goodbye somewhat enviously, seeing the coming term as a succession of beach games and midnight feasts.

All too soon we were there; unloading an overstuffed Tuck-box (bravely banned by several of today's schools) and searching under the seat for Simon's small leaving gift, to be opened when we'd left for home. After an interview with Matron, he'd been whizzed off with the other 'new bugs' to his dormitory, to unpack, supported by Andrew Phillips, who had travelled down with us. Smilingly, we'd been waved off. Attempting to heed the advice of 'Don't draw out the goodbyes ' I kept my own smile firmly fixed until out of sight. On our way to give Watchet the once-over, the floodgates opened and I sat overwhelmed and grizzling, convinced that sending one's much-loved offspring away at such a young age probably qualified us for some obscure child-cruelty order. Such is the misery and guilt of Mothers: Fathers appear to have more sense of proportion about such things. I suspected that any tears on Simon's part would be saved for the privacy of his bed. Whilst an exceptionally sensitive child, he'd never been one for displays of public waterworks.

Watchet turned out to be a quaint little town; calm, unhurried and steeped in history and with an amazing natural harbour. That particular evening, the breeze was sharp : but it was only April. The surrounding countryside was exceptionally beautiful; soft green fields and rolling hills, punctuated by small villages, many of them medieval. Much of the area had featured, two or three years earlier, in the rollicking film 'Tom Jones' with many of the crew housed in 'The Foresters' our chosen B & B for the night. After a couple of hours exploring, taking-in the 'patch', to which we'd be moving later that year, we returned to the Foresters for supper and bed. Roll on August.

Chapter Fourteen

ST. D'S' SEEMED TO HAVE BEEN A GOOD CHOICE. Simon seemed cheerful, had made two or three friends, complained little about either the school, the staff or his diet - which though stodgy - sounded wholesome and plentiful, and now and again, visited Granny P, with Andrew. That first week, I'd telephoned every other day and then we received our first letter: a little brief, but as OK as one could hope for. (Unlike a poor friend, whose son, at another school, instead of writing 'Dear Mummy and Daddy', had begun 'Dear Major and Mrs - my

Simon & G on raft at Pansanjan Falls Philippines 79/80

bed is hard; my porridge is cold. Your loving son...' Oh ... How we missed ours, but comforted ourselves by blessing the proximity of the beach to the school, the fact that it would soon be moving-day, and that we could hang on to Dom - if she liked - until her twelfth year.

Now old hands at the game, we arrived without incident, in Watchet, on a sunny day in late August. Our quarter, the usual three-bed, red-brick, metal window-framed (another freezing winter) slightly larger estate-type house, was sparklingly clean; such a bonus meaning we could start on the boxes almost immediately. Once unpacked, despite noticing that we were sorely in need of a visit from the decorators, overall, we decided, everything could have been far worse. In Sutton, we'd acquired a little furniture of our own, at country auctions, and Mother, having once again moved house, during our trips South had been kind enough to hand on not only unwanted goodies of her own but others, gathered from the mass of antique shops and stalls in Brighton and Hove, no doubt flirting madly whilst beating down any hapless male dealers. No one drove a harder bargain with more wit and style.

The previous occupants of our new home now lived - following promotion - immediately opposite, in a similar house but with four-beds and a larger garden. Soon after our arrival, they popped across to introduce themselves and having thanked them for not having to scrub before unpacking (nowhere near as uncommon as one would imagine) daringly mentioned how startled we'd been upon finding a series of deep holes in both front and rear gardens. Somewhat shamefacedly, they admitted to digging up their recently planted new rose-bushes. 'We were damned if we were going to leave them'. Fair enough.

G. was now, officially, on leave. Something of a rarity in our lives. In my entire time as an army wife - twenty four years - he never once, not ever, took his full entitlement. However, within eight days of our settling in, he announced one morning 'What about a holiday'. Just like that. The final decision was coastal West Wales, a favourite with us both and where I'd spent time as a child. Within 24hrs. Mr. Fixit had booked us into what sounded like excellent farmhouse accommodation, which as well as being close to several lovely beaches and the small town of Cardigan - home to several family friends - was less than a three hour drive away.

And so began the first of a series of visits to Penrallt Ceibwr Farm, a great establishment held together by the hospitable Fletcher family, for many years uncomplaining hosts to children and pets, young and old, and providers of homely surroundings, comfortable beds and fabulous food.

On day four, installed happily on a beach, digesting our delicious packed lunch, I spotted a lone figure in a blue uniform carrying, what appeared to be a large pair of black boots. Every few yards, the figure would stop and bend to speak to various people who all appeared to reply with a shake of their heads. Alarm-bell time again. Hadn't there been something on the car radio concerning Gen. Franco of Spain, threatening to invade Gibraltar... I sighed. It had been good while it lasted. As the figure came closer, I nudged G.

'There's a man in blue on the horizon and I think he's after you'.

'Rubbish' he said, easing himself up onto his elbows.

We listened as he addressed the male half of a nearby couple 'Are you Captain Pettifar'?

'There you go' I said brightly, seeing the remnants of our holiday float slowly off into the hinterland. G. rose to his feet.

Delighted to have found us, our policeman smiled, before saying slowly and gravely, as if about to announce Armageddon. 'I've notice, from the War Office. You've got to get back to barracks as soon as you can. They didn't say why... Must be serious though'. Upset for us all, but mostly for the children, my own reaction was far less restrained. 'Oh, bugger bloody Franco'. G. looking puzzled, turned to me, saying 'Who mentioned Franco?

The following afternoon we were home, digesting the regiment's 'new tour' order. Six months 'Unaccompanied' in Gibraltar.

G, as Quartermaster and mover-in-chief, soon unfurled his wings and for the next two weeks or so, flew frantically between office, Stores and home, whilst I attempted to salvage what remained of the holidays. There had been scarcely time to get to know people, although those we'd met couldn't have been more friendly or welcoming. Virtually everyone was new to us as G. had now become part of the Royal Warwickshire Fusiliers (shortly, due to Government cuts, to merge, along with three other regiments, into The Royal Regiment of Fusiliers).'The Warwicks' as they were known, had, in fact, only recently returned from an emergency tour in Aden, so by comparison, we had little cause for complaint: not that G ever did.

And there was plenty to think about. Dom would soon be starting at the local Primary and just days later we'd be returning Simon to St D's for the start of the Winter term. Soon, it would just be Dom and me, although Mother was now en route. But how Dom would miss her Daddy. Plans for her fifth birthday, just 48hrs. after G. would have left, included the usual party, so as a diversion, we brought it forward.

The day prior to his leaving, G was having a little diversion of his own. I'd popped upstairs to help him pack, watching as sheepishly, he folded his D.J before laying it inside the large suitcase.

'And what will you needing that for?' I murmured. 'The C.O. said we'd probably need it. There's a casino'. Of course. Much later, I heard that the evening following their arrival, to a man, the officers had all decided to give it the once-over.The C.O, a pleasant, sociable chap, had thought it a good idea to meet as many of the locals as possible.

Mother, having surveyed Watchet and given it her firm approval - 'Pretty little place. Very quaint' had returned to Hove, whilst Dom and I were soon absorbed into patch life.

Playmates around her age were mostly boys, which seemed fine with her, and school, a short walk away, was judged as 'OK'. Our next door neighbour, funny, eccentric Pam, still a good friend, was fast becoming a regular coffee mate, as was Shirley (previous occupant of the house) and soon we'd been christened 'The Three Little Maids from School.' Also, there was Liz, newly engaged to one of the subalterns, who, whilst born locally, at that time worked and flat-shared in London, regularly spending weekends in Somerset with her mother. Meanwhile, Dom and I had joined the local library and were jogging along, but for our daughter, the sun really only shone again once G. had phoned home a few times. He'd also written, so we were well up to date. 'Over there' sounded fine. Franco, having realised the Rock wasn't his for the taking, had calmed down a little, and the diplomats got on with being diplomatic. Maybe 'the tour' (lovely expression: made it all sound like a week's jolly to Llandudno) wouldn't run it's full course, after all.

Come October, word went round that a large apple farm nearby desperately needed pickers and was offering work, depending on the number of baskets filled, at around three or four pounds per day. A group of us, including one young and pretty new wife - married just a month - decided to sign on. As things turned out, at the end of our two and a half weeks stint - solid with laughs - we'd probably have qualified for parts in 'The Darling Buds of May', which I was re-reading. Both the setting and the weather had been idyllic and the trees, their heavy, lower branches skimming the ground with just about the lushest harvest for years, made for easy picking, whilst the farm owners and their family, a friendly lot, had shared our labours. As we'd gained speed, many baskets were filled and when one day, someone bravely piped up that her fussy husband had peevishly ventured the opinion that 'Apple picking wasn't exactly a very proper occupation for Army Officers' Wives' we all snorted loudly and granted her instant permission to 'Spend every penny you've earned on yourself'.

All too soon, our Indian summer faded into monotonous downpours, reminding us that the West country's reputation for dampness wasn't entirely a myth. Dom, having acclimatised to three years of Midlands 'bugs' was, in her first school term, now gathering the full force of whatever our corner of Somerset had to offer that particular week, spending less and less time in the classroom and more on our sofa, snuggled up in a sleeping-bag. With the winds seemingly blowing straight through the house (such were the window-frame fittings) I built up the sitting-room fire to hothouse proportions, heaved in the oil heaters from the garage, for upstairs, and in true British fashion of the times, our fronts fried whilst our backs froze. As we moved into mid-November, Dom was fast becoming bored with her sojourns on the sofa, and as TV was heavily rationed, it seemed a good idea to get her reading. Following yet another course of antibiotics, we went off and bought the first half-dozen of the Ladybird learn-to-read books. Always eager to move fast, Miss Speedy proved an apt pupil, soaking up instruction like a sponge. Within three weeks she was virtually there, racing through the remaining six books before progressing to simple stories.

The downside to this, however, was that in what was fast becoming the '60's norm, many schools had developed what they called 'Family Groups,' i.e. larger classes of pupils, aged between five to seven years, who were all taught together at the same pace. But, once it became obvious that Dom read well - very well for her age - she was put in charge of 'listening to and helping the others'. At five years of age. Used to what was fast becoming an out-of-date practice, that of 'streaming', or maybe even a pupil being 'moved up', I had problems with the new system and following a quite friendly, though unsatisfactory chat, with the form-mistress, in an effort to prevent the possibility of upsetting repercussions, it seemed prudent at the time not to take things further. Better perhaps, that G visit the Headmaster (by reputation a difficult man) when he returned. (He did, and received a loud and lengthy dissertation on 'Interfering, impertinent, parents.')

Soon, tentative plans for Christmas were discussed but G. as usual, had some of his own. 'You can all spend it here' he'd said blithely, half-way through a phone call. 'You can 'Indulge' with the children. I'm borrowing a flat... The fare is just £10 each, from RAF Lyneham. There's a flight on 18th Dec. and I've arranged for you to receive a form... Fill it in, send it off and if you don't hear you've been allocated seats, don't worry!' There was more. 'The form will state firmly that (quote) "If by 16th Dec. you have not received specific notification that your application for indulgence passage(s) on Flight ? leaving for Gibraltar on 18th December has been granted, you are instructed that on NO account are you to report to the Movements Office at RAF Lyneham". He continued 'Just ignore that. They never really know the score till the last minute. Trust me..' And so the decision was made - MOD or no - we'd go.

Five days before the deadline, we'd heard nothing and I began to twitch; even more so when the temperature plummeted. That morning,

Dom, always an early riser, rushed excitedly into the bedroom. 'Mummy, get up, there's snow everywhere. Really, really deep. It's lovely.'

Trying hard to at least look as if I shared her excitement, I drew the curtains on an eerily silent world, the muffled sound so often the result of a prolonged, overnight snowfall.

N. Somerset had swapped hemispheres. As far as one could see, the countryside sparkled: all white, exquisitely so. 'Yes, love, it looks gorgeous'. Unable to stifle a sigh, I switched on the radio. 'Parts of North Somerset have been severely hit by deep, overnight snowfalls with more expected throughout the day... Several roads are blocked, including the A38 and 39.' Leading straight to Simon's school. With permission to collect him a day early (in 48hrs time) I'd organised as much as possible for our trip. 'Please' I prayed 'After the Wales fiasco, please let's get this one together.' Christmas cards and gifts had long been sent off but it looked, bar a miracle, as if we'd be going nowhere. After more snow, which, as forecast, froze overnight, I called St. D's. 'Please reassure Simon that somehow, we'll be there to pick him up, on Monday, as promised .' And how, exactly, was that to be accomplished? The white stuff looked set to last forever. But somebody had listened. By Monday morning, a thaw had set in and Dom and I, after a call to the AA, set off - complete with snacks, drinks and a spade. One never knew... We couldn't wait to see Simon again.

The C.O. of the regiment at that time, Col. Joe Blackstock, an extremely kind man, had, true to form, insisted the children and I be driven to RAF Lyneham, by his driver, in his staff car. With luggage kept to a minimum - a mini-stocking for the children plus one 'good' present each (a microscope and a 'Tiny Tears' doll) plus something small for G., the lovely, Corporal J, packed us in. In no way convinced that 'We'll be seeing Daddy tomorrow' I'd had to explain the situation as clearly to S and D, as I could. Whilst desperate not to prick their bubble, I'd also had to be honest. 'So far as I know for sure, we have not yet been allocated seats and might just have to drive home tomorrow. We can only wait and see. We'll need to sleep somewhere tonight so, at Dad's suggestion, I've booked us all - provisionally -

including Corporal J. - into a pub on a roundabout, just outside Wootton Bassett...But first of all we have to go to 'Movements', at Lyneham."Even though you're not supposed to'? said S, looking worried ...'

With the roads more or less clear, we arrived in just over an hour, and after leaving the children with Cpl J. I found my way to 'Movements'. There, a young Welshman, after taking all G's details and checking the list, said with a big grin and a broad accent.

'You 'aven't been called forward, 'ave you?' He grimaced. But you're all right. Reely lucky you are. Just one spare seat. 'One' I croaked. 'I need three. There are two children desperate to see their Daddy - in the car; with the driver.' He seemed impressed. 'Oh. A driver' and I explained that whilst husband was only a lowly Captain, our CO had offered his car and driver and we'd be spending the night in a pub, near W. Bassett.. .Just in case etc... 'Don't worry. I'll find you somewhere here. All in one room, mind.' and on seeing my face added. 'The driver can stay on camp. Don't worry. Cut-off time is 5am tomorrow and take-off's at 7:30. Someone will bang on your door at 4:30am and then you come and report to this desk, see. OK?'.What a star. He even allowed me the use of his phone to cancel our B & Bs.

As promised, our summons came early. After dressing rapidly, I lurched off, bleary- eyed as if hungover (not alcohol but cigarettes: ten years later life changed totally when finally tobacco-free, waking-up no longer involved feeling either drunk or desperate to lie-in). Then 'Mrs. Pettifar. Plus two?' I nodded. 'Three of the Navy haven't turned up. You're on. You'll be flying on a Brittania and take-off is at seven thirty. Please have your luggage ready for collection'... Ready? Ecstatic, the children, beamed with delight at the news. Then - a Brittania? With so much to think of, the fact that this was to be our very first flight hadn't really registered. Indeed, the entire up-in-the-air business had always struck me as unnatural, but whilst anxious, it was vital not to appear so and to try and emphasise the luck and excitement of it all. Finally - we were off - and up.

Two evenings later, at a party, I was asked 'You must have been on that Brit? Tuesday morning? The one that overshot...The pilot was taken ill and his new co-pilot had to get it down. Only his second 'go'. So that was it. Although later, G. true-to-form, had barely commented on the children's remark 'It seemed a funny landing, Daddy' apart from 'Mmm. Gib:one of the more interesting runways'.Totally clueless and lacking experience, I'd simply looked around, trying hard to ignore the pair of rosary-clasping women opposite, whose restrained whimpering and frantic signs-of-the-cross, hadn't quite escaped our wide-eyed children. My explanation had been 'Some people just don't like landings'.

The days were melting fast and with G's passion for leaving no stone unturned, we'd been steered rapidly around just about every accessible corner of the Rock - plus one or two which I, with no head for heights, felt might have remained better left unseen. We shopped at the local Liptons supermarket (v. 'homey', Gib.) and having bussed across the border to Algeciras, returned with a rich selection of locally produced fruit, nuts and veg. And there was, of course, the usual obligatory trip to the apes, which the children (both having the best time ever and behaving impeccably) found fascinating. 22 Dec. G's birthday, was spent at home and on catching my remark that we'd be 'treeless, husband was promptly despatched to seek out 'Something green and real - a bushy, tallish plant would do.' That evening the three large palm leaves resulting from his foray sat firmly fixed with stones into the largest available pot, when I remembered the red cellophane ribbon and two tubes of silver glitter - remnants of a card-making session, with Dom - nestling in the base of my handbag and scooped up in one sane moment before leaving home. Adorned with a mass of shiny, red bows, sieved icing sugar and glitter, and finished off with some lights, the slightly eccentric result sat cheerfully in a corner of the hall.

Christmas Eve was celebrated in the packed cathedral with a very beautiful Service and once back at the flat, we assessed the children's gifts. Fewer than usual, but they were having a great time and we'd heard no complaints. Mid-morning, on Christmas Day we set off for the Symonds - our Medical Officer, Gary and Lorna, his wife (today living in Kew and still the hosts with the most). Having tied the knot just weeks before the emergency, they'd sensibly decided to roost together for the remainder of the 'tour' in a small flat, near town. Somehow, that day we ended up numbering twelve or fourteen for 'the meal': furniture had been shuffled, added to, removed, and with the final permutation sorted, plus borrowed cutlery and china, we sat down to a delicious, relaxed and memorably funny lunch.

Due to leave Gib. on 5 Jan. we arrived at the airport in good time, but after a few hours of 'Sorry. Problems' were told 'Very sorry. Twenty-four hours delay.' Having hosted a large party at our borrowed flat in return for all the generous hospitality we'd received, our one remaining day had been spent returning all to 'March Out' standards - a full scouring (including - oh joy - the oven). There was no chance of us returning there for even one night's B/B...Once again, it was Col. Joe to the rescue, with supper and beds for us all. Goodbyes were hard but we kept them short and after a few hearty shouts of 'See you in March' we were off.

England, we heard, was conveniently in the grip of a severe freeze. Our car, a basic but sturdy and luckily, roomy estate (we'd also be dropping off the wife and three children of a member of G's staff) had apparently been driven to Lyneham by another visiting regimental wife, two days previously, and been left there for me to drive us home. Good. Unfortunately, it was discovered to contain just enough petrol to 'Maybe clean your teeth, Maam' words spoken by the sympathetic chap-in-blue who'd handed over the keys. Once again it was R.A.F. to the rescue, and with a tiny top-up from their station pump and directions to an overnight garage (a rarity in '68) we set off into the night, surrounded, as we'd first arrived, by icy roads and banks of snow. Our trip of a hundred or so miles would take about three hours, but all depended on the conditions. My own wasn't brilliant, but probably the result of cigarettes, late nights, jollies, greed and stress. Luckily, the children seemed fine.

With Simon back at school, and happily, close enough to be picked up and brought home for the occasional Sunday, Dom and I once more settled into our lives. Provided weekends were planned, time drifted by uneventfully, even the long evenings, as by and large the television of the late '60s and early '70s; not having yet discovered 'reality' produced a considerably wider-ranging selection of good, interesting viewing. As well as the Sunday night high- light, the unmissable 'Forsyth Saga', there were engrossing plays and serials, funnier sit-corns. and superior documentaries: plus excellent childrens' programmes, few of which bear comparison with today's dumbed-down offerings, with its series of constant repeats.

Two or three weeks after arriving back from Gib., in an effort to escape the combination of howling gale and snowflakes wafting through our loose window-frames, a friend, plus Dom and I, had just abandoned the dining-table to finish lunch on our laps in front of the fire, when the doorbell rang. Rushing in, Roger, husband of Ronni,due any day to produce her No3 in as many years - explained 'Our phone's out, Bev. Think we need an ambulance.' An hour or so later, he returned, panicking quietly. 'No vehicle, Bev.' I sped off to check on Ronni, who, as a tightly disciplined former dancer, was bearing up valiantly. With no sign of help, it seemed vital to try and assess developments. No doubt there, and with a few silent pleas of 'Doc. please Lord' I scrubbed my hands and helped Ronni onto the bed - narrowly avoiding the two-bar electric wall-fire. Just seconds before our unflappable GP, Paul Biddell, strode into the room, a delicious cuddly bundle, later named Bella, appeared. Surely one of the swiftest arrivals ever. Taking immediate charge - congratulating Ronni and turning to an emotional me, he said 'Don't go, Bev. we may need you'. Then 'Roger, come and meet your beautiful daughter'. In the words of a certain journalist 'What happened next, you couldn't make up'. As the bedroom door opened, Roger's entrance was preceded by his sliding in a diaphanous, lavishly flounced and highly flammable cot, whose folding metal legs skidded to a halt in front of the now red-hot electric wall-bars. Swiftly, with flames reaching for the ceiling, we all yelled 'Fire'. Paul grabbed Bella and our two late arrivals, the ambulance-men, having spotted the blaze from outside, rushed in, complete with extinguishers. As the room quietened, Paul concentrated on Bella, and Roger on Ronni, until suddenly we heard loud, but distorted noises that can only be described as 'pushing' sounds. Roger, looking up, muttered something like 'Oh my God. It must be Lumpus' and promptly disappeared. Lumpus, the more vocal member of the family, a chatty African-grey parrot, who, in a tissue-paper walled downstairs room, having heard it all, was treating us to a recital of his very own. Some time later, missing the family whilst boarding with us, he said nary a word - bar a few piercing trips down memory lane - re-living his 'labour'. (Bella, one of our God-daughters, is now a successful sculptor, happily married and living in Oz.)

G. returned in early April and after the first week or so of settling in together, we reviewed the state of our finances... Back to the 'Sits. Vac.' Young Lady Receptionist required. Interest in Art preferred.' said the ad. 'No Saturdays'. That evening, curious, I called the London number. The delightfully camp but charming voice said 'I'll be interviewing on April 23' and named an hotel in Minehead.'

Damn. 'The 23rd 'is really rather tricky' I explained, being St George's Day, when 'Monty', the esteemed Field-Marshall Montgomery. would be with us to take a special parade, solely to mark the merging of four regiments which would then become 'The Royal Regiment of Fusiliers'. The parade was to be followed by an official lunch and a large Ball in the evening. We'd be hosting a houseful. The reply was remarkably insouciant. 'Don't worry, darling. Try and fit me in between drinks. I'll be there until six and look forward to seeing you. How's that?' Who could possibly refuse.

St. G's Day arrived, happily a dry one and after the parade and lunch, Husband decided that I could just about manage a quick trip to town, returning before our house-guests were due, and to save cruising round, he'd drive and wait in the no parking area during my interview.

And so began a friendship of over forty years with Ken Wynn, artist and illustrator, one of whose several claims to fame included producing the original drawings for the Pepsi-Cola ads. Ken was one the kindest, most generous, talented and modest of men. Short and dark with collar-length wavy hair, a small beard and moustache, his tilted dark eyes never failed to spot an attractive woman at 100yds. We sparked immediately, but conscious of time, my queries were few and apart from being unable to work the required hours, due to Dom's school-run, I left rather short of information. The job - Receptionist to a group of five pastel-portrait artists - involved making appointments, framing pictures (with a staple gun), taking the money - and keeping the peace. 'Where? Said G, 'And how much would you be paid?' Sheepishly, I confessed. 'Sorry, not a clue on either count' but with the hours being wrong there had seemed little point in planning ahead. Next morning, however, a call from Mr. W. 'The job's yours if you'd like it'.

Two weeks later, having first dropped off Dom, I slotted into Butlins car park and strode off towards the well-signed Regency Ballroom. A real 'first.' Sometime in the late '40s, a popular film 'Meet the Huggetts', in which an East-end family take off somewhere similar for a week's break, had left me begging my mother to 'Pleeze - may we go to a holiday camp'. A tentless week in a minefield might have met with more enthusiasm. But twenty years later, here I was - feeling ridiculously excited. 'Go diagonally to the far corner' Ken had said, and you'll see a sign saying 'Portrait Studio. It's not large'. True: maybe five and a half metres by two. I knocked on the counter to announce my arrival. Behind it, against the wall, stood a tall stool - my pitch - and behind that, in a row, were five easels and five small stools, each lit brightly from above. Ken, plus three men and one women, were already setting-up, and after warm greetings, introduced me to the others. He then produced 'the book,' explained the simple-sounding system, and after a few practice shots with the staple gun, reviewed the price-list. That first morning turned out to be surprisingly busy and by 10:30 we'd had our first sitters.

Watching the process of a twenty-minute (or so) portrait being produced from scratch, in pastels, a medium I'd never used in my amateur efforts on the drawing front, was a riveting experience and by the end of day one, it seemed that the job might be advertised as 'Art lessons for free' rather than real work. At lunchtime, having piled everyone into our crumpet-wagon (a friend's description, due to it's bench seats and steering-wheel gears) we'd driven off to a pub, the group soon emerging as almost the friendliest, easiest and off-beat lot I'd ever met. An interesting hour was spent pooling our 'Landing in

Butlins' stories: mostly holiday jobs for everyone, bar Ken (a busy freelance illustrator) and Rod - whose other life involved artificially inseminating cows in Sussex, descriptions of which caused much hilarity. It seemed it would be 'all change' on the work-front, every two or three weeks, leading to a tremendous contrast in styles which taught me much about technique, as well as the application of simple rules, such as not drawing teeth, or smiley faces ('You'll soon become bored with toothy grins on your walls' Ken would tell the clients).One delightful older gent, on being informed 'We don't draw teeth' promptly took out his full set, popping them in a pocket before resuming his pose, complete with a wide toothless grin, before then being asked politely to 'Please relax your face'.

But one particularly warm afternoon lingers forever. Built-like-an-Oak Nick, a handsome bearded Scot, with thick, shoulder length wavy hair and black eyes, having completed his portrait and finding his client apparently asleep (common with the older sitters) upon closer inspection came over to me and softly whispered 'Bev. I reckon my poor old bugger's on an everlasting holiday. I think he's dead. What now? ' And then 'Who's going to pay?'As no-one ever dies in holiday camps ('bad for business') bodies are removed as unobtrusively as possible. Trying hard not to appear too solemn to the waiting customers, we watched as our silent client - complete with portrait delicately balanced on chest 'A nice touch don't you think?' said Ken - was wheeled away in a chair. There were days I ached from laughter. Soon after joining the team I'd willingly have given up the weekly f10:00 wage so generously paid by Ken for my services (a whole five hour day) and worked for nothing. Also, two, or sometimes three times a week, staff perks meant that both children could accompany me to work where, under the beady eye of the hard-working Redcoats, they not only enjoyed the pick of the two pools and a string of organized activities, but also the pick of the amusements. Time passed swiftly as each working day produced something new; not only from the job, but as captive audience to the ongoing stream of Regency Ballroom entertainment. I soon found myself riveted to the brave and spirited participants of the morning Keep-Fit classes, the intensive

'Old-Tyme' dancing sessions; the competitions for the best looking 'Dad and His Lad' and the awards for Glamorous Grans and Knobbly Knees. There was also an extra prize, when a statuette would be presented from the male Redcoats to the 'Most Popular Female Camper of the week.' Luckily, any parents remained in blissful ignorance as to the necessary criteria qualifying their 'little girls' for such a prize; clapping heartily as that particular week's well and truly bowled-over maiden would totter up to the stage, usually on her best white stilettos, to blushingly receive her trophy... Such scenes are impossible to forget and any Juke-Box favourites of '68 - Gary Puckett with 'Young Girl', Stevie Wonder's 'Isn't She Lovely' or Bobby Gentry and her 'Ballad of Billie-Jo' (usually coinciding with my morning sprint to the far end of the ballroom) now whisks me back to that jokey summer - which had also left us with several new and interesting friends.

We kept up with Ken throughout the Winter and I did another three months for him the following year, unable to complete a full season as sadly, our time in Somerset was coming to an end. A new posting: two years in Berlin. Exciting, but for the first time, it would mean leaving Simon at school without our being just thirty miles away. On hearing the news, before the house was stripped and stowed into 'the boxes', Mother and a friend joined us for a couple of week's holiday, which they enjoyed enormously. In her usual fashion, Mama floored us all by spotting Gevrey-Chambertain '59 in the local grocery store, promptly buying the remaining two dozen bottles. At the equivalent of £1:50 each it was probably the steal of the century.

When Butlins closed at the end of that season, Ken started a similar, and highly successful business on cruise ships, which continued for some years. He then decided to move house, from Hampstead to Brighton, where, along with his illustrative work, he produced a brilliant series of paintings devoted to Hunting and Horse-Racing, subjects in which, as a true countryman, he'd long been interested. We stayed in touch, meeting up often over the past 25 or so years, during which time - as a 60th birthday present - he also painted G's portrait, in uniform; now hanging in our downstairs hall where it is much admired. Sadly, at 89, he died, having, in his seventies, fought and won a fierce battle, with Non-Hodgkins Lymphoma. A truly generous spirit who, throughout our many years of friendship had never been heard to speak a single unkind word about anyone. Romany, his ever-youthful, long-standing devoted girlfriend, organized a loving and memorable funeral, where he was remembered with deep affection and much hilarity by his many friends.

Packing-time again. The move to Berlin produced several interesting moments in our lives, due mainly to G's participation in the regimental exercise (in France's Champagne country) turning out to be considerably more voluntary than I'd been led to believe. Something to do with his never really fully appreciating the joys of dismantling the house and the subsequent filling of the boxes. Arriving home just in time to screw on the lids less than a week before we were due to leave the country, was, in wifely eyes, not one of his better ideas, particularly as certain key facts (such as 'But why were you there?) have never been answered, to his advantage.

Best Choccie Cake for Boys (2 loose-bottom cake tins 3cm deep)
30grm.cocoa, 100grm. golden syrup, 75g light muscovado sugar, 1 teasp. Bi-carbonate-of-soda, 100grm dark choc, melted in bowl over simmering water and cooled,125grm diced unsalted butter, plus some for greasing tins, 2 separated eggs, 1 teasp. vanilla essence, 150 grm. plain flour, pinch salt. Preheat oven to 170c(fan) and grease cake tins.

Place cocoa, syrup, sugar and 50ml water & bring to boil, whisking till smooth, stir in bi-carb. Mixture will froth up :leave to cool, maybe 30 mins. Blend butter with egg yolks until pale then blend in melted chocolate followed by cocoa mixture and vanilla. Blend in flour and salt. Transfer to larger bowl and fold in stiffly beaten egg-whites. Divide evenly into tins, smooth surface and cook until just shrinking from sides of time 20 or so mins. FROSTING: Melt 200grm dark choc.with 30 grm. unsalted butter over pan of simmering water, stir until smooth. Combine 50grm cocoa with 2 tabsp. golden syrup and 100mls water heat to almost boiling point, whisking constantly. Combine with melted choc and slowly whisk in 90mls double cream. Sandwich cooled cakes together, then spread on top and sides.

Chapter Fifteen

WE CONSIDERED THAT THE BEST THING regarding a new posting taking place two thirds through the school holidays, meant that the children always had a picture of 'home' before starting a new term, ensuring that when they actually thought of us - as we were assured they did from time to time - home-life fell into place. My own erratic childhood was paramount in deciding that with Service life, in itself already disruptive enough, security, surely the best of gifts, always came first. We lived in hope.

   Berlin, August 1969: a divided city to which every adjective and contradictory phrase in the book might have applied. Having not yet had access to East Berlin, our first impressions were of a city steeped in history: vast, grey, dark, light, empty, proud, sprawling, grand, beautiful, ugly, decadent, sterile, ancient, modern, sophisticated, quaint, still, pulsating, licentious, law-abiding, underpopulated, solemn, cheerful, too cold, too hot, cruel, sentimental, vibrant, cosmopolitan, xenophobic, cocooned, imprisoned, sombre, insular; totally fascinating and often, deeply melancholy with remnants of the last war still plainly visible. The area towards the Wall and the railway station, close to the old Jewish community, had remained almost untouched since '45, due to a few years still remaining of the agreement which allowed previously-owned family property to be reclaimed. But we felt surprisingly welcome in a city, which despite its chequered history, still boasted a surfeit of fascinating and beautifully preserved architecture, as well as the contrast of several exciting new buildings. Not only was the place stiff with culture - museums, galleries, wonderful libraries and research centres - there was an abundance of markets, restaurants, clubs, cafes, hostels, food stalls, hotels, interesting side streets, and back streets - housing small, interesting boutiques, kneipes (student bars and pubs), more bridges than Venice, and, in a country noted for its lack of - a surfeit of deliciously dry wit and humour. G. having first been there with the regiment (and Fusilier Mickelwhite/Michael Caine) a year or so after the war, naturally found it much changed from the horrific bombscape of '48/49.

Our quarter was in Charlottenburg, one of the city's greenest and most attractive areas, in a small road off Heerstrasse, a broad six-lane highway. Semi-detached and light, with three stories, parquet flooring, four good-sized bedrooms, a well equipped kitchen ('fridge containing a welcome-pack: with beer) a spacious 'through' sitting-to-dining room - and joy of joys - a large, warm, dry, cellar, complete with a well-proportioned, deep, porcelain sink and a long wooden airing-rack. Laundry and storage in one: luxury. Every window, each double-glazed, had outside metal shutters which, once dropped into position from inside, ensured security and warmth. In the garden was a (newly mown!) lawn, a small paved terrace, and three mature oak trees, two being ideally sited to take a Badminton net. We were delighted with everything and as Dom and Simon 'bagged' their rooms we unpacked, impressed, as never before, with the immaculate cupboards.

Being part of the advance party meant a wait for boxes, so with no frantic rush to set-up house, G., having already driven us from Hamburg Docks to Berlin, spent an hour or so digesting the German road-rules before taking, and luckily passing, his 'tick-test'. That first weekend we explored the city where everything appeared so much bigger, faster, taller and wider than in England: hmm - my own tick-test could wait a while. Soon however, with the arrival of the battalion, normal life resumed. G. allocated the quarters whilst the children and I found our way around the local shops, markets and general locale; also to Spandau, just a few k's away, where good friends, Liz and Steve were living. Frieda our newly recruited cleaner, as an old-hand well used to military families, spoke fluent English and fitted in well. By this time I'd also passed the test and deemed road-worthy, driving everywhere: Very Carefully. But really, my mind was concentrated on Simon's return to school. As an 'Unaccompanied Minor' he'd be well cared for on his flight back and met at Luton by a lady from that great company 'Universal Aunts' (does it still exist?) who would then see him off to Somerset. But as usual, it's the mothers who feel guilty and I couldn't wait to be told he'd arrived safely.

Berlin, as a posting, was perhaps the most social in the book. Due to the four-power agreement, the steady stream of both official and

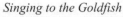

Brunei, Jan 80,
Dom, Bev, Simon,
Charlotte

non-official parties, would usually be attended by several nationalities, most of which spoke English, but our school French along with G's limited German from previous postings, would have to do for a while. Although it wasn't really a problem as Germans all learn English at school and were usually happy to show it off .

Next came the shopping. With our new freezer gracing the cellar, I began to plan menus. Entertaining within the battalion was no problem but one felt obliged to move things up a peg or two when feeding the French, although as G. was still only a lowly Captain, our lives were simple and undemanding in comparison to those of the upper echelons. We joined the Officers' Club, where facilities included a large pool, tennis courts and inexpensive menus in both restaurants and bars, and the Education Centre and Library, in Spandau. There,we had a choice of courses in just about everything from Russian and Mandarin to Floral Art but simplistically, I plumped for Pottery. Am no real shopper, but due to the foreign-exchange shopping and club-membership rights, with both French and U.S. Forces, our choices turned out to be excellent, entitling us not only to use the Pavilion du Lac restaurant, but also to take advantage of the Economat. Here were great cheeses, pates, escargots, patisserie and amazing wine and beer bargains: and Hermes scarves for £5:00: then retailing at £12 in UK. The American PX offered a rare assortment of goodies including a fabulous selection of linen and books and the children knew that shopping there meant king-sized burgers and sodas at their cafe, Harnack House. With cheaper spirits, make-up and scents on sale at the large NAAFI, along with the choice of the German supermarkets, each day offered several new and interesting ways of boosting the European economy. Indeed, some non-working wives, yet to hear the phrase 'Retail Therapy,' might easily have earned themselves degrees in the science of shopping.

With both children at school (and, due to the complicated structure of the Berlin Budget, the services of a full-time cleaner employed at advantageous rates) it was time to find a job. Within days, thanks to the grapevine, I'd become part of the Families Medical Centre, in Spandau Barracks, as a part-time Chaperone and Receptionist, working for the lovely David Lord, a kind, down-to-earth Lancastrian, whose lively wife, Leslie, occasionally filled in as locum. The medical staff were a humorous, if totally irreverent, lot and most days produced a fair share of laughs:essential in a serious business. David insisted I sat in on daily surgery (wives and children only) which initially-fearing someone might object - had proved uncomfortable; but no-one ever did. Unsurprisingly, my medical knowledge grew rapidly, particularly regarding female and childrens' ailments. All extremely interesting and - had I been a hypochondriac - worrying; although the most useful advice ever was 'Jumping to unqualified conclusions causes stress and wastes energy'.

About half-way through November it began to snow. And snow. Small flakes, large flakes, wet, powdery, glistening white or pale grey: every size and shape the Almighty could muster: regularly and enthusiastically, until 1st May, a fact which sticks firmly in the memory as, 1st May being Allied Forces Day, we'd sat - rigid with cold -watching the huge Parade, and cursing, as yet another sprinkling of white stuff covered the stands. Then very gradually, it stopped. The temperature rose a crack or two and by the time the last line of soldiers had marched briskly off, a slender shaft of sun had appeared. And that was that. But the house, and we, had been warm throughout, even on New Years Eve, when temperatures had fallen to 25 below. It had been a great Christmas with open house and lunch on Boxing Day for a steady stream of friends. We'd enjoyed the fabulous Christmas markets and both children had made the most of their first shot at outdoor skating - with Dom - due to her incredible sense of balance, catching on fast and first. But favourite had been an evening at the Christmas equivalent of one of our fun-fairs where the selection of super-sophisticated rides and amusements had left us not only giddy, but gasping.

Before long, Simon was on his way back to St. D's, but being the shortest term, just toward the end of March, he was home again, for Easter, arriving just days before G. left for Schlesweig-Holstein. So well-timed, these Exercises. That holiday, we sledged, walked and almost wore out the Pick-a-Stix, Draughts, Monopoly and just about every board and card-game we owned, although Simon concentrated mainly on his Airfix models. Interestingly enough, despite the non-stop assault of the elements, super-efficient Berlin with snow functioned as well as Berlin without snow; although we heard recently that times have changed.

Within three weeks, Spring had sprung and we began to prioritise the requests for summer visits. Sometime however, in early June, a chance introduction at a party, to Dick Norton, then Head of the Berlin studio of B.F.B.S - the British Forces Broadcasting Service - had - following his interviewing me on 'Mad Moments of a Market Researcher' for a programme - resulted in a totally unexpected job offer.'Come and join us. I can't pay you, but you sound really good. Am prepared to take you on as a trainee?' Convinced he may well regret his decision, such opportunities had to be seized.

We were a small team. As well as Dick and various males reporting on sport, there were two other women volunteers who mostly filled in for the 'annos': the five minute local announcements read 'live', twice daily, prior to our linking-up with the BBC for the news broadcasts following the one and six pm pips. We also had an expert sound engineer, Walter: what a pro. There was much to learn and coming across as professional was essential. Dick's faith was touching, but with little of my own, the fact that money wasn't an issue came as a great relief. But, writing as the original half-wit when dealing with anything remotely technical, those first two afternoons found me floundering with the studio clock - different - until one got the hang of it. My first spell 'live' would be reading the local 'annos'. but those initial, pathetic attempts ended by my either overrunning for a whole minute or having an entire minute to spare: seconds, it seemed, were fine, but not minutes... something to do with the way the clock hand finally flipped over. Dick - later discovered to have invented the word 'impatience' - couldn't then have been kinder; a real Mr. Cool, putting it all down to nerves and teasingly asking the others 'Need a minute? Just ask Bev. She usually has one to spare'. After two afternoons dithering and almost mute from feelings of inadequacy, I finally got there, dismayed at the effort required to produce just five minutes of perfectly-timed, uncluttered speech.

Next came U.H.E.R lessons. (The UHER, simple to use and much beloved of old hands, due its fantastic reproductive qualities, was/is, a solid, square, portable tape recorder. It also weighs a ton). However, due to a long and unfortunate history of sabotaging electrical goods (have since decided am not 'earthed') it also scared me rigid. But Dick, whilst an excellent teacher was also a confidence booster. Slowly, after a concentrated few days spent sharpening my interviewing skills, he came up with 'There's a group appearing next week, at the Deutschlandhalle: Jethro Tull. Know anything about them?' There were real advantages to having a son whose interest in the pop scene was blooming fast and being a fan anyway, I relayed what I knew. Impressed, Dick murmured 'Excellent. They're yours. OK? We'll get you a Press pass'.

Studio instructions were 'Be at the Kempinski (then No.1 hotel) by four on Sunday after noon, and find the Roadie. He's your way in so be nice to him...And any you meet in the future.' He turned out to be a lovely guy, instructing me to 'Follow the green coach to the venue and we'll do it there'...

At the rear of the building in the now dark car-park sat two coaches, both green. As one of them moved off, I slipped in behind. Some time later, obviously en-route to Tegel airport, I remember thinking 'Something wrong here'.The vehicle ahead which I'd doggedly pursued from the city, did not contain a pop group: or indeed any group. In fact, limited interior lighting indicated that it was probably empty. Omigod. Stupid, stupid bloody prat... A frantic glance round and with all toes neatly crossed, the car and I - having made the swiftest U-turn in history - moved smoothly in the opposite direction toward town. Thank-you-Lord. Once at the Deutschelandhalle, having greeted the roadie with a smooth 'Thought you'd like time to get the feel of the place' I was introduced to Ian Anderson, the group's leader. What a dream; Mr Loveliness himself, who - for the uninitiated - plays a wonderful flute, mostly whilst standing on one leg. No one in the pop world could have been a more fluent, charming, gentle and articulate respondent. (Still occasionally 'gigging' but also fish farming in Scotland).

'Well done, Baby doll' (gosh) was the following morning's greeting from Dick. 'All good stuff. And the sound quality's fantastic. Now we'll edit. You'll soon get the hang of it.' Quite so. It's true. Fear really does concentrate the mind. A few days later Dick announced 'I've written a script for the new programme we were discussing.' In, On Berlin', a focus on interesting city happenings which would also include interviews. 'Here's your copy. Let me know what you think... We go out on Tuesdays at 5:30.' First one next week' (it was now Thursday). 'You'll need to sort out the interviews.'

The programme, pacy and interesting, worked well and we went out hiccup-free. Kind words from the powers-that-be, in Cologne, meant everyone was happy. Dick produced three more programmes, and having suggested I 'Might like a go at the fifth' (the result of which he subsequently approved) he promptly announced that he and wife Pam, were off to Spain, for a break. 'You'll be in charge. But if you're unhappy about doing the programmes live, Walter will record, on Mondays. I've already spoken to him'. To my flippant 'Oh yeah' he'd said 'I'm serious. You're more than capable of running the show. It'll be fine.' G. No.1 critic, was delighted.. ' He obviously has faith' (that word again) 'Clever you'. I flinched, feeling anything but. Dazed, more like. Thank God for Walter.

As Dick and Pam intended buying a holiday-home during their trip, Ashley and Tanya, their children, were to remain in Berlin but when child-care arrangements collapsed G. and I agreed that the children could stay with us. Dom and Tanya, whilst not exactly best friends, tolerated each other well enough, and Ashley, a blonde, affectionate six-year old, whose huge blue eyes belied a thriving streak of mischief, was no problem either.

One afternoon, toward what I fondly imagined to be the end of my time 'In charge' Walter, having studied the script for week three remarked 'You've written here 'And this time next week, Dick will be back in the chair...' I nodded. 'Right'?. 'Wrong, Bevee.' he replied. 'They do not return for two more weeks' and mentioned a date. 'But he told me they were away for just three weeks...' Knowingly,Walter shrugged. And grimacing, added...'Not so. But we are OK. Yes?'

Summer hotted up, so along with work and our bulging social life - any spare time saw me either hurtling Dom off to one of her many activities, or in the kitchen, feeding the freezer. With a cleaner, a reliable baby-sitter, Angelika, and an extremely economic food-buying system called F.R.I.S. (Families Ration Issue Supplement) we considered ourselves extremely fortunate. (F.R.I.S.- a system whereby all Service families based in Berlin were able to buy certain subsidised tinned foods, fresh meat and groceries, stemmed from the time of the Berlin Airlift, when in 1948, the city was isolated from West Germany by Soviet and East German action, cutting all road and rail links between West Berlin and the remainder of Germany. The city was supplied by air with food and other necessities including, believe it or not, coal. The Western Allies built and maintained stocks of these supplies even after the blockade ended in case it should happen again. The stock of fresh items needed to be turned over regularly; hence 'FRIS'. This system continued until the Western allies left Berlin.)

As with any reporter, stories are many and varied, but one of my most unforgettable involved 'The World-Champion Yo-Yo Player.' We'll call him 'Mr. F'. News of his visit and subsequent performances were all down to Dom. who, arriving home from school one day announced that the highlight of the following afternoon was to be a Yo-Yo Demonstration. The possibilities of a cracking five minutes radio loomed large. I rang the studio. 'All yours, Bev,' said Dick.

Next day, having first cleared arrangements with the Headmistress, I arrived as morning school ended and was soon introduced to a tall, slim, American. He appeared clutching a yo-yo and immediately hoisted my attention by performing a series of highly dexterous and clever tricks at the same time talking non-stop, carefully taking me through each movement. Ah...Yes. This was indeed serious stuff. Something of a gift was Mr F. Having so far glimpsed neither the tiniest trace of a twinkle in those dark, skinny eyes nor the merest twitch of a lip anywhere on his lantern features, it became obvious that our warm-up stood no danger whatever of being invaded by so much as a split second of either humour or irony. Life is real. Life is earnest: especially when accompanied by a yo-yo. After toe-dipping with a mildly jokey reference to 'practice' (the particular stony ground on which it fell being strewn with boulders) there was nothing for it. Off we went, each thoughtful reply accompanied by yet another 'trick'. Some of the old tapes survive, but sadly, not this one.

'To begin, perhaps you'd like to tell us something about the history of YoYo?

'Certainly. Yo-yo goes back to ancient Greece, but was played all over the world. In one of your British museums there is a picture of one of the Georges of England, lying on the couch playing with his yo-yo. Maybe you've seen it?'

Disbelieving, thinking I'd misheard, I shook my head. Then, 'You have very flexible hands. Do you need to do anything special to keep them in shape. Exercises, perhaps?

'Oh yeah. I keep a selection of toys, rubber toys, which I use every day.'

'What sorts of toys? Can you explain exactly how you use them'.

'Sure. Special rubber balls and cylinders; made from tightly compressed rubber.I squeeze them hard, alternately; to keep my fingers strong and supple."

'And your family?Your wife? Children? Are they interested in playing yo-yo?'

'We have no children, but my wife plays really well. I've taught her a lot and we play together most days. She seldom travels with me but I keep up my practice alone'...

After about fifteen minutes, we stopped. Needing a loo on arrival, I was now desperate when he suddenly requested I play it back. At last. His face relaxed in the direction of a smile. 'Great' he said, nodding his head as I closed up 'Yeah. Great'.

Later that afternoon, Husband's answer to it all was to quote 'Honi soit qui mal y pense' - the regimental motto (Evil be to him who evil thinks). Indeed: our yo-yo-ing friend must have been, as they say 'As pure as the driven.' Next morning, Dick rang me at the clinic.

'We're almost wetting ourselves here. Pure gold, Baby doll. Pure gold. The problem is what to cut.'

Bless you Dick. But Mr.F had come perfectly gift-wrapped, with the largest of shiny bows. At a drinks party, a few days later a friend remarked 'Driving up the Heer strasse in my new Merc, with you and the yo-yo man on the radio ... V-e-r-y dangerous... I could hardly see for tears.'

Towards the end of that first year with BFBS, Dick often offered me the choice of 'interviewees'. With Berlin's constant stream of visiting personalities - from world politicians (his province) to legendary superstars - aware that my sketchy grasp on current affairs might be better left unaired, I, by and large, embraced the popular. Most memorable were the yummy Neil Diamond, whose ambition it was to 'Learn to tap-dance'; Johnny Cash, the man in black; so-polite Englebert Humperdinck and Michael Bentine, the sweetest of all; plus Stephane Grappelli, Dana, that year's Eurovision winner (now a politician) and several pop groups; often classically trained chart-toppers who, to a man were friendly, chatty and fun.

One morning, G announced 'Sunday's free - we're on the train'. Ah. The train: now consigned to history but then highly recommended as a relaxing day trip. For a nominal sum and available to all British Forces families from Berlin, this daily, return train journey between Berlin and Helmstedt, a small town on the West German border, had come about as the result of the Berlin Blockade, when each of the Western Allies reserved the right for a daily freight train and passenger

Phillipines, Manila, 79, Simon, B/ev, fronting Jeepneys

train to travel back and forth between East and West: all meals provided. Both our young seemed keen, so off we set, each with a good book, boarding in time for a continental breakfast in the pristine restaurant car. After lunch and a two-hour stop in Helmstedt (a typical, suburban town) we started for home, and nursery tea in the restaurant car: two boiled eggs and soldiers, followed by pastries. Happily, we'd all enjoyed it, missing little in Berlin but a day of non-stop rain.

That second year we suddenly became everyone's hot holiday spot; advising friends to 'Book before July: after then, we pack'. The phone buzzed constantly. By now, as old Berlin hands, we had a varied itinerary and apart from the galleries and museums, offered Peacock Island; days on the river Havel; a bus of part of 'The East', taking in Treptow Park and the impressive Russian War Memorial; and evenings at the opera, or maybe a night-club or student kneipe (where only I was to be offered a politely-refused 'joint'. 'It's the long hair' remarked G). Or sometimes we'd have a day at the famous zoo, where inmates included woolly pigs. And, of course, there was 'The Wall': that long, bleak, loathed stretch of misery which stood only to endorse man's terrible inhumanity to man.

Sometime in May, the rumour that mid-August would again be jumping-off time became fact, with a posting order to Catterick, in North Yorks. Back to reality then; although exactly what that might entail we were yet to discover. Initially, our bleats were predictable. 'Bound to be bloody cold.. .Freezing in the North' and 'Bet there's no central heating... And what about FRIS? (convenient attacks of amnesia instantly banishing all past groans re. the quality of the 25p per pound rump steak - today's money - mainstay of many a curry lunch and dinner party Bourguignon and Stroganoff)...'And there's my lovely cleaner.. .And babysitter... And the extra cash? ...Oh. And what about the Economat...And our cheap booze. We'll be back to unjoined-up meat and tinned Tuna ... And what about the opera?' So it went. How very spoiled we'd been.

We'd also miss the zany 'Rowan and Martin's Laugh -In', shown on American Forces TV, in which the then new, and gloriously ditzy Goldie Hawn made her debut - as well as the Christmas classic James Stewart film 'It's a Wonderful Life.' For whatever reason, there seemed to be a lot of 'leavings'. But - our children would be in the same country, which made up for everything.

My time with the medics would soon be over. They'd been a great bunch to work with, kind, skilled and witty and we had a jolly get-together one lunchtime, with sweet speeches, exchanges of gifts and Nigel's 'special' G&Ts. (gin, the odd iceberg, almost half a lemon and a glance at the Tonic label). I'd learned a lot: it was always interesting but occasionally daunting, being not without its tricky moments. But the two years had seen much hilarity: better maybe, left where it happened, in the surgery.

Working for Dick had been tremendous fun. There would probably never again be the opportunities of meeting and speaking to so many interesting people - famous as well as infamous - and I was grateful for both his knowledge and his patience. There were occasions when work and social life inevitably clashed, causing some scrambled arrivals and gnashings of teeth (from G) but somehow it all came together; including one interview with a very accommodating gent. which, due to my not checking the hastily-grabbed (and minus tape) UHER, had needed double coverage. But the entire experience had been invaluable. Dick had drilled me well and these days - a hundred years later and still more inclined to listen than to watch - I sometimes find myself thinking 'Ouch. Bad edit' or 'We'd never have got away with that'. Once, reporting from the Berlin Dog Show - hardly of universal interest - my suggestion that one half of a married couple 'Hang about' whilst I questioned the other, caused a certain coolness at editing time.'We have standards' Dick had muttered, glowering. Nevertheless, his gift of a reference was the best, glowing even - and when I tentatively asked if he thought there might just be a niche for me in local radio, he suggested I send a tape (to be assembled by Walter) featuring my ten best pieces, to either Tyne-Tees or Yorkshire Television. 'You could manage a TV reporting job easily. No problem.' Flattered, but suddenly silent, having never once imagined such dizzy heights, it occurred to me that inside appearances, to a real audience which until this moment had barely featured, would require effort, not to mention real clothes. For the previous two years, invisibility,whilst holding forth from the cosy depths of a small radio station, had been guaranteed, and occasionally, when pushed for time, arriving at the studio with a towel covering my wet hair, Sir's reaction had been little more than a raised eyebrow and a wry 'Glad to see you could make it.'

But Dick had standards, which we all recognised, despite his reams of wicked anecdotes, from school-days at Stowe with a naughty George Melly, to hilarious moments throughout years of radio and television. Consequently, outside interviews produced my shiniest front and Pam - his Irish and unique (3rd) wife, initially nailed by his stunning good looks and 'The voice: who could resist it?' - had more than once congratulated me for 'Getting the best out of the old bugger'.

With just over a month to go before we left, some good friends unexpectedly decided to join us for a week. Fine, but as both children would shortly be home, shopping time was short. In those last few days of freedom, I endeavored to float the Deutschmark, buying up sets of elegant E European glasses, bed-linen and towels to last a lifetime, and from the Economat, tins of escargots and marrons (and two sneaky Hermes scarves). These, plus various non-perishable goodies from the German supermarkets would be just a few reminders of how spoiled we'd been.

G began assembling the boxes, breaking off now and again to murmur 'I hope you've got it right'... Me too. Having plucked a figure from nowhere when asked 'How many boxes?' I'd replied brightly 'Oh. Thirty two or three should do it 'Winter kit first, books, spare toys, memorabilia and Simon's letters from school, etc, etc, until, all was finally slotted in and accounted for in the 'Move' notebook. Remaining were table-lamps, the scrapbooks, some china, cushions, pictures and bed-linen, to prevent the house appearing too institutional.

Whilst the children and I were flying home, G would drive, the extras all safely stowed in our elastic-sided wagon. Relieved, days later, we waved the boxes goodbye and set about rearranging the house. Our immaculately packed and labelled crates would be stored in the camp for the massive container move to Catterick, due sometime over the next two weeks.

Twenty-four hours before our friends left for England, we were hosting the final 'Roulette Supper', for about thirty people. 'La Syndicat de Gazelle d'or', as it became (the regimental mascot being a gazelle) had been taken over by our officers, almost on arrival, from those of the outgoing regiment. A great success, it had been run from within the Club, just one evening per month, with players limited to club members and guests and regimental wives - except that we weren't allowed to cash in our chips. Stakes were also limited, with profits split equally between the club and regimental funds. That evening, dashing around, refilling coffee cups, I took a phone call. Somehow, expecting bad news, the message failed to fully penetrate as calmly I replaced the receiver and whispered to G. standing nearby 'The garages housing the families' boxes are on fire; you all need to get down there immediately'.

Sadly, the majority of the families lost everything they owned in that fire. Having had their crates stowed in the camp, the possibility of fire had simply never occurred to anyone. Arson, whilst suspected, was never proven, and as the Crown cannot be sued, recompense in any form appeared unlikely. But enlightened Husband spent the night in the barracks, with his staff, devising and producing 'loss' forms which were then delivered to families whose crates had been stored and destroyed, with a proviso that they must be filled in and returned to barracks within twenty-four hours. 'That way' he said 'Reports of non-existent losses will be kept to a minimum. Leave it any longer, and some will perhaps use it as a chance to claim extra cash.' We had always taken out extra insurance to cover our moves but our claim was refused on the grounds that our property had been in storage and not in transit.'The families we felt most for were those without insurance and where, perhaps for the first time, a wife had been able to work in a country that offered such a great choice of affordable goods.

The Ministry of Defence, however, following a full investigation, agreed to award each family a compensation payment (ours was £500) which, being totally unexpected, was better than nothing. Also, the Mayor of Charlottenburg had shown supreme consideration by kindly opening a fund for the regiment, from which we all later received a donation. I couldn't believe how lucky we'd been by saving certain irreplaceable items for the car journey, much as G. had complained at the time 'You've plenty of space - why not pack them? (Oh yes: the energy expended, filling those endless boxes. For years afterwards, unable to find a particular item, we'd realize it had probably 'Gone in the fire'). But there had been no loss of life. As for not packing the scrapbooks. I had no rational explanation then, and I've none now. Despite the - still smarting - loss of Simon's letters from school, both children's first shoes and other tiny treasures, the scrapbooks had been saved. For us, that really made up for everything.

Almost time. There were endless farewell parties, finishing with two marathons of our own. Frieda and I then took over the house, cleaning-through together, until G. remembered the attic. After my flat refusal to wet-mop its floor, thick with accumulated dirt, dust and squirrel droppings, I agreed to 'Sweeping only', whilst Frieda, then on the wrong side of sixty, was excused attic-duties. All mine, this one. Clad in tiny bikini - the August of '71 being amongst the hottest on record - I flew up the loft-ladder, plus broom; to emerge almost three hours later - black, sweat-streaked, boot-faced and furious. 'That's it. Never. Ever. Again', before moving off swiftly to soak and sulk. A morning or so later however, as G left toward Ostend, our loaded wagon bulging, I said 'You know. I've the funniest feeling we'll be back.'

Pork Stroganoff (for 4)

6oo grm. Pork tenderloin: trimmed and cut into stir-fry strips.
1 med. onion chopped finely plus 3 cloves garlic, crushed.
220 grms sliced mushrooms
2 and a half tabsp. Wholegrain mustard
4 tab'sp. Brandy or white wine.
250grm. Crème fraiche
2 tabsp. Chopped parsley.
2 tabsp. Oil and a little butter.

Melt butter and oil together and add pork, onion and garlic: cook for 3/4 mins. Stir in mustard and mix well. Add brandy or wine and bring to boil. Remove from heat and add cream. Return to stove and heat through. Serve with rice and a green salad.

Chapter Sixteen

As the train pulled into Darlington station, both children and I decided we rather liked the look of Yorkshire. Met by G., already installed and unloaded, we caught up on the previous couple of days whilst taking in the scenery on the drive to Rawlinson Road. Although still a Captain, G had been allocated a Major's quarter. At the end of the short, cherry-tree lined drive, stood a low, two-storied, red-brick semi, separated from our neighbour by a high hedge and fronted by a thriving rockery and lawn, prompting a 'Great' from Simon. 'Space for a Badminton net.'

'Apart from a double-aspect sitting-room, a utility-room and a fourth bedroom,' G had replied, when quizzed on the homeward journey 'The house follows the usual pattern... Sorry. No central heating. But it's on the cards...' Ah. 'And I've made up all our beds. But before we go in I'll just mention that decorators have been promised. Due in about three weeks.' Ah, again...But it had a friendly look. At least from the outside. Once inside however the hands of friendship remained firmly clenched as we surveyed our new living quarters, succinctly cursing the previous occupants whose two, perhaps three years worth, of accumulated dirt and dross was all too evident.

A year of real change. In less than a month, with Dom at the local school, and Simon in his last but one term at St. D's. late September found G. preparing for the first of the regiment's Belfast tours. I suspected he'd been warned sometime prior to us leaving Berlin - such moves being planned well in advance - but considerately, had said nothing. And so began the start of the soon to become familiar pattern of what the family referred to as 'Bog-Trotting'. The regiment would remain in Catterick for almost four years, although we were posted - a Staff job for G - after three and a half. During this time, six tours in Northern Ireland would have been completed, plus exercises in Denmark and Canada.

As several of these tours turned out to be closer together than one might have expected, welfare problems grew rapidly. That first year, with the men away for both Christmas and Easter, some families, having bravely arranged short summer holidays, were forced to cancel as, after just weeks back in England, the men were again en route to N.I. for an 'Emergency three weeks, or so' - the 'Or so' turning out to be another full four months.

With the house scoured, painted and boasting the novelty of carpets and curtains which for once, failed to clash, our limited spare time before G. left, was spent exploring. Close by, situated at the edge of the beautiful N. Yorks Dales,was Richmond, a small, ancient, friendly market town, whose famous bridge spans the picturesque river Swale. After two years of big-city life we appreciated the change, immediately falling for the broad, surrounding stretches of wild countryside, delightful small towns and villages, and exquisite ruins, all of which oozed history.

Those first months dragged less than expected, although, once G. had gone, each day began and ended with the first and last available news broadcasts. As the branches of our six cherry trees shed the last of their leaves, so began the usual struggle to heat the house. Our pungent and unattractive oil heaters, now replaced with equally pungent and unattractive calor-gas heaters, were heaved in from the garage and set up on hall and landing. With a good, open- fire in the sitting-room, we'd be fine. There was also Christmas to consider. Cards inevitably took forever as our list of friends expanded, but this year it looked as if the annual struggle to get the overseas bundle out first, might actually happen. Also, it seemed that our evenings, easily inclined to drift into non-stop TV, might be better occupied making new decorations. Dom, her friend Sally and I, spent hours covering polystyrene balls with glue, glitter, sequins and 'snowflakes' cut from white edging fabric, which, hung with gold string from the light fittings, festooned with strands of ivy and evergreen,produced many compliments as well as suggestions that we set up a stall...What with those and the patchwork quilt I'd begun, we were turning into a regular little cottage industries. There was also the housework. Due to 'Low funds equals no cleaner' the Marigold's and I kept things going, reasoning that this particular house had probably never been so clean for years. Far more fun was catching up with friends recently posted back to the regiment, resulting in hours of news, gossip, endless coffees and days spent in auction rooms where brass-monkey temperatures threatened to finish us all off completely. (Note: anyone considering strip-tease as a living might first wish to try a spell 'oop North' where the art of layered undressing really comes into its own.) Coffee mornings and Wives' Club also featured, as did ferrying Dom to and fro. She missed G badly, often popping into our bed during the night, but he managed to call most evenings, always before her bedtime, never failing to mention that nothing in the media was as bad as it looked, and minimising the hardships. After Christmas, we'd agreed Dom could begin weekly sessions on the military dry-ski slope, as well as joining the local stables. They would be nowhere near as well-equipped as those of Berlin, which as well as the indoor facilities had also had the pick of some of the most trustworthy ex-police horses. These having been 'retired' to the military riding-school, managed the young perfectly and, aged eight, Dom was regularly seen perched on Nautilus - a full nineteen hands and one of the steadiest mounts ever.

Simon, first to break up, appeared at Darlington Station, taller, slimmer, scarcely recognisable from half-term and with a startlingly deep voice. I recall regretting how swiftly time was passing. But he appeared happy and it was wonderful to have him back. Almost thirteen, he'd be off to 'big-school' in April. Sherbourne, our first choice, had been abandoned as being too large, so we'd almost - depending on Common Entrance exam results - settled on Bloxham. Andrew, with whom he'd attended St. D's, was then in his third year there; grousing little and doing well. We'd visited twice and as well as the Headmaster, had met and liked several members of staff. The atmosphere had been friendly and relaxed and the boys pleasant and helpful. The school itself, medium-sized and situated in the pretty village of Bloxham, had a fair record and little evidence of hothouse pressure. Once again - we lived in hope.

With snow forecast, the next move was the tree hunt.All Christmas plans, naturally, were overshadowed by G's absence, but we decided that stockings would be opened as usual, with all other presents saved until the 30th when he'd be home, for turkey, celebrations and a precious four days R and R' Rest and Recuperation. Christmas Day was to be spent with good friends who would then join us for Boxing day. How lucky we were.

7.30am We love a parade
Prior to a Palace reception with
friend and neighbour Anne
Matthews (left)

The tour ended in March and again, life resumed the mantle of normality - although one was never quite sure for how long. In this case; not long at all. Back they all went, for a spell just long enough to negate half the Easter holidays. The remainder was spent sorting out S's kit, for Bloxham, which he'd now seen and approved. Soon, it would be just Dom and me..

And then came our lovely Pandora: a not only beautiful, but also beautifully behaved, ten-month old, yellow Labrador, reluctantly passed on via friends of friends, following an overseas posting. It was love at first sight and problem-free; bar her twice yearly 'season' when she'd be sought out by Dougal, a black Lab. just two years older and living nearby. He'd appear, almost cross-eyed with lust, to camp on our front doormat, assessing his chances. These came just twice; the first, during G's second tour, amid a spell of R & R, when Pandy's spectacular, early-morning leap through our open bedroom window to her panting sentinel below, found me draped over the sill, fearing either a dead or badly injured dog. Instead, the only evidence of her waywardness was a perfect set of skid-marks on the damp lawn below, and two tails - one black and one tan, disappearing around the fence. That night, our exhausted siren returned, non the worse - though probably pregnant. Luckily, the vet was ready to oblige with a hefty jab of morning-after mixture.

Despite our unpredictable lifestyle, I decided to put some real effort into getting work on the agenda. With both G. and S. absent, intentions of sounding-out either Tyne-Tees or Yorkshire television had long been abandoned. Life at home with Dom needed to remain as stable as possible and even in the unlikely event of either company being willing to take me on, it would have been totally unreasonable to have expected any concessions regarding working hours. Instead, I wrote to BBC Teeside (Now Radio Cleveland - or perhaps it's the other way round)) enclosing my tapes and Dick's glowing reference, and astonishingly, received a quick reply suggesting an interview. After time with the Controller, Allan Shaw, I was offered a job as a reporter/presenter. However, with no back-up, I needed to consider the worst scenario: negative but necessary, there being no spare cash to consider paid help. The possible combination of split shifts, bad weather (N Yorks. specialising in freezing fogs) and Dom., maybe at home for the odd sick-day off, it seemed only sensible to offer my services as a freelance (Stringer).That way, whilst nowhere near as interesting as joining a studio team, any promising stories nearer home could be investigated, as well as my being around, as usual.

It was soon obvious that whilst natural curiosity and an ability to communicate has its advantages, my gentle probing of the locals produced little beyond gossip; occasionally riveting, but of little use. With whistling cows and Satanism thin on the ground that year, unless the surrounding countryside suddenly yielded either oil, Saxon treasure or an emerald-mine, opportunities for interesting interviews would need to be sniffed out with the zeal of a starving bloodhound. There was little 'airworthy' material to be gleaned from the weekly paper and with the men away, few chances of military happenings. But, aware that the kitty needed a top-up and with 'must try harder' as my mantra, I ignored the sense of backsliding and decided to sign up with a couple of Market Research companies. The certainty of flexible working hours, combined with a need to keep my hand in, were too good to ignore and would at least cheer-up the bank manager, possibly paying better than the BEEB (never famed for its largesse). Happily, pre-Berlin, having graduated from 'the field' to the more interesting world of unstructured interviews, the tyranny of 'quotas' and repetitive questionnaires were now firmly in the past.

Within a week or two, as local stories began to surface, the first Mkt. Research assignments rolled in. Next was a call from the studio saying that Irish actor - Dermot Walsh - handsome stalwart of many J. Arthur Rank productions of the '40s '50s and '60's, was about to begin rehearsing the part of 'Scrooge, in the town's forthcoming production of Dickens' Christmas Carol, due to open just before Christmas at Richmond's exquisite Georgian theatre. A phone call later and sounding delighted to be asked, Mr.Walsh agreed to be interviewed, saying how much he looked forward to appearing in one of the oldest and brightest jewels in Yorkshire's historic crown. (The theatre, built in 1788 by Actor /Manager, Samuel Butler, had originally housed an audience of under 100 and for reasons unknown, was closed in 1848. In 1963 it re-opened and funding found for a full restoration and extension programme, resulting in seating for over 200 people.)

This past decade, with the Northern Irish problem still occasionally making the news, I've thought often of my meeting with the (sadly) late Mr. Walsh: probably then in his late forties - tall, slim, with dreamy black eyes, long(ish) dark wavy hair, and charm by the bucketful. That winter, due to various problems, I'd taken him home for tea, following rehearsals at the theatre (where sub-zero temperatures made every clearly spoken word a triumph) a gesture, which, whilst happily toasting crumpets, he sweetly assured me would never be forgotten. After completing the interview, I took a phone call in the hall and returned to find him studying a small book, found on a nearby table: 'Four Months in Winter', published earlier that year by the regiment. The book covered the day-to-day life of seven hundred soldiers set in the urban situation of armed strife which existed at the time of that first tour in Belfast. My awareness that any reference to the situation quaintly labelled 'The Troubles' to a Southern Irishman - who was possibly both Catholic and a staunch Republican - might, but for his obvious interest in the book, - prove unwise. But as the anxious wife of an army officer involved in the conflict, I decided - rightly or wrongly - that this was perhaps my one chance of questioning a member of (possibly) the opposition. Hesitantly, I first explored and established the direction of his loyalties, before listening intently whilst this humble - but immensely arresting man - educated, well-read and totally lacking in bigotry (have since learned he read Law at Dublin) spoke quietly and calmly, becoming neither heated nor strident, never once attempting to influence or persuade me in any way toward his views, nor to push me into apologising for my own. Finally, when asked his reaction to the merciless violence, his diffident reply had been a helpless shake of the head.

True, he was an actor, handsome and charming; but speaking as one of the not-easily- impressed, and with my opinions still firmly in place, it was impossible not to respect his quiet sincerity. I offered him the book which he accepted gratefully: 'I was about to ask if you'd mind me taking it...' If only G. had been there. That would have been an exchange well worth hearing.

That summer, heavily-pregnant friend Liz, suggested we take a break 'No further than two hours drive, just in case'. Simon and Dom, again disappointed at G.s absence, needed something to look forward to, so after considering the possibles,we settled on Arnside. The AA book promised an unspoilt, attractive, small estuary resort, not far from the Lakes, so, as good army wives, we planned a 'recce' and one morning set off with children, Pandora, and a substantial picnic.

Despite the child-age variation, no day could have been more perfect. We had it all: cloudless sky, hot sunshine, light breeze, an interesting beach with rock pools and enough sand for comfort. Having agreed that a weeks' stay would be about right, Liz decided to ask her mother, Mary, to join us'. Soon, we'd found and booked our week in a fairly-priced comfortable-looking B&B, beginning the following Sunday, and left a still-sunlit beach to head for home. The only drawback had been the 'No dogs' rule, but Pandora, happy in the car, with her own bed and blanket, would be fine too.

Half-way to Arnside it began to rain: not threateningly, just gentle misty, summer drizzle, till unloaded, installed, and full of tea and cake, we groaned as the sky darkened and the downpour gained momentum. Optimistically, Mary remarked 'Oh well, we may as well get it all over with tonight,' producing the instant lively riposte from our unforgettable Scottish landlady 'Och. Not at all. It could be in for a wee while here, you know... ' Speechless, we'd gazed unblinkingly across the table at each other. But there was more. Whilst an accomplished cook, our hostess could have outshone every competitor in any contest involving the spoken word. By day two, Mary and Liz almost forbade me to so much as look at her. 'She'll never stop if you show any interest in anything she says or does. Try and ignore her.'

But our chatty friend was right. Bar the odd, thin streak of sun, the rain continued, and with the unspoiled locale offering little but the lush countryside - all seen through a grey mist - we'd set off each day for the nearest castle, country house or museum. These trips, whilst fine for Simon and me, did little for Dom. though to be fair, she seldom complained. Picnics were out, so apart from a successful afternoon at a local cinema showing 'Born Free', it was soggy dog walks, punctuated by endless coffees and snacks in a selection of 'Country Kitchens and Cosy Cafes': often anything but. A pool would have been a boon, and today, maybe Arnside has one, but agreeing we'd been bravely (if foolishly) over-optimistic on the weather front, there was nothing left but to make the best of things - and in retrospect, it could all have been much worse; and at least we had seen it at its best. Also, to be fair, we were treated well. The house was spacious, comfortable and well supplied with books games, jigsaws and cards, plus a good selection of freshly cooked, plentiful meals. G. called regularly; uncomplaining as usual despite his restricted lifestyle, while I admitted that 'Yes, the weather was wet but we were all fine.'

And then it was time for the off. Leaving Amside more or less as we'd found it, enveloped in mist and rain, we'd dived thankfully into our cars and made for home, rattling towards Yorkshire, Radio 1 at top decibel. A few miles on, the skies lightened and gradually, Summer emerged. Our children, cheated of their week of sun and sand, had - with each other - probably been at their scratchiest ever, resulting in my letting rip one day with a brisk barrage, which had amazingly, produced almost instant calm: whilst Anna, Liz's bright, feisty three year old, had, sometime on day two, turned into Sally Sunshine, causing her mother to remark disbelievingly 'Is this really my child?'

De-dogging the car took forever. There may have been remnants of mud and sand left on Arnside beach but we doubted it:although being alone each night can't have been much fun for a sociable pooch. But the following summer made up for everything, when, with G. home for once, we accepted the offer of some kind friends to borrow their recently inherited, four-storied period house in lovely Elie, a small town on the Fife coast. 'Make as much mess as you like and do take the hound' they'd said 'One day we hope for enough spare cash to move in and renovate. Until then, it's holiday kit and we want our friends to enjoy it.'

Oh bliss. With the house situated just yards from a beautiful beach, we rejoiced. Simon, keen to fish, was ecstatic, soon finding a spot by the sea-wall where daily, he'd reel in a heap of delicious, herring-sized Saith - crisply fried ambrosia of which we never tired. There had also been a small dinghy for messing around in. And the weather? Well-toasted, we'd returned to a soggy, grey Yorkshire, our appearances producing a mixture of envy and amazement 'Lucky buggers. We've had a fortnight of rain here'.

Meanwhile, the months rolled on. The previous year, along with the rest of England, Dom and I had sat through the miners strike ('Oh lovely, Mummy, we'll be able to watch TV by candlelight'). Having - a month or two previously - refused to swap the sitting-room open fireplace for a garish, electric flicker-flame piece of nastiness, we'd scored - supping happily on foil-wrapped baked potatoes and a selection of one-pot meals cooked over the coals. That summer had also seen us blessed with central heating. A cause for celebration indeed, but joy was short when after just a few weeks - almost overnight - the £17:50 which had first filled our 200 gallon oil tank, became an unbelievable £57:00. It was back to the calor gas and kerosene'.

Catterick it seemed, was loved and loathed by all in equal proportion, but we decided the often dire weather was well compensated by the surrounding countryside. Spoiled for choice we explored the Dales, Barnard Castle, Ripon, Harrogate, York, Fountains Abbey, the museums, Bronte country, Scarborough, Whitby, Holy Island and Robin Hood's Bay, whilst a bemused Liz would remark 'You're the only people I know who will drive 95 miles to the coast in the morning and 95 miles back in the evening'.But we actually accomplished the previously unknown - two consecutive gorgeous summers, when, joined by a good friend and her three daughters, we seldom travelled further than Richmond, spending hours on the banks of the Swale, chatting, reading and sunbathing, pooling our picnics - often finishing off with huge juicy peaches, bought, due to a glut, at knock-down prices from the local greengrocer. And we swam. In a Yorkshire river! In August and early September. Looking back, it seems scarcely credible; though Dom and I were delighted for Simon, who, due to holiday in Cyprus at the home of a schoolfriend, had been forced to take Foreign Office advice and stay at home when unexpected trouble created unrest on the island. Now fourteen, a head taller than me, and something of a looker, he'd learned fast to feign ignorance when two of Dom's older friends would appear 'Just thought we'd pop in' to sit, gazing silently and adoringly opposite where he'd be reading. Each girl had promised Dom their favourite possession in exchange for a lock of his hair 'You can do it when he's asleep...' He was changing fast and already smoking. Our proviso of 'Preferably never, but never indoors' resulted in Pandora's legs becoming shorter by the day as she was hauled off for yet another trip around the block. But at least it meant he puffed less..

G's spells at home seldom lasted for longer than eight or so weeks, the longest being eleven – due mainly to his always being on both the advance and rear parties of any move; but we relished his presence when, for a while, life resumed a semblance of normality.

Mother and Celeste, always good company, visited regularly, and as usual, with enough to do, we jogged along, at the end of each day so thankful that we were still a complete family. Each tour was an ordeal for everyone and always a reminder, that less than half way through the very first, in '71, a friend, had been shot and killed.

Officers wives, particularly those of senior ranks (G. was now a Major) are expected to set examples, help out when necessary - especially on the welfare front - and assist the Families' Officer when domestic problems surfaced within a husband's Company. On the whole, difficulties were dealt with internally, sometimes with advice from a friendly GP, but it was important to realise that, whilst all more or less in the same boat and in sympathy with each others' problems, we also needed to remember that largely, we were considered privileged with better quarters, higher incomes and cars for which we held licences. Many senior wives also had the benefit of experience, aware that frequent separation, combined with cash shortage, housing issues and little relief from the strain of caring for young children might result in depression, illness, and occasionally, real tragedy. During our time in Catterick, one particularly chilling example involved a young soldier's wife from another regiment, who, obviously desperate had - for whatever reason, in her husband's absence - simply walked out and disappeared, leaving her year-old child alone in the house with the family pet, a large Alsatian dog. Due to the involvement of Social Services in this sad case, which took place shortly after that of Maria Coldwell (another shameful episode from the '70s involving Social Services, child-neglect and death) following the usual inquiries, questions were asked in the House, but the results were again, never made public. That tragedy had led to me interviewing the then Tory MP for Richmond, Mr.Tim Kitson, Prime Minister Edward Heath's PPS. but as in the Maria Coldwell incident, relevant information never reached the public and to the present day, remains under wraps.

Work, both for the radio and otherwise, had gained momentum, but as expected, pay cheques from the BEEB were soon overtaken by those from other sources. In the main it was enjoyable and I even had one real scoop: the only UK interview with a local farmer, when a military vehicle from a Cavalry regiment, stationed nearby, had become stuck in a stream on his land. After two weeks of preventing the removal of this new and expensive machine, his lack of co-operation had made both the national press, and the TV news broadcasts on three channels. Draining my reservoirs of persuasion in the process, I finally reached his better nature at 7:30am one morning, in a misty field - his choice - only to end up the equivalent of 'spiked' - laid to rest without so much as an airing when - when for whatever reason - he'd capitulated, just prior to us making the 6pm news.

That year also included the big trip to Buckingham Palace, when Mr. Modesty announced 'I'm getting a gong. An MBE. To my startled 'For what?' he'd answered 'Oh. You know, nothing specific. The usual stuff...' We didn't know but were delighted that his hard work had been recognized. He'd returned half way through a Belfast tour and, with S and D on 48hrs. special leave from school, had whizzed us all off to old friends in London to celebrate. We'd appeared, ready for inspection (not really) groomed and spruce; both children gleaming even me, resplendent in new kit, despite friend Liz's swift reply when quizzed as to 'What's Bev wearing?...She's bought a new pair of jeans'.

The palace was certainly impressive, although G's expectations of 'flunkeys with coffee' never materialized. Proudly, we'd watched as our pristine warrior was 'done'. And the answer to the question that everyone asks afterwards? 'The Queen had said "Have you come far?

It was then off to Hertfordshire to celebrate with lovely cousin Shiela and her family.

Some weeks later, supper began with 'I've been offered a Staff job in Berlin, working from the Olympic Stadium. We'd be on our own this time: no regiment.. Seldom does one get a second chance at such a sought after plum. Although my enthusiastic hugs and kisses of congratulation were slightly tempered - this time, we'd be leaving both children behind.

So began the big hunt for Dom's senior school, the one positive aspect being her apparent eagerness to actually go (I say apparent now as her/our choice failed to live up to expectations). Cousin Sheila suggested we try and restrict our search to the Hertfordshire area, and as one of Dom's friends was shortly due to start at a convent in Letchworth, we arranged to view, along with two other schools recommended by friends. The convent won - and she'd be off in September. It would come all too soon and I was dreading it. Now almost twelve, she was affectionate and good company. There was a lot to miss in that sparky personality.

Happy, that first evening, at her enthusiastic waves of farewell, we'd driven off, hopeful that the shock-waves of boarding (being neither E. Blyton nor 'Butlins') might penetrate slowly. As it happened, with her usual stoic approach to life in general, we heard few complaints. Instead, I was the pathetic one. With G. back in Belfast, Pandora and I rattled around together, consoling one another.

The joy of half-term passed all too quickly and by Christmas, both children, at twelve and almost sixteen, had moved on fast. So full of news, wit and chat were they that once back at school, it was hard to accept that our next reunion wouldn't be until Easter, in Berlin.

In an attempt to arrest my packing fever, Liz suggested we sign up for a short course – Upholstery.'Just one afternoon a week'. She took to it like the proverbial duck, diligently transforming what had once been a wreck, whilst I did my best on a Victorian armchair - £10:00 from a friendly local dealer - working at snail's pace: but still with us and still comfortable. Meanwhile, Liz and Nick, her partner, having both gained degrees in Antiques Restoration, now own and run a thriving antiques business in Somerset, where he's 'Clocks and Carpentry' and she deals expertly with the upholstery side.

Chapter Seventeen

BERLIN IN '75 WAS DEEP IN THE THROES of Baader-Meinhoff, and a very different place from that which we'd left almost four years earlier. Security couldn't have been tighter and no-one does it better than ironically, Germany and Israel. But we soon adapted to flashing I.D. Cards just about everywhere and decided it was good to be back.

Once installed - this time in a major's quarter - larger and closer to the Grunewald (the forest) G. sorted the vagaries of his new job, whilst I, relieved once more of housework by our legendary new cleaner, Irena, filled the freezer, breaking off only for coffee which we drank together in the kitchen. She, one of natures great communicators, had voluntarily and complete with dictionary, decided to take on the role of teacher, helping me to sort out the language. I swear those comical, daily fifteen minutes or so, sessions, taught me more than any structured class could ever have done, and while grammar featured little, my idiom and vocabulary swelled. Irena, short, round, dark, chatty and naturally humorous, and I, had hit it off from day one, but speech was essential and gradually, together, we made verbal sense. Fascinated by my manic, but methodical catering sessions, she'd help me transport endless dishes to our new king-sized chest-freezer, in the cellar, where, making the most of the (still thriving) F.R.I,S, we stacked starters in compartment one, mains in two and puds. and cakes in three, along with the odd pack of canapes and smoked salmon sandwiches. Dinner-party menus had now risen a notch or two, with richer fare. Delicious: but healthy? Not a hope. Instead, the butter, cream and booze were sloshed in with abandon and thinking back, can only hope not to have killed anyone. Posted above the freezer were lists of the clearly labelled contents and any removals were crossed off immediately; the intention being to keep topping up. Reflecting on such daunting efficiency, am delighted that the need for such disciplined effort has long since past.

One day, about to house a batch of Coq-au-Vin, I took a call.

'Hello' - an American voice - 'Mrs Pettifar? Milly Sibboly here. Just

G Brunei 79 Water Village behind him

to say there'll be eight of us for lunch tomorrow, and not ten.' 'Eight?'.. just eight. Is that OK?'...

'R-i-g-h-t.' In the shortest time we'd met so many people: French, German, American - even the odd Russian. The brain bounced into overdrive, dredging rapidly through recent happenings but not a glimmer of an 'American' lunch emerged; although a split second later I'd planned the menu and about to break the minute's silence, heard the voice at the other end say tentatively.

'Mrs. Pettifar? Mrs Valerie Pettifar? A-a-a-h. Being immediately off the hook I cooed back cheerfully 'That's not me'.

We'd been mistaken for the other Pettifars - in almost twenty years our first namesakes - met briefly, just a day or two earlier, at the nearby R.A.F. Station. .

With both children back at school, life hotted up. Through Trixie, a friend from our '69 tour, we collected several new friends, mostly European, but also a handful of Egyptians. This interesting International group all spoke at least three languages fluently, sometimes more, slipping graciously and swiftly into whichever tongue happened to be appropriate. (Such expertise certainly puts the British habit of speaking more s-l-o-w-l-y and loudly than usual, as if to a halfwit, to shame.) Invitations for drinks, lunches and suppers, were endless, plus opportunities to retune our opera ears. With the Arts heavily subsidised and opera considered in no way elitist, seat prices, in both East and West Berlin, were low in comparison to England, although the venues varied widely. East Berlin's opera house (where the Allied dress-code stated Mess kit for foreign military men and evening dress for women) whilst smaller than the re-vamped modern structure in the West, was also older and impressively more elegant, being exquisitely decorated in white, gold and delicate shades of blue. Performances varied, but were usually of a high standard, although we became used to seeing something other than the programme advertised.

Increasingly, we discovered more of Berlin's many and varied leisure activities but on Sundays, would sneak off early, first to the YMCA, for the papers, before moving on to Wintergarten - a huge, elegant glasshouse restaurant with the best buffet-breakfast in town: three or four juices; teas, coffees, selections of just about every conceivable cold meat and cheese, plus boiled eggs, fresh fruits, Danish pastries, breads, croissants, crispbreads, butter and preserves. Unlimited grazing at around £6:00 per head (and from a recent report, still thriving.)

We'd been back just a few weeks when a chance meeting with someone called Bob Pearson, a friend of Dick Norton and now his replacement at the Berlin studio, led to an offer of work, and whilst the word money featured 'small' it would be good to keep my hand in. And as usual, there would always be someone interesting to interview. The studio, having recently been overhauled, smelt strongly of fresh paint, new carpet, plastic and 'electrics' and - as during my later interview with the 'Stones' - I was finding it increasingly difficult to concentrate, seldom leaving the building without a headache. Outside work was fine, so I volunteered for 'More out than in, please...'

During the summer holidays the house throbbed, with friends from both offspring's schools staying and others constantly in and out. Dom learned to sail whilst Simon and friends - thanks to the network of military buses and excellent public transport system - familiarised themselves with the city. Combined with the facilities of the Officers' Club pool and our cellar, now theirs, they were extremely well catered for. As promised earlier, the cellar underwent a makeover and we winced as walls - and ceilings, thanks to a lissom sixteen year old - sprouted innovative patterns of black hands and feet. There was no shortage of parties for either them or us, but for theirs we remained firmly in situ, appearing briefly, but unexpectedly, just a couple of times during the evening, no doubt placing ourselves firmly on their hate list. These days, with teenagers of their own, they understand why.

That Autumn, I morphed into 'The Tattooed Lady', working mostly in Brigade HQ, (the building originally built for the '37 Olympics) selling tickets for the Berlin Tattoo. Produced by the world's 'Tattoo Genius', Major Michael Parker, it was about the most popular event ever housed in the city, and took place regularly every two years. With virtually no time to give the offer much thought and under the impression my duties would amount to the equivalent of selling raffle tickets to the Military, it was a shock to find myself employed by a non-English-speaking German boss who operated solely from the Deutschlandhalle. There were a few things to sort: different seat prices for different performances on different days, as well as student, child and other concessions, and everyone clamouring to change their tickets once it became known that Prince Charles would be attending on the final evening. Also, at least half my customers would be German when, on Saturday afternoons, I'd be selling on the Kurfurstendamme, from 'The Tattoo Van'. Rapidly, my little sessions with Irena came into their own and whilst seldom a swift thinker, and virtually innumerate, I somehow managed to sort the Montags from the Mitwochs, the Dienstags from the Donnerstags, and the Sonntags from the Samstags - at the same time, working out the final D.M. costs of seat selections. After that first afternoon in the van, it became obvious that the majority of my salary would be going toward - what would surely turn out to be - a massive shortfall when it came to totting-up time. Somehow - incredibly - it all worked out, with not a single extra Ffennig needed for the final total. To this day I've no idea how. It had felt like the longest eight weeks of my life.

Next came my launch into the world of The Berlin Bulletin; a small, English-language paper, varying in content between eighteen and twenty-four pages. Published weekly, on Fridays, it had a circulation of somewhere between four and four a half thousand copies, and served to keep the Military and the Embassies up to date with local news, details of concerts, cinema and TV programmes, plus a page of small-ads. One of the two regular staff, was dear Klaus Endtler, installed on Day 1 (sometime in '48) without whom - those first few weeks particularly - I'd never have coped. Apart from the pasting-up, Klaus handled any cribs from the German Press, the photographs, and the small ads., and over the years, had worked with a series of English female assistants whose duties involved producing a couple of regular features, commissioning copy, dealing with proofs and re-writes and generally acting as assistant-editor. At holiday times we stood in for each other, leaving as much 'in hand' as possible. Acting as our 'Beaverbrook, the delightful Brigade Commander - Brigadier Charles Grey, sadly no longer with us - had the final say on anything remotely controversial. Thanks however, to his great sense of humour, that particular year we both briefly managed to gain the unexpected displeasure of our big boss, General Roy Redgrave (otherwise known as 'Daffodil') when G, having realised that The Bulletin came out on 1 April, and never known to resist an opportunity, had popped up with 'Something for your Bulletin...' His 'Tips For Tourists and 'New Environmental Laws' included 'All parked cars considered to need cleaning by the recently-formed 'Clean-Car Services' will immediately be 'booked' and cleaned. The fee will be D.M.20...' and 'The first day of every month is Taxi-Training Day in the city. When the driver holds out his hand for the fare, shake it warmly and go on your way'. The Brigadier's reaction, a loud whoop and a firm nod, was later to gain him an unexpected thumbs down, and me, a firm snub. We decided that 'Daffodil' usually a humorous man, had probably had to deal with a possibly embarrassing, complaint - or three.

Sometime in June, having, with difficulty, secured an interview with the Rolling Stones, I'd nervously found, within minutes of entering one of the Deutchlandhalle's tiny dressing-rooms, my train of thought dissolving. As Mick Jagger patiently began to answer my first question and Keith Richards - Mr. Loveliness himself - made quiet, gentle offers of 'Come on Darlin' 'ave a drink' (forever establishing himself in a corner of my memory as something of a gent.) my second question sort of 'hung'. The title of the album, Black and

Blue, the group's most recent release, had distressingly escaped me, floating off somewhere into the hinterland of the heavily scented air. The next day, after editing, we'd somehow ended up with a reasonable four and a half minutes, but had I reacted more positively it could have been better (All was revealed several years later, when, following periods of ill health, I was diagnosed with multiple allergies to a surprisingly wide variety of foods and chemicals. I recalled G's reaction that evening: 'You reek of pot. Where have you been?')

Half-way through the holidays, with Simon's lovely Lindsay now swapped for lovely Charlotte (eldest daughter of friends who lived opposite) hours were spent in his room as they studied for A Levels; complete with joss-sticks, Patti Smith and David Bowie: obviously no deterrent to the full set of A's, later gained by each (were we the proud parents). Any spare time was well-catered for by G's brilliant holiday scheme 'Earn While You Learn', which employed teenagers at a small hourly rate. This saw Dom rushing off to catch the 6am bus for the Officers' Club, where she cleaned the pool changing-rooms, whilst Simon became part of 'Removals and Exchanges'. We felt it was good training for them both and they were grateful for the extra cash when later we took off for three weeks of bliss - the longest ever of G's leave breaks - to a large mobile home in the South of France.

Sometime in mid-March, my lack of pioneering spirit - untested since the births of both children - was about to surface, with G's news that we'd been offered a 2/3 year posting in Brunei, on the North West coast of Borneo. 'We'd be leaving in November,' he'd said. His enthusiastic delivery deserved an equally enthusiastic 'How exciting Darling, that sounds lovely'... Instead, Miss Cautious replied 'Convince me'. (At that time with growing teenagers, often more needy than young children, it seemed just a step too far). The Husband would need to work hard at this one, honing his propensity for casting the very brightest glow on everything to its finest edge. Although it was obvious that the Runes were already cast. He began. 'Fantastic beaches; heat - a bit humid - but you like the heat; friendly locals and the children will join us for all holidays, as usual.. And it's a really good job.. .And we'll be able to travel all over the Far East... I'll be attached to the Sultan's army, training other Quartermasters... Really don't want to feel I'm too old (48) to do a 'funny' (long- distance tour).We get a large - Rent-AND-Utilities free - three bedroom bungalow. 'Imagine, we can save money' and other perks include a live-in amah and generous allowances. And 'There's a NAAFI ...'

Silently, Miss Negative took over. 'Bugger the NAAFI... Rent and utilities-free accommodation: why? (Bribery?). Children on the other side of the world; an Islamic country where Pandora wouldn't be welcome - and anyway she loathed the heat - Ok for me perhaps, but as 'the chest' hadn't been good that year, humidity might be a problem. Bugs would be in a league of their own and doubtless, after Berlin, where everyone was too busy, so would the gossip. Echoes of S. Maugham's atmospheric tales, featuring bored, alcoholic ex.pats. who seemed mostly to loathe each other, surfaced swiftly. Then, shamed at my negativity... 'Oh well. If it's really grim at least we'll be together ... And S and D might enjoy an adventure.. .Who knows. So might we.' Then came the mind-concentrator. 'You might like to know that the alternative is N. Ireland. And I've already refused Nigeria...' Ah. 0...K. There was just one proviso. The children would need a base in England. Before leaving, we'd have to buy a house.

In early June, with our exit from Berlin set for mid-September, accompanied by Charlotte, we set-off for a crammed week in UK, stopping first to collect Dom from school to shop for the half-term she'd be spending in France. She looked well, but really wanted to join us... On then to Bloxham, to stay with old friends nearby, after watching S. take a talented lead in the school's production of C.P. Snow's, The Masters. Next night there was the school Ball,where, dancing with S's Housemaster, I was asked to try and persuade our son to accept the offer of Head of House, followed the next term by Head of School, both of which he'd turned down - reasoning that the work needed for either post would hinder any chances of his getting to Balliol. Next stop, before Guildford, was Brighton, for a hopeful meeting with an estate agent found in the Sunday Telegraph (I recalled a Roy Brooks - estate-agent ad. from the '60's: 'The only thing keeping most of the property in Brighton standing is the fact that the woodworm all hold hands'). Swiftly, after dismissing several dreary flats, we settled on a light, pleasant, undistinguished (bar the purple sitting-room walls) three-bed terraced house, in a quiet street.

Surprisingly, bar Charlotte's suitcase detaching itself from our roof-rack - involving a 100 mile drive and probably a few bad moments for the policeman who'd received it from it's Irish finder (this was '77) all had run smoothly. Our endless lists and errands completed, we'd covered over 2,500 miles.

Work, as ever, fitted in with frantic weekends of Sunday brunches and curry lunches nudging us toward the inevitable.Sadly, our stalwart Irena was about to retire to care for her invalid spouse so as a diversion, we accepted the offer of a friend to mate her handsome, well-born Golden Labrador. Monty - young and raring to go with Pandora, who accommodatingly had just come into season. But after less than a 20 second 'union', P. all snarls at this attack on her person, took off in the direction of home. Weeks later however, with her again, bloating and lactating, the vet 's verdict of 'Alles ist fantasie' (phantom) found us, the next day, amazed to discover our panting hound guarding three very new baby boys. Expecting more, Dom, Charlotte and Simon - complete with doggy manual - took on midwife duty and the next few hours were punctuated by the arrival of numbers four, five and six - the last of the litter, a second little girl, being the smallest. Next morning, with Pandora in need of attention, Dom and I, complete with a boxed set of babies, once more set off for the vet - subsequently a most unhappy man when presented with my 'Alles ist fantasie ja? Fur zie, Ich habe sex kliene Geistes.' (For you, I have six little ghosts). Our fee for the previous visit (over £100) was refunded in full, the only 'Fantasie' having been the x-rays. During the next few weeks, mother and rapidly-expanding babies, lived happily, during the day, in a large cage, which we moved around the garden and soon, complete with appropriate jabs and authenticated pedigree forms our 'young' were advertised in a daily paper. They sold all too quickly, and whilst goodbyes were a wrench, Poppy, so christened, the last, prettiest and still the smallest, hurt the most. Although, having talked through Brunei yet again, it looked as if Pandy wouldn't be coming with us either...Our forthcoming stay in the Orient was fast losing it's already limited appeal.

As Celeste - now a fully-fledged grown-up Banisters' Clerk - had spent Easter with us, Mother and a friend were our final guests before the big pack. While Dom and Simon continued their day jobs (leaving evenings free for parties) I, now unemployed (and replaced at the Bulletin by an ex. Daily Mail professional) succumbed to a frantic call from the studio. Richard Asprey, now the BFBS 'Man in \Berlin' - by then a good friend having been in situ. for six months or so - simply said 'Help Bev. Please. Shiela is off to London for emergency surgery.' So followed three whirlwind weeks, featuring two interesting interviews: one with Schering - the pharmaceutical company, then testing a 'Not yet successful' male-contraceptive pill (can't you just hear it 'You're alright tonight Darlin', I'm on the pill...) and the other with a lovely guy, Len Richmond, who had spent a happy three days researching 'Berlin's Gay Hotel Scene. 'Riveting radio' we were told; along with the usual complaints regarding the subject-matter. How tame it all seems now.

Meanwhile, Simon and Charlotte, complete with a full medical kit and instructions covering everything from earthquakes to sunstroke, plus G's AMEX card (for emergencies) were in Turkey, staying for part of the trip with the family of a young Turkish friend of Charlotte. Having wondered if we'd ever see them again, we were ecstatic at their on-schedule return – tanned - and flea-ridden from the previous night's sojourn in a cheap 'hotel'. But whilst bursting with news of their adventures, S. first had to open the big 'results' - still intact despite our itchy fingers. What a star. 3A's and 3 As's. At last he'd be able to count on hatching the first of his plans for Oxford... Catching up, later, we were delighted to learn of his refusal to exchange curvy, blonde Charlotte for an - apparently sizeable - flock of sheep, and touched at both their descriptions of the poverty-stricken, but immensely generous hospitality of their hosts. On their final evening, both scrubbed and shiny (pre.the flea-pit) they'd used, as pro. G's instructions, the still-untouched AMEX card, for a slap-up meal in Istanbul's best restaurant; somewhat to the consternation of the maitre'd, who had no doubt suspected it stolen.

After three weeks of generous farewell parties, following three of our own, we were ready. All spares, white goods and garden furniture, had been passed on, sold, or ditched, and our 35, rigidly-packed boxes were somewhere on the high seas. The children flew off to school two days before we moved into Edinburgh House, and Pandora, now passed on to good Berlin friends, stayed until the last possible (howling: me, not her) moment. It's impossible to leave an animal 'on loan' for almost three years, especially as June and Wolfgang loved her almost as much as we, so the arrangement was 'See you all sometime in '81'...

We'd lost track of last-minute callers covering our final 24hours in

Edinburgh House, but by 7am the next morning, a Sunday, there we were, loaded and ready - the belly of our snug Ami 8 Estate, almost grazing the tarmac. Sheila, Charlotte's mother, had said 'You'll never do it: SO much kit...' Making for the Avus, our exit road, we passed Jo's Bierhaus, wide open, as usual, for breakfast; but maybe it never closed... Already feeling nostalgic, we reached the Avus, only to discover it lined with barriers for the annual 24 hrs. motor-race. Despite all the meticulous planning, that particular event had somehow passed us by. Deep breath. The Ides were not good. On then to Am Postfenn and 'The Corridor'. (It seems impossible for me to have written so much concerning Berlin without previously describing it, but on glancing back, it appears so.) The Corridor, covering some 50 miles or so, was East Germany territory, and as such was naturally policed by them. It was also the entrance and exit route used specifically by the military when entering and leaving Berlin. The rules stated that speed limits must not be exceeded, and that each journey never took less than two hours. Just to make sure, all vehicles were logged at start and finish, at checkpoints then manned by the Russian military.

Two hours later, maybe just 12 ks. from 'finish' we broke down. There we sat, waiting for a British Military vehicle (E. German aid being 'disallowed') to bale us out. Finally, having been 'fixed' we fairly sped along. Hours later, however, around dusk, following a loud clunk, we steered gently into a safe position, once more sitting quietly, debating our fate. But - Hallelujah. Within moments, a cruising rescue vehicle, with flashing lights, slid in behind us and after a fractured conversation, we were hooked up and bounced, at the end of a short tow-rope, some 70 miles or so, to a Citroen garage, alongside which stood a small hotel. All for around £35:00. Having slept and breakfasted, whilst our split fuel pipe was swiftly and oh-so-efficiently renewed, we were, once more en route, arriving at Ostende just in time to wave off the ferry: literally.

Spinach, Cream Cheese and Prawn -
or Smoked Salmon - Roulade,

Serve as Starter, or part of a Summer buffet.

Heat oven to 190c and line a 12x8 swiss-roll tin with lightly greased Bakewell paper.

Four separated eggs.2 level tabsp. grated parmesan cheese. 1 med tub cream cheese + 200grm.drained Prawns ('Maine' are best' from 'best' supermkt.) or 200grms.smoked salmon.200grm cooked, chopped spinach.

175grm drained weight cottage cheese.30grm each of butter and plain flour and a little milk. I med-sized finely chopped onion, softened in a little oil

Melt butter, stir in flour and then milk to make small quantity of thick-ish sauce. Season well and set aside. Blend spinach with one generous tabsp. sauce and the egg yolks and onion - season with pepper and grated nutmeg and fold in parmesan and cottage cheese.

Fold in stiffly beaten egg-whites. Spread mixture evenly into tin and bake for 15 mins. Remove and cover with clean T towel - cool, and invert onto a table: T towel at bottom.

When cold, trim edges. spread over cream cheese and prawns or smoked salmon. Make a nick about 4cm along roll-up edge and roll roulade. with help of t. towel

Decorate as desired and serve in slices.

Chapter Eighteen

PASSING THE FAMOUS ROYAL PAVILION, gleaming in the strong September sun, Brighton welcomed us in; it's vibrant atmosphere almost tangible. We'd made 23, Coventry St. in good time and as G. began to unload, I opened the front door. Oh...We'd forgotten Mr Rentokil. Our heavily masked assassin was diligently going about his business - as they did and probably still do - in a haze of pungent chemicals (immediately, I visualised a surreal heap of gasping woodworm, tiny hands still tightly clasped). G, now alongside, bearing suitcases, muttered 'Hmm. Can't stay here tonight'. Unloading completed, we left Mr. R. to his work and fled, to the nearest 'phone box, sure that Mother and Celeste would be delighted to put us up. But not before a little detour. Whilst our Yorkshire auctions had seen us 'fully furnished' we'd never got around to the beds. But Brighton had them all and with delivery promised for the next day, we whizzed off to Mother and Celeste, in Guildford.

Once back at 23 and installed (sort of) we opened all windows and made for the local Hire shop. A trestle table and four plastic chairs later, plus the necessary painting kit, saw us about ready to start. Meanwhile, I dug out kitchen china and linen, the remainder of which was probably bouncing around somewhere on the South China Seas. That evening, after excellent, local fish and chips, desperate for sleep, we staggered upstairs.

By the weekend, with a working 'phone, the house re-carpeted, the painting completed and Simon, Dom and Charlotte due any second, we decided that the following Monday morning, rather than hand over the £500 quoted by the Yorkshire company storing our furniture to deliver it to us in Brighton, we'd book a small van and collect it ourselves.

Luckily, our family reunion - brief, but so very joyful - had set us up for the doubtful pleasure of a frantic, almost six hour drive, severely hampered by a duff vehicle whose gear stick, refusing to stay put, jumped out of position at every corner (the one at Hyde Park proving particularly interesting) plus an indicator wand which now and again simply fell off. Having 'phoned earlier and arranged to choose and buy curtain fabric, in a favourite shop in Barnard Castle, we arrived late. The accommodating owner, however, supported over many years by hordes of Service wives, simply said warmly 'Welcome back. Loove...And you joost take as long as yer like.'

The next morning, finding ourselves alone - all storage-company staff having mysteriously vanished - we 'broke stack' and filled the van, whacked after a merry evening with good friends who had not only put us up but also sweetly killed the fatted calf. Following another tortuous drive, we finally reached home at 11pm. G. couldn't wait to deal with the car-hire company, who in the end, actually refunded - plus extra - their entire fee.

Finally, we were ready. With nothing left to be done to our re-decorated, re-carpeted and re-curtained (tacked and lined by me, but due to the machine being electric, sewn by G) we were now fully packed, and in my case waxed and truly hacked (off). UK Christmas cards and presents had been bought, written, wrapped, labelled and stacked at the home of our lovely new postman friend opposite, who'd offered to act as caretaker, as well as promising to mail everything on their given dates. Ron and Elsie Rook were the kindest, most generous neighbours imaginable and we were so exceptionally lucky to have had them as friends.

Only 48hrs earlier we'd seen both children off to their destinations, and ticked off the endless lists of endless tasks. With a simple cookery book in the kitchen, piles of tinned supplies and a notebook in the hall containing local shop opening hours, instructions re. fridge, heating, phone, fuses, TV, plugs, water mains etc; plus 'Things to do on arrival and Before leaving'. We'd hoped to have covered everything, having settled purposely on an urban area with easily accessible shops, takeaways and launderette. It was now simply a question of leaving them to it. G. as usual, had the right approach. 'They're not babies (by then 15 and almost 19) and they'll be fine. Stop worrying.' Not a chance.

Meat Loaf (for 6)

Turn oven to 180c.

You'll need 1 mug white breadcrumbs and 1 kilo finely minced, or ground, meats - pork and beef work well.

Place in bowl and add breadcrumbs

To 2 tabsp. hot oil add 1 large finely chopped onion, 3 cloves crushed garlic, 2 grated carrots and 3 or 4 chopped mushrooms - when soft add to meat and crumbs. Break in an egg, a splash of Tabasco or sweet chilli sauce, plus a dash of soy sauce and a pinch of salt.

Using your hands, mix everything together but try to avoid squeezing the meat.

Turn into a loaf-tin and smooth top.

Serve hot with a well-seasoned tomato sauce or sliced cold with a spicy pickle or chutney.

Easy Pasta Sauce

Slice 175 grm mushrooms and fry in scant mix of butter and oil, Add 3 cloves crushed garlic and season well with salt and pepper. Stir in med. sized carton sour cream and a third t.sp. Nutmeg. Heat through and add to chosen, cooked pasta.

Chapter Nineteen

'STEAK OR LOBSTER MADAM?' smiled the steward in first class, who, considering it was now 2am, looked remarkably lively. We on the other hand, following a seven hour delay, neither felt nor looked remotely so. The airline had done its best (along with the Sultan of Brunei who would be footing the bill) as, with nine of our fellow fliers, we'd taken advantage earlier of 'Dinner - plus whatever else you would like from the 'Tavern in the Sky' - and had, on the whole, enjoyed an amusing evening with a thoroughly entertaining group of people. No doubt the fizz had helped, but time had flown and for a while, stopped me wondering how the children were.

Eyes closed, I leaned back in the spacious seat, trying to relax and as the day's events lined themselves up neatly for inspection, my train of thought gathered speed. There had been the final once-over of the house, resulting in a mad dash to the shops for plastic wood to fill a previously unspotted hole in the back door; then the goodbyes to Mother and Celeste where our car now waited to be passed on to friends. Next, up popped the cab-driver who, spotting my distress, had looked concerned and dealt swiftly with our heap of luggage. Well. No going back now. I tried to feel more positive. As G settled down to snooze, I watched enviously for a moment, wondering at the apparently built-in ability of the military to sleep: anytime, anywhere.

First stop had been Kuwait where we'd waved off the interior designer: a fellow diner who had recently sold her house on the Kings Road for an impressive £79,000. Having just bought ours for around a sixth of that, we were very probably the most impressed of all. The next stopover should have been Kuala Lumpuar but due to 'Running late' (and what about those who actually lived there?) on we flew. Within what felt like seconds later,G. pointed to the window. 'Lots of bright lights. Must be downtown Singapore. Take a look...'

Leaving the aircraft, the heat and smells of the Far East immediately enveloped us, although the atmosphere felt very different from that of Bahrain, twenty years earlier, where, for whatever reason, I'd soon felt at home - something I never did in Brunei. G. had remarked how different the two places were but as a 'Korean Veteran', whose R&R periods had been spent in Tokyo, he was way ahead of me.

Met by G's soon-to-be predecessor, we taxied off to the Mandarin Hotel, in Orchard Road, Singapore's equivalent of Park Lane. There, in the vast, much-mirrored reception area with its tastefully-sited plots of lush indoor jungle, we were welcomed as if old friends and due to our original booking having been released, were gravely offered a suite. Assured our identities hadn't been confused with V.I.Ps, G accepted their suggestion with aplomb, smiling widely at the 'We so hope you'll be happy'. (As I recall, this lush little penthouse pad, previously occupied by Muhammad Ali, might easily have accommodated three separate families.) 'Make the most of it' murmured G, as we'd settled into one of the pair of Queen-sized beds... But there wouldn't be time. Within hours, we'd been whisked to the airport and placed in the loving care of Singapore Airways.

Had anyone have asked, I'd have imagined we were landing in Surrey, so un-tropical had our destination appeared from the sky. But after the swiftest and actually slickest, transfer from plane to cab, just a short drive saw us soon dropped at Angs Hotel, our home for the next few weeks: later christened 'Angst' when the air-conditioning broke down. This brown, seven or eight-storey building at the edge of Brunei's capital town, Bandar Seri Begawan, whilst unprepossessing in appearance, far exceeded expectations. Our en-suite double room had comfortable beds, a phone, television, clean linen daily and an excellent laundry service. Hefty amounts of guesswork went into mealtimes, but what the menu lacked in translation it made up for in versatility and soon, with time and a certain ingenuity,we were working our way through a fine selection of both Chinese and Malay dishes; as well as some of the best pepper steaks ever.

Our 'Pre-Brunei' Information Pack' told us that this small Muslim state was ruled by His Highness the Sultan (now His Majesty) who, after attending Singapore's International School, went on to Sandhurst, where he had been accepted for Officer Training. Once back at home, the tough Sandhurst course would have helped him tremendously when dealing with affairs of State. Particularly impressive was his title and a letter to him from one of his staff-officers, of whom George was one, would need to begin with his full title, some five lines long.

Initially, Brunei, roughly 30 miles long and 20 miles wide, comprised dense, lush jungle. Over the centuries, however,with increased development, larger kampongs (jungle villages) and towns, have gradually been established and since the discovery, sometime in the '50's, of oil - and later, Silicate Sand and natural gas - the country has become significantly more prosperous. Naturally, this has resulted in a higher standard of living for the mixed population of Brunei-Malays, Chinese and a few - usually older - Europeans and Antipodeans who, at the end of a working contract have been granted Royal permission to remain. They could do worse. A birdwatcher and butterfly hunter's paradise, along with the unhurried pace of life, exquisite coastline and fascinating flora and fauna, Brunei is perfect for those opting for the lower-tech. life - although in the steamy, enervating climate with average humidity at 95%, the joys of the 'Air Magicianer' (so-called by a friend) would be sorely missed.. During our time there, travel facilities improved monthly, but today, a thriving tourist trade exists for those seeking a holiday with a difference.

That first evening, following a better-than-average dinner, had been spent watching 'Poldark' on TV. How very surreal it seemed. The next morning, Sunday (in a Muslim country, a normal working day) we taxied into Bandar, a small town, full of shops; mainly open-fronted and offering just about the most comprehensive selection of goods we'd ever seen in one place and it was soon obvious that the occasional request for a particular item - having already produced the smiley reply 'Finish already'- usually turned up after a diligent search. Stocktaking was obviously not a priority, if indeed, it existed at all, but as everyone appeared totally unhurried, who were we to even consider it. Even the livestock appeared unruffled. We'd watched in disbelief as a plump hen on a market stall had stood patiently, emitting no more than a brief squawk whilst wrapped in a sheet of paper and secured with a rubber band before being solemnly placed, parcel-like, under the arm of a waiting customer.

G.'s working hours soon took on a life of their own with early mornings and late evenings leaving him just enough time to shower and change before supper. Combined with the job, he was also trying to fit in the language course; never completed due to pressure of work. By now, we also had a car and thanks to the cheap petrol, motoring cost little; although a spell behind the wheel might liven up the day no end with our licenses encouraging us all to 'Drive more or less on the left'.

Luckily, some old regimental friends living nearby, the Hamptons, now on their third contract with the Royal Brunei-Malay Regiment, soon made contact. Delighted to see some familiar faces and immensely grateful for their kindness over the next few weeks, we listened intently to 'the life and times of Brunei' some of which was good, some not. They treated us to long, lazy Sundays on their boat, anchoring for a few hours on The Spit' - a 'brochure beach' complete with monkeys, a few miles further up the coast where G. caught-up, from Bahrein days, on his water-skiing. The sea was the warmest ever but the advice was that no dip was complete without plimsolls, due to the odd Stingray, Stone-fish or Sea-snake...

Later that week, in G's absence, I found myself, after an evening spent with Zoe and Tony, on the receiving end of another previously unspecified but quite unforgettable little extra. Having stepped into the lift, I'd been immediately joined by a middle-aged Chinese man. Having replied politely to his 'Good evening' and two or three questions, at the 7th, floor I'd nodded and left. Reaching our room along the dim, gloomy corridor, silent but for the restrained hum of the air-cons. I'd jumped as my new acquaintance appeared beside me. Smiling, as if offering a treat, he said 'I come with you. Yes? I velly much like to make love to Eulopean woman.' In the briefest of seconds my heart and mind raced together. 'He may have a knife...Had I been too friendly? As a foreign woman in a Muslim country, if attacked, I'd probably be tried for enticement ...' Silently, I pleaded for help until, from nowhere, a calm British voice (mine?) said reasonably. 'No, you may not come with me. Please go away'. Parrot fashion, he repeated his request as firmly, I repeated mine, adding. 'You are offending me. I find you very offensive. Please go away...' Finally, murmuring 'Velly solly. I go now' he turned, drifting toward the lift. As the doors clanged, I flew into the room and whilst wedging a chair under the door handle, offered aloft garbled prayers of thanks.

Soon aware that we'd pitched up in a land of daily water rationing: 5:30am -7:30am - 5:30pm 7:30pm - regular electricity cuts and a 'phone-system that was totally hit and miss, due to the wires being strung between the trees - a la Christmas lights - instead of buried neatly underground, we adjusted our minds and accepted that all three never actually worked together; and as G. gently reminded me, he could have accepted a posting to Nigeria (swiftly turned down after some friendly advice to 'Go if you like, but don't bother to unpack'. In that first five weeks, with G. at work, the change of pace felt odd. Used to rushing, we realised that here, the word simply didn't translate. Naturally, we missed the children but otherwise, had few complaints. Until the air-conditioning system failed. With the stifling atmosphere in our room barely stirred by a free-standing fan (courtesy of an apologetic manager) sleep disappeared. Rapidly, I developed a severe neurosis as the emergent wildlife, now unrestrained by the icy blasts from the air-con., appeared en-masse. Taking it in turns to doze, we'd lain prone, index fingers poised on the button of our cans of insecticide: pungent powerful and long-since banned in Europe, which, whilst leaving us with severe headaches and nausea had little effect on our unwanted guests. Bedside lights blazed as, after an incident, that first airless night involving bare feet (mine) and a mangled cockroach, I'd insisted 'Lights on all night. OK?' Instructions for playing host to an uninvited selection of rats, spiders, centipedes and ants - plus several unidentifiable (to us, anyway) strays, which judging from their sizes existed solely on the Malay equivalent of Shredded Wheat and Carling Black Label, had, it seemed, been excluded from the pre-arrival info... 48hrs. later, with taps and showers reduced to intermittent dribbles, our remaining sense of humour nose-dived. In such a climate, the combination of restricted lighting, no water or 'air-magicianer' plus the rapidly increasing numbers of 'visitors' the prospect of staying put became a deeply unattractive prospect until, thanks to G., with our allotted quarter still in the hands of the decorators, we were offered an alternative 'Just for a few weeks'... And so was move No1 completed. Simplicity itself, really. Transferring from the hotel involved little more than re-packing the suitcases and popping them into a large cab. It was moving out, three months later, that was to prove so memorable.

Large, newly-built and hallelujah, clean, our temporary residence, one of three, was reached via the novelty of a jungle track off a main road. With four bedrooms and baths, a large kitchen and sitting-room and balconies from most windows, we were so grateful to move in and amazed and excited to find that everything actually worked. The recently installed beds, bamboo sofas and chairs (termed collectively and accurately as 'Hard Furnishings') would eventually move on with us to our final? Brunei home and until our kit arrived, we'd make do with G's borrowings from barracks. Oh joy. Within days, both children would be home.

And then we were four...How they'd grown. Where had they come from, these two very different people? Excitedly, we'd exchanged news and driven them leisurely around Brunei, anxiously hoping that if after Berlin, the sun, sand, Christmas festivities and 'newness' of an exotic posting, might compensate for the loss of the rather more sophisticated delights of the past three years.

Christmas came - spent on the beach with friends, barbecued turkey joints, a pudding, nose-protectors, paper-hats and bikinis (visions, we women were) - and went. Shortly after new year (featuring a very overcrowded 'Dance' at Angs), Dom. then fifteen and eager to show off her tan, flew back to school for the Easter term, leaving a large space. Simon however, at the beginning of his gap year, decided to stay for a while, having first found a job helping out at a local school. Gradually, we settled for life in the slow lane, enjoying the club pool, the beach and leisurely boat trips out to the Islands. Indeed, the phrase 'chill out ' might have been coined for us alone. The decorators' smiling assurances of 'We finish soon' began to matter less and less.

With little warning, the monsoon season started and the days shortened. They were also dim, damp and gloomy and such was the scenario that there were times I expected to find S. Maugham installed in our sitting-room, banging away at an old typewriter, or Sadie Thompson sprawled senseless on the terrace. The acrid smell of mould outdid all else, whilst along with the increased electricity cuts, the drains, unable to cope, overflowed constantly.

Fungus sprouted overnight on the unlikeliest surfaces and several homeless snakes - along with the outsize rats - sought refuge... I began to long for warmth, sunlight and a green field of buttercups and daisies.

And then, moving time again. 'This Thursday?'..Ah. 'The day after tomorrow'?.. 'The men will pack.' said G. Ever the sceptic, I began making lists, having first suggested that Husband and Son collect cartons from Chop Wah Ho, the local supermarket. Despite arriving with just clothing, we'd lately managed to acquire a few extras. (Chop Wah Ho was, and probably still is, an amazing Chinese emporium, where, along with a wondrous selection of kitchen-kit and foodstuffs, American, Chinese and British, stood ten large freezers, three of which held duck-webs, duck feet, and chicken feet: a lesson in economy and adventurous eating to us all...)

At seven a.m. on Thursday, the sun - unseen for weeks - shone brightly. 'A good omen' I thought optimistically. At nine it still shone brightly as we waited patiently for the 'Due at eight' movers. At least, I waited: Simon was on a half-day driving lesson whilst Entan, our bolshy amah - who so far had done more or less as she'd pleased due entirely to my failing to get to grips with the language - had announced that she was 'Going to new house': she'd actually meant ours, but such was her manner that we'd gained the impression she'd taken off for a position that suited her better. G. - leaving earlier for the office - had backed out of the door with a 'Don't worry, you'll be fine, there'll be ten movers'. Ten? We'd obviously be out in no time. As the morning wore on, the sun wore out and it began to rain. Predicting a short, sharp shower, I gazed at the dismal vista: maybe G. had meant the following week? Unlikely. Had we possessed a phone, no doubt he'd have rung to check on progress...From the overnight bag I accessed a paperback and settled down to read until, somewhere around eleven, through the curtain of rain, I spotted a battered open?- oh yes - truck, pull up outside. But a truck was a truck and we were so far behind that anything by way of reliable transport would have been welcome. Greeting the five (five?) movers with bottles of Coca-Cola (first things first) I examined the form handed to me by the spokesman and inquired politely - whilst they settled themselves on the sofas and downed their drinks - whether or not they had sufficient protective covering for the furniture 'As the truck appears to be ...Open.' Warily, they'd glanced at each other, saying nothing, under the impression, perhaps, that an immediate demonstration of atom-splitting might be required. Next, following a loud, animated discussion in Malay, together, they beamed genially back at me, as slowly and deliberately, I was told 'Soon - rain go. Furniture dry'. Now why hadn't I thought of that? Deciding to make a start, I tentatively began directing operations, beckoning everyone upstairs, at the same time wondering how to keep the mattresses dry once they'd been loaded. A lecture on splitting the atom might have been easier after all. Then: ah...the original plastic mattress protectors were downstairs in a spare carton and the open ends could be secured with the pegs I'd whipped off the line with the morning's (wet) washing. Such is happiness.

In the main bedroom stood a selection of cardboard boxes, along with four suitcases, three holdalls and a couple of dozen or so black sacks, each containing clothes or cushions. To a man, the heavier-looking stuff was ignored as they each took one black sack and gingerly descended the stairs, as if transporting priceless porcelain. Having soon fitted the two single mattress covers, I struggled with the double as the stately procession trooped back into the bedroom. Ten movers would have been good. Five? Well; maybe we'd get away tomorrow. Glancing up through a mist of perspiration at five speculative pairs of eyes, I squawked 'Help' indicating the slippery polythene mass. Smiling and nodding benignly by way of reply, they instantly formed a chain and in strict slow-motion, began dealing with the remaining black sacks. Finally,with everything loaded, bar the furniture, and desperate to leave before dark, I realised that the workers were now in a huddle, pointing to their watches. Then our Breadwinner returned.'Thought you'd have been at the house ages ago' he said. 'I waited almost an hour. Simon's there too... Entan has been and gone. Joining us tomorrow apparently...but I wouldn't hold your breath'. Then looking around with a puzzled expression, he added 'They don't seem to have got far...'. Suddenly our mover-in-chief advanced, looking seriously unhappy and still pointing to his watch. 'We go now, Tuan. (master). Come back Saturday.' I watched with interest as Husband moved into full negotiating mode.

Our sizeable bungalow was spacious and light with a large sitting/dining room, three en-suite bedrooms, kitchen and a long outside terrace, bordered by (tropical) grass. It was also freshly decorated and clean - thanks to Simon and I having spent the previous week working together - assisted occasionally by Entan; inclined to regard her job as not only voluntary but also part-time. 'Something's not quite right with this division of labour' I'd remarked acidly to S. one day, to which he'd replied sagely 'Mum. Entan just thinks we're crackers'. True. But whilst her departure headed the current 'Pending' list, her notice could wait: my priority was getting in and settled. Then, even the (occasional) extra pair of hands would be better than none.

With the boxes unpacked, life moved on. The curtains - a hundred yards or so of unbleached calico needed to cover two 35ft glass walls

Fussen Bavaria, January 1981: G&B

of sliding-doors - had been left with the multi-talented camp tailor. At less then five old shillings a yard (25p), I'd worked on the principle that volume over quality cancelled the need for lining - and fading wouldn't matter. Once finished and hung, the surprising results brought forth several comments of 'Gosh. Raw-silk..' Having immediately confessed my thrift, the idea caught on and soon the local store was forced to re-order (at only a very slightly inflated price).

With Dom home for Easter, Simon decided he'd fly back to

England with her, move into our little house in Brighton and find a job. How quiet it would feel. But he had the right idea and now needed to earn more than the local school had been paying. Whilst sad to leave his class of smiley ten-year-olds (so eager had they been to learn English) reality - and Charlotte (still No.1) were beckoning.

Having both S. and D. home together, the latter bursting with news and chat, had been fun We'd obviously been missed, but true to form, Dom never once complained. But it became obvious that a kindred spirit or two would lighten the unfamiliar environment and the saying that 'It's people that make a place' had seldom seemed more apt. G. - Mr. Fixit - suggested a party. 'Teenagers only, and big brother (parents to be holed-up in bedroom, plus books; visible only for meeting, greeting and the good- night curfew). And the guests? The next day, bravely clutching a list of 'phone numbers, secured by G, Dom rang every military household with a teenage family. We admired her spirit, listening gratefully as the list of acceptances grew. Simon, older, with a driving licence and a few job contacts, had fared better and already improved his social life.

Owing hospitality, apart from a Christmas Drinks gathering we'd held back, due mostly to the moves. So: back to the lists and menus, later helpfully revised by Zoe (our oracle) on a basis of ' Not those with those; they've fallen out.' We were also advised that when entertaining Brunei Officers and their wives, some of which were closely related to the Royals, invitations to informal suppers were inclined to be easier than a formal dinner-party, when a last-minute cancellation might sabotage a complicated seating-plan. Getting it right was vital; although, Royal or not, the personality of the average Brunei-Malay came across as slightly diffident, good-humoured, family-oriented and by and large, uncomplicated.We soon realised that misconceptions involving time, or a sense of urgency, were simply down to culture differences. Indeed, in such a climate it was amazing that anything worked at all.

As the settling-in period passed, along with my lifeline of adrenalin, it was time to take stock. Slowed down by the heat, even filling the freezer had become an unwelcome chore. The local NAAFI - strongly scented with mothballs and Shelltox - did its best, supplying the usual basics, but for extras, it was back to Chop-Wah-Ho, where new freezers held not only a good selection of meat from Oz. but also an expanding array of assorted goodies. How lucky we were, too, that the fish market was so well-stocked with the finest ever seafood. Sieving weevils from the flour, oats and breakfast cereals brought back memories of Bahrain, as did the lack of fresh milk, but UHT milk was plentiful and, when heated together with an equal quantity of de-salted butter and whizzed through the blender a few times, passed as a very acceptable substitute for fresh cream.

The children's absence, plus that of Pandora (now 'replaced' by 'Chan', a handsome and affectionate male moggie) left a whopping gap and I decided to join the odd afternoon session at the Families' pool, leaving Jenny, our replacement for Entan, ironing: not only our clothes but - much to her friends' amusement - the weekly delivery from England of tightly-rolled 'tissue paper' editions of The Telegraph. Sadly, my brief desire for exercise soon diminished as 'the chest' problems (variable, but lifelong and ever-present) increased. As usual when below par, my antennae grew, producing a strong sense of not only paranoia, but also an indefinable edge to the atmosphere, particularly when advised, at a girlie lunch, by the two inseparable and apparently, leading hostesses, to 'Stick with us. We'll tell you who's worth bothering with and who to stay away from'...Gossip naturally flourished, but to a new girl, names to faces meant little as the airways buzzed with the latest 'Have you heard'? But - whilst never above a bit of scandal, the funnier the better, I trod warily and so with little to contribute, I contributed little.

Aware that the combination of homesickness and unreliable health produced excellent misery food, I resolved to get a grip, dump the negativity, stop scratching the thin skin, and make the best of it, supplementing my diet with regular doses of Paracetamol, Vitamins and some Homeopathic remedies picked up somewhere in the markets area of Brighton. No doubt there were also others who felt like hitching a ride out on the next available Jumbo. So with little inclination and even less energy for trying out either tennis court, Stables, Bridge or Mah-Jong sessions, thanks to G. - still on his 'extended' working hours - I began helping out in the library, two or three times a week. This provided moments of wry amusement, due mainly to some of the young soldiers not having quite got the hang of the term 'lending library.' When requested to return their previous borrowings before taking others, they would smile sweetly with a 'No understand'. Fair enough. Three copies of 'Photos of Marilyn' are probably still out there somewhere, along with several lavishly illustrated travel books, but at least they made use of it all, which after all, was what really mattered. Shortly after taking over the exceptionally generous book-buying budget, G. discovered a new company in UK - 'The Good Book Guide'- recommended by one of the Sunday papers. The Guide gave excellent service, proving to be reliable and fairly-priced, and after leaving Brunei we continued to support them (pure bliss at Christmas). Some years later, with G. retired from the Army and living in South London, we visited their H.Q, in Battersea, where for a while, having taken up their unexpected job offer, I became part of the team .

The official front of our tour comprised a mixture of intermittent cocktail parties, lunches and regular parades, always held on the Padang (Parade Ground) at 7:30am. There we'd sit, well before the sun reached full-beam; wives suitably clad, hatted and shod (no flip-flops) and never yellow: reserved for Royals - alongside our gleaming toe-capped men, all pristine olive-green, razor-creased uniforms topped off by a small - and on the whole - flattering, gold-braided regimental 'Sungkok' hat. To the strains of the regimental band, we'd watch as the Sultan, a handsome chap, proudly inspected his rivetingly immaculate soldiers: probably the shiniest of us all. Now and then, when various dignitaries visited, the regiment would 'Beat Retreat' which - for the uninitiated - usually takes place in the early evening. It involves the well-rehearsed band, interesting displays of complicated marching patterns and skilled drumming demonstrations. All often followed by a cocktail party in the Mess. When attended by HRH, alcohol was never served in either the Sergeants' or Officers' Mess, but to some degree (says Miss Greedy) this was compensated by a selection of delicious canapes. Official lunches, usually large and held outside, meant segregation of the sexes, Buffalo curry and and warm orange squash - and if it rained - we'd get wet. Luckily however, the downpours - mostly short and warm - did little damage; bar one memorable event involving a crowded reception at the 'Istana' (Royal Palace) with friends, Ann and Rob Matthews. That evening, due to several visitors' cars limiting the usual parking facilities, just half-way through our brief walk to the Istana, suddenly began the most monumental waterfall-type drenching ever, leaving us all resembling joint winners in a fully-clothed diving contest. Lacking shelter, there had been little option but to keep going and having reached the sanctuary of a cloakroom, Ann and I, helpless with laughter at our mirrored reflections - flimsy underwear clearly outlined through the delicate silk of our dresses - managed no more than swift repairs to hair and face before joining the men. Seconds later, we'd stood, praying for invisibility as our Royal host passed with his entourage. The husbands performed their very sharpest salutes as any notion that our clinging-to-every-curve-sprayed-on frocks might just have escaped the Royal gaze, promptly dissolved. HRH, having moved forward no more than a yard or two, suddenly turned, and stopping briefly, looked quizzically back at what was/is perhaps, the oddest-looking quartet ever to have graced the Royal presence.

A favourite game when posted to a new country was 'Spot the CIA Man'. In Berlin, oddly, it hadn't taken long but in Brunei, we hovered. He turned up at many civilian parties as well as a few military ones, but his cover was excellent (all total conjecture on our parts, of course, but fun). The social set-up for such a small place was remarkably varied, with an interesting pecking order: top of the list being anything involving Royalty - mainly 'The Polo lot'. 'The Boss,' as HRH was fondly known, spent much of his leisure time on the polo field and played well. The best kit, along with the best mounts, no doubt helped things along nicely, and at regular intervals, clutches of ponies, would arrive from the Argentine, attended by some of the most jaw-droppingly gorgeous grooms whose good looks often outshone those of their female companions.

Then there were the Engineers, Teachers and Palace staff, who seemed to socialise together, and The Medics' - an interesting, good-humoured and hospitable group, many of which ended up as good friends. The only hospital, then a smallish hutted complex - now replaced by a larger and far superior establishment with excellent facilities - became a familiar part of my life during this tour, although I strongly resisted all invitations to 'Move in for some tests', preferring to visit when required. My Outpatient care was second to none, being in the skilful hands of one (now Professor then, Dr.) Ashley Woodcock, a truly kind, caring physician, who treated me until he and |Fiona, his lovely wife, returned to England, just shortly before us. We're still in touch and it's wonderful to see how his expertise has not only won him world-wide recognition for his research in the minefield known as Asthma, but also a Nobel Prize.

Finally came 'The Military' - who popped up everywhere - an odd mixture of all three Services - Army, Navy and Royal Air Force - each - probably for the only time throughout history - wearing almost identical uniforms. And to this day I can't really explain why.

By the end of our first year, G. approached by his boss regarding my - intentionally not mentioned - time with BFBS, managed to land me with the production and presentation of a weekly, half-hour radio programme on 'The Royal Brunei Malay Regiment'. A sort of 'What's On' in the R.B.M.R and a totally new venture. The interest and directive had come from 'above' and my name put forward by an old ex-Berlin colleague of G's. Refusal, it seemed, was not an option. With phones often down, the ability to set up interviews by the usual means seldom existed, resulting in long, hopeful, but often fruitless drives followed by teeth-sucking return journeys of frustration, at having to find an appropriate 'filler'. By the time we reached No 3 edition, scripts had become a sort of 'Take Your Pick' for this weeks' news from the RBMR'.

Another gripe was the lack of an editing machine, which, having been long broken and lacking the services of a sufficiently specialist engineer, quickly discarded, meant we worked with a sharp razor-blade; once common practice (but not in my day). Once, I'd have made the best of it all but at that time, the equilibrium was in a state of quiet uproar and liable to revolt. Later - when asked to consider a second series of 'General Salute' (our programme) - I decided that the energy, patience and enthusiasm required - even with the help of the team we'd managed to gather, had simply melted..

My inability to cope further was due, in part, to a new regime involving large doses of powerful medication which seemed to be affecting my memory. Writing as someone whose recall has usually been reliable, looking back recently through the scrapbook covering that particular time, many events featured in photos and notes might well have happened to someone else. There are, it seems, side-effects to pretty much every chemical.

Meanwhile, Simon was nearing the end of his first year at Oxford, and, it seemed, loving it all, despite the hard work (the word 'Mods' seemed to crop up a lot). With both he and Dom. home for the long

Summer break, we ignored instructions from friends to 'Go to Penang, in Malaysia' and instead, took off for a break in Manila.

Well used by now to bumpy flights, due to the volatile climate, this one to Manila was no exception, but with memories of a recent, bouncier-than-usual ride, from Singapore still fresh, G and I exchanged sceptical glances. The trip in H.R.H's personal aircraft, which, as a 'turbo-prop' machine had lacked the power to get us above what had felt like the end of the world, stormwise, had left Gus, our pilot - also our next-door neighbour - to fly through it. The sudden screams of panic as cabin baggage bounced into the aisles from our overhead lockers when a sudden drop saw us lose some 1,800 feet (so we heard later) popped up in conversation for some time to come.

Masala Prawns (for 4)

28 raw prawns, cleaned and de-veined, larger than our natives, but not huge!

2 med-sized minced onions

1 tin chopped tomatoes

2 t.sp. Dried coriander

1 t.sp. Garam Masala spice

Half tsp. Chilli powder + 4 garlic cloves & piece fresh ginger minced or grated finely

Salt to taste.

Mix coriander, garam masala spice, chilli, salt and prawns and leave in fridge for 1 hr.

Fry onions, ginger and garlic gently together until just brown. Add prawns/spice mix, then tomatoes and pinch of sugar. Add cup of water and heat gently until prawns cooked.

Serve with plain boiled rice.

Chapter Twenty

THE AMERICAN INFLUENCE IN MANILA, our chosen holiday spot, featured large and maybe still does, but apart from a hairy day at the impressive Pansanjan Falls - around which G. and S. swam (resisted by both Dom and I) it's the traffic one remembers. Although at the time, along with the locals and without a second thought, we frequently and happily lurched our way - on the broadest of highways, unmarked as |I recall - from one end of town to the other - travelling in Jeepneys. These oddly but aptly named vehicles, were Jeeps, left behind from W.War 2, which having been brightly decorated and 'elongated' to take extra seating, doubled as buses, leaving the Maltese buses, which so many years before I'd christened 'dodgems', positively staid by comparison. It was in a Jeepney, I believe, that we toured the sites, accompanied by a non-stop lecture on 'Imelda, Our First Lady' (and lest-we-forget 'Queen of Shoes') delivered by our female guide in the deeply reverent tones of a nun describing the life of the Blessed Virgin. Indeed, such was her fervour that this particular convent-educated person had sat rigidly to attention, wondering if perhaps the correct completion of a questionnaire might be a proviso for eventually being allowed off the bus and back to our hotel (where a notice on the back of each door stated 'In the event of an earthquake, guests are requested not to use the lifts'). Incidentally, the word 'shoe' reminds me that our one shopping trip produced little apart from table-linen and the guilty purchase (how-could-such-shoes-sell-for-so-little) of three pairs of elegant, ladies high-heeled sandals at - £1:50 per pair! But as G. remarked 'Even a little spending helps the economy'. The true state of the country was all too evident, providing food for thought, as apart from the well-maintained Catholic churches and 'Hotels' area, where the staff probably earned the equivalent of our weekly paper-bill, much of the city appeared run-down, fragile and impermanent, as if the slow push of a finger might send entire buildings toppling to the ground.

Later that year, by way of contrast, when the lovely Trixie had returned to Berlin having spent five weeks with us 'helping out' after looking me over on arrival and announcing 'You are ill'; I shall stay and look after you ' - I accompanied G. on a business trip to booming, bustling, shiny Hong-Kong, where the smell of money was almost tangible and no conversation complete without a reference to it. Flying in - for those who never have - left our Gibraltar-landing, standing; if you get my drift... Nothing has ever quite beaten that first gentle, if heart-numbing descent, through a narrow gap, flanked on both sides by tall apartment blocks where residents,we were told, seldom give so much as a second glance to the vast, noisy machine temporarily blocking their light.

That particular visit - just overnight - led to a longer stay the following year, when along with four other couples, we took up the offer of a three-day cruise aboard a visiting Royal Naval ship, the Sir Percivale (seen years later on a TV report during the Falklands War). For a nominal fee, we'd be fed (and how!) watered and comfortably accommodated: lucky us. With our flights back to Brunei organised and a room booked by a kind friend in the Officers' Mess of a barracks there, we climbed aboard, complete with books and G's supply of Kwells. Coasting gently through tranquil waters on our first night, all went well, but the following two evenings found us dining alone with the ship's officers, our companions prone in their cabins as in a suddenly corkscrew-like ocean our vessel had become a giant see-saw. Somehow, in that tropical weather, a doped-up G. had remained happily and totally together; quiet but vertical.

Once ashore, regimental friends took over. Shortly to complete their two-year posting, they knew it all and as co-bargain-hunters, kept us well in the black. Hong-Kong, then a shop-aholics Nirvana, had no comparison and the next day, even I did my bit, at a certain fur emporium. Wanting a casual, three-quarter length coyote coat (From G, for Christmas) to wear with jeans, my choice was firm; much to the Manager's horror, who tried every ploy to change my mind. 'Dog?.. Why you wear dog? Why you WANT dog'?.. Then cajolingly 'Lady like mink. I find you good skin. I have best skin. I show you '. My reply of 'No thank you; a fun-fur: not mink' produced despairing looks and much head-shaking. We were quite obviously tasteless English plebs. But we were there to be served and soon, my measurements noted, an assistant appeared with a pile of soft, lush-looking coyote skins. 'Coat for fitting in two days: ready in four'... Well. On then to 'Sam's' where it was G's turn for the tape-measure: three days for a new suit; bespoke and a third of English prices... Too good to miss'. Next came the famous Stanley Market, where, having scooped up stocking fillers for the young, we found a pair of large, plain white, ceramic table lamps - complete with handmade silk shades (which turned up later in Brunei, exquisitely packed; transport arranged by a kind friend). A visit to H. K without inspecting the bling is almost impossible, although happily for G., baubles not being my thing, that was all we did; apart from wondering whether or not an equivalent word to 'subtle' existed in one of the many Chinese dialects. Some of the jewellery had been startling, both pricewise and in design. To prevent any flagging on the shopping front we stopped now and then, to refuel, stuffing ourselves with delicious Dim Sum, Spring Rolls and juicy King prawns (no holding back, you understand) Due however, to a generous business contact of G, back in Brunei, who at intervals, treated us to long Chinese meals - ten to fourteen courses of such unforgettable delicacies as Sea-Slug, Sea-Cucumber and Sharks Fin Soup being the norm. - we stuck firmly to simple fare.

On our last afternoon, needing a couple of inches off my hair I found my way through a maze of back streets to a local hairdressers, having decided that a non-European establishment might prove more interesting than a salon at one of the large hotels. The bemused-looking, non English-speaking proprietor understood my simple mime and having been shown a chair, I sat waiting my turn, fascinated as the shouting increased and the noise levels escalated, surmising that the loudest explosion could well have passed without comment. Mesmerised, as the entire room spun with life and movement, I spotted a young woman arrive, holding a tightly-swaddled and obviously new baby: probably a boy, judging from the rush of enthusiasm. 'Mama' was, I guessed, a valued customer as within seconds, her bundle having been promptly seized by a member of staff for what appeared to be a lively game of 'Pass the Parcel' - she'd then been installed in a comfy chair and with each hand and foot placed in a small bowl of water, waited for her 'Maniped'. Ten out of ten on the entertainment front. And the haircut was fine. Again, one marvelled at the sheer effeciency of the Chinese.

With just a few months left of our posting, G was promoted to Lt.

Colonel - something of a coup for a Quartermaster - there being only eight Q.Ms to hold that rank in the entire British Infantry. His job was going well and his Trainee Quartermaster's Course flourishing and with twelve decorative local ladies comprising his office staff (whom I'd christened 'Daddy's Butterflies' it being highly unlikely that he'd ever enjoy such a pleasant view in a military environment again) he'd considered his time there well-spent. Indeed - his only real complaint regarding 'work' was the fact that in Brunei, the word 'Manyana' failed to fully express the sense of urgency that it did elsewhere

Our final Christmas went well, split around several dining tables, but mainly those of Ann and Rob Matthews, our next-door neighbours, and our own. The assorted selection of similarly-aged young rubbed along well together, including Charlotte - still Simon's No.1 and now up at Exeter. She 'd arrived looking blooming and left almost a month later looking more so. She and Simon (happy in his second year - producing features and poems for 'The Cherwell' magazine and preparing to produce his first play) enjoyed their exotic break together and made a great couple. Very much the proud parents, we hoped that his Oxford life was - more or less - as hiccup and debt-free as it appeared.

Dom, having produced a very decent crop of O's ('Bet you didn't expect that'...) was keen to act and eager to try her luck at R.A.D.A. but I'd be dishonest to admit it was a choice we applauded or encouraged (the words 'acting' and 'security' seldom seem to pop-up favorably in the same sentence).Whilst fully aware of her talent, we'd only recently heard from friends that their would-be-actor son's application had been rejected, with advice to 'Go away and live a bit : try again when you're twenty-one.' So Business Studies College it was, in the hope that some healthy qualifications would turn-up enough well-paid work to cover future 'Resting' periods. But as a friend once said ' You don't ever need to worry about her succeeding: she can't fail... (She and her husband now run their own highly successful Marketing Agency).

We'd intended fitting in more trips, but plans for exciting forays up Mount Kinabalu, or a week in the Cameron Highlands were abandoned. My health improved, thanks to the daily cocktail of increasingly memory-numbing pills, though never quite enough to keep either G. or my lovely medicine-man, Ashley, completely happy.

But up was up and there's usually a funny side - in this case the discovery that my abstinence from alcohol had produced the interesting rumour that I was, in fact, a recovering alcoholic. It was generally accepted that 'A sneeze in one area becomes Pneumonia in another' so for a while, I ignored it; particularly as the weekly ration of folklore varied widely, depending on the source. Tales of rampant musical-beds, bribery, near-murder, alcoholism and fraud filled the airwaves; often featuring just a tiny element of truth, especially the funniest ones. These might just occasionally prove to be 'Gospel', easily filling a book of their own. But not this one.

Whilst packing, I took stock, reflecting on days with friends, in the jungle where the selection of Technicolour birdlife sometimes seemed have to appeared straight from a Disney cartoon : visits - complete with cigarettes, beer and small gifts - to longhouses; each accommodating maybe 90 Iban families, who, whilst speaking little English, joyfully devoured - courtesy of a large TV set and generator - several imported English programmes - No 1 favourite, unbelievably turning out to be 'Are You Being Served'; weekends in Singapore, thanks to special rates in the Mandarin; and the odd night or two in Labuan, a small island, a few, bum-chiselling miles up river in a flat, military speedboat whose solid metal seats ensured 'ouch' at every bounce. But to G; now a seasoned helicopter passenger, it was the frequent, spectacular jungle-journeys that he'd miss most on returning to the real world. S and D had been 'up' a couple of times, as had a French friend, whose unexpected arrival, whilst on a business trip from Malaysia, had pleaded to share that day's flight with Dom and Trixie. He has since remained totally unaware of how very near he came to experiencing the lush vegetation of Brunei at closer quarters than anticipated, when a nearside door, having suddenly flown open, had led to Trixie - probably his most ardent non-fan - sitting very firmly indeed upon her hands in order to ensure his spending the remainder of the afternoon actually inside the vehicle.

Thanks to Jenny, our handsome amah from the Murut tribe, without whom I'd never have coped, our visitors, mainly military, had been well-looked after. Parties and parades had punctuated our leisure time, more of the former than the latter, and suppers for forty were not uncommon, although in such a climate, 'simple' was the password. Time seldom appeared to hang although I could be wrong, having produced   this Brunei chapter with the invaluable help of the appropriate scrapbook. We'd made many new friends and whilst we were all to take different tracks over the coming years, not for one second did any of us imagine that the multi-talented, bright and beautiful Lynette Lithgow, then a journalist and TV presenter with Radio/Talivishen/Brunei would, some twenty years later, be featured in and on the world's news, after being found brutally murdered -along with her mother and brother-in-law - in Trinidad, her homeland. Since leaving Brunei, Lynette had become a familiar face on both BBC and Granada television, but finally decided, after taking a degree in Law, at Oxford, to turn to writing. It was during her stay in Trinidad, whilst researching the career of an eminent retiring, local Judge, for a book, that she lost her life so tragically. Later, we were privileged to join over three hundred members of her family, friends and work colleagues, at a beautiful and intensely moving Memorial Service at Southwark Cathedral.

And then we were done. After the usual round of 'farewells'; nineteen consecutive evenings of entertaining and being entertained, plus an apparent 'first': a great party thrown for us, plus guests, in the Polo Club, by the generous Brunei Officers: a totally unexpected and much appreciated gesture. Before moving in to spend our final night with Ann and Rob, we handed our 'adoptee' Chan, to good friends, Adrian and Juliet Hughes, where he was subsequently treated like royalty, and locked our sparkling house.

A generous leaving gift from H.R.H. to his departing officers, was three nights at a Singapore hotel of their choice, before flying back to UK. With the pick of the menu and the wine-list at the elegant Shangri-La, we might have had it all. Instead - knackered and talked out - in between brief, last-minute gift-shopping sorties - we could be found on our vast canopied bed, reading, dozing, or half-watching trash on television, sticking firmly to room-service and dining on the simplest fare: beer and steak sandwiches for G : milk and 'tuna-fish on-brown' for me. Our bill must have been one of the lowest ever received by the Palace.

Chapter Twenty One

G. VIRTUALLY COMATOSE FOR THE ENTIRE RETURN FLIGHT, remained so and I, as usual unable to sleep, chewed over the next posting - a Staff job at HQ BAOR Rheindahlen, in N. Germany. It would be new territory for us both and 'NOTHING like Berlin' friends had warned; but perhaps, still preferable to Belfast. Returning to life as we'd known it would probably seem odd, but we'd enjoy trying. I decided, instead, to just think of the children, due at the weekend. Grateful that several of their half-terms and weekends had been spent with Celeste and Mother, in Surrey, we were anxious to be a family again although they, as we'd seen (not without a pang) at Christmas, were now young adults

Whilst England in freezing February holds few charms (but more in a coyote coat) we were ridiculously grateful to be back. Our little house, full of flowers (and a bottle of fizz from the children) had held up well and S and D had worked especially hard to ensure it all looked pristine; how very lucky we were that they'd proved so reliable.

Before rushing off to buy a car we hired something small for the first couple of weeks and made for Oxford. Simon, who had kindly booked us in for three nights at the 14th century Turf Tavern, pulled out all the stops to give us a memorable three days. Seen mostly through the bitterly-cold mist, we were squired in and around that special city, introduced to his friends and on our last evening, invited to dine in Hall. Who could help but feel proud. He'd worked hard to earn his place and deserved every second of his time there.

Dom, then over half-way through her course, in Tunbridge Wells, was also pulling out stops and anxious to 'Get out there and start earning'. She was already showing a sound business bent but, anxious and wanting the best for her, we felt 'All in good time'. Meanwhile, we skittered around Surrey, |Berks. and Kent, catching up on family and friends, thanking all profusely who had helped out in any way during our absence.

In March we celebrated Simon's 21st birthday, recalled with a certain clarity as, due to G. being half-way through a bout of 'flu and the rest of us nurturing heavy colds, the family meal out that evening would scarcely have qualified as anything remotely approaching a celebration. Also, despite advanced warning of Simon's plan to visit the local barber, the impact on us all when a pale-faced, dark stranger appeared for lunch, had been sheer bewilderment. Lost for words, we viewed our once light-brown-but-now-deeply-black-haired son with amazement (the words 'Punk' and 'Goth, we knew not but soon realised that black-haired son = deeply green parents). Wisely, G. kept v. quiet indeed whereas my foolish, puzzled and impetuous comment of 'Being dark doesn't really suit you' - earning an immediate - 'It's not supposed to' did absolutely nothing to improve the shining hour.

With the house 'virtually' sold (a v. special word 'virtually') G.-having been whizzed off almost two months early to Germany due to ' a problem' - was now well installed at H.Q, Rheindahlen, about which he'd been strangely quiet apart from mentioning some 'Really nice people'. Due to return the evening prior to 'Exchange and Completion', he arrived as I zipped up the last holdall and over supper from the local chippy - finishing as we'd begun, on day one - we decided to leave the no-longer-ours but gleaming No.23 (carpets and curtains cleaned, cooker immaculate etc.) sometime around noon the next day.

D-day. With plenty to think about and never more ready for the off, my pangs of anxiety - multiplying steadily since 6am - were pushed briskly into a corner until finally, bowing to the inevitable as we stripped the bed, I murmured 'Sorry. She's not going to show...' 'She' being our prospective buyer, a writer of historical novels whose every demand had, so far, been met. G's testy reply of "Oh for heaven's sake, she's not due till eleven', whilst warranted, went nowhere. On the dot of 10:30, Mr.Ely, our kindly, one-man-band agent, the epitome of old-world charm and helpfulness, arrived bearing the necessary stack of paper, his ginger moustache twitching as he sensed my, probably, by this time, toxic anxiety. At twelve, following a garbled phone call from a certain madam - the word 'Bankruptcy' featuring large - 'That 'as they say - 'Was that'. Miserably, we re-instructed Mr. E., loaded the car and set off for Newhaven.

'Nice Rice' Serve with a Green Salad.

This is mine own and a great favourite with the young.

1 large onion, 2/3 cloves garlic, 1 med.-sized red pepper - all finely sliced or chopped and sauteed in a little oil until soft.

Med-sized tin Tuna, in oil – drained and flaked

Med. sized tin pineapple pieces: save a quarter of the juice and mix it with 1 tabsp. tomato puree, 1 teasp. Mustard and 1 teasp. Pepper sauce (or 2 teasp. Sweet chilli sauce).

Handful roasted but unsalted cashew nuts, or raw pine nuts

Half-teaspoon ground ginger or piece fresh ginger; grated or finely chopped.

3 teasp. Dark brown (muscovado) sugar.

Allow 75grm long-grain rice per person and cook as usual. Leave to cool. Then, using large fork stir in all other ingredients. Any odd meat or fish may be used in this dish: smoked haddock,bacon, ham, chicken or pork. Re-heat thoroughly before serving

Will serve 6 healthy appetites.

Chapter Twenty Two

OUR FIRST NIGHT IN NORTHERN GERMANY (where, it seemed, the language bore little resemblance to the more harsh but clearer tones of Berlin) was spent with the Gunnells; kind, regimental friends, with whom it was lovely to catch up. G., already installed in our clean, four-bed and problem-free new home, with its immaculate garden and terrace, had stowed the kitchen kit, seen the boxes in and made up the bed, leaving the next two or three days clear for establishing 'home.' Shortly, Dom would have completed her course and be returning to Germany with us for a while, when we drove back to England for her 'passing-out' day, in a week or so's time.

Meanwhile,we explored. A curious place. There we were, a short drive - less than a half-hour - from the Dutch border town of Roermond, set amidst acres of 'Armyland'; streets and streets of houses, each dwelling varying little from that of its neighbour. I couldn't have felt more disorientated had we set up home on an ice-floe. But to be fair, Rheindahlen Camp had everything one could possibly need and subsequently, we weren't remotely surprised to discover that several of the younger, lower ranks, on short postings of a year, or less, had never once ventured off the camp during their entire tour; despite a reliable and apparently inexpensive, public transport system. This seemed sad, but possibly the security offered by the camp - something of a 'Little England' - combined perhaps with a lack of confidence, language skills and the usual cash shortage, ruled out, for some, the desire to even take advantage of organised shopping trips to nearby Dusseldorf and Munchengladbach. Natural curiosity aside, the immediate locale, with its vast, well-stocked (from Oxo cubes to cars) N.A.A.F.I. plus a few German shops and cafes, really offered just about everything on the retail front. There was also a sports centre, complete with pool, ice-rink and indoor ski-slope; two cinemas; a theatre, banks, hairdressers, beauty parlours; an excellent Education Centre with a varied selection of classes; a thriving up-to-date library;

a couple of garages, a tailor and the odd dressmaker. The experts had obviously done their very best and with B.F.B.S. Television - then a fairly recent and welcome extra - showing favourite 'Soaps' along with several popular sit-coms. and serials from home, most tastes - including 'whoopee', Radio 4 - had been catered for. Indeed, one might have been living anywhere (just slightly) out on a limb, in England:which was possibly why the thought of venturing further afield was - for some - just really not important..

G's departure from 'Quartermastering' was different and initially, demanding, but as usual, he simply beavered away quietly,without complaint, remarking on the luck of having such helpful staff and 'A good guy at the top'. As his working days gradually shortened to normal, we began on the usual round of returning hospitality, already having met several interesting new couples with whom we're still friends.

Dom., now home - and lovely it was to have her there too - soon became part of a group of teenagers, all living nearby and either beginning Gap years, or waiting to 'Go up'. After a few days, she announced that they were all planning to do a six-week stint at a local cherry-bottling plant: Mon-Fri 7am-4pm and that 'Kate, the General's daughter will pick me up in the mornings at 6:30'. Luckily, early rising had never been Dom's problem. Soon, she was returning home for tea, heavily stained with the dark cherry-juice and worn-out, but delighted to be earning. We felt they were lucky to have the work-experience - and the cash - and enjoyed hearing the often comical, but typically cold-hearted teenage feedback, regarding the 'awful' senior staff. Soon however, she began to make 'London -type noises as in 'I'm sure I could easily get a job in London - and share a flat...' True. But we were not encouraging, and she stayed another couple of weeks or so, joining us, and a group of friends on a weekend river trip on the Rhine: recalled as noisy, crowded and hot - but scenic.

Dick Norton, my 'B.F.B.S. mentor and boss from our first days in Berlin, in '69, was now top of the tree in Cologne, where he and Pam lived in an old, impressive German house. Less than an hour's drive away, he'd soon been on the phone. 'Don't stay in that God-forsaken place at week-ends, come and join us. Anytime. Someone's always having a party'. We did, often, although never once whilst making for the 'Nortonry' did we take the same route. Miles of new autobahns saw to that: criss-crossing at regular intervals 'a la Spaghetti Junction' each one (I swore, as navigator) specifically designed to confuse any motorist, cartographer, or travel writer...'Nortons before dark' was always the aim: anything later and we'd have been there yet. But it was fun to catch up again, especially when a party included Pam's Indian food. Schooled by the personal chef of an old friend of Dick, the Maharajah of Baroda, her party table was simply the best. Steaming dishes of delicious chicken, lamb, beef, prawns and vegetables - some strongly flavoured, others less so - came with home-produced pickles and relishes, along with rice and several trays of assorted Indian breads - all of which, as if by magic, appeared in a constant stream from Pam's gadget-filled kitchen. At that time, a home-produced Indian meal meant just that. Even in '70's Berlin, the 'Takeaway' or curry restaurant was a rarity and supermarkets stocked few spices beyond nutmeg, cinnamon and one or two ready-prepared curry powders. Luckily, Pam's supplies were regularly topped up with pungent parcels from India, the contents of which would be painstakingly ground with pestle and mortar prior to each of her marathon cooking sessions.

September, and it was back to London for a few days to help Dom. celebrate her 18th birthday. Eager to spread her wings, she was now working as a P.A. on the fringes of the City and flat-sharing, in Kensington. Always good at keeping in touch, she rang us most days, and luckily, seemed to be enjoying both her job and her new life. Whilst we missed her sparky presence we were only too aware that the limited charms of Northern Germany scarcely featured when compared to those of the great metropolis.

One of the best things about our latest - and, I suddenly realised one day, our last!- posting was the absence of 'The Exercise'. For the entire year, G. - bar expeditions around and about - remained at home. The surrounding terrain, mostly flat (but lacking the charms of Norfolk) held few delights, but one Sunday trip lingers. Sometime in late October, but still warm and sunny, G. decided to show me Vogelsang, an hour or two's drive away, making no mention beforehand that during the war, much of the area had been devoted to the planning of producing 'Fine specimens of pure Aryan youth'; tall straight-limbed, blonde and blue-eyed gifted youngsters, as perfect in every way as possible. These were to become the future of Germany, whose continued, almost medically supervised, procreation would eventually create a 'Super-race': bright and unmarred by any form of physical or mental abnormality...' I still recall the odd drop in temperature as we pulled up outside wide metal gates fronting a long drive, at the top of which stood a large, grey building. Pulling at my light jacket I looked around, saying 'This is the strangest place. The sun is shining but I'm chilled; it's so silent. What went on here?' Waiting until a puzzled G. (who felt nothing untoward) had finished explaining the history of the area, my only reply was a muttered 'May we go now.' The pall of imagined Frankenstinian activity combined with my over-sensitive nature had been shocking and unsettling.

That particular time in our lives might even be described as static; with Simon in his final year at Oxford, Dom. in England and we two rattling round in a comfortable house, in a foreign country (which felt anything but with its regular supply of' Woman's Hour and The Archers'). G. worked hard and amazingly, announced he'd joined the weekly 'Hash', a sort of slightly straggly, cross-country run, requiring both energy and enthusiasm. Meanwhile, I cooked, drank coffee, met friends and now and then, scribbled a little: doing nothing to excess, accomplishing little and as a result ending up feeling disjointed and odd. 'The health' continued with the usual round of medication; presenting nothing new bar a lack of energy.

We'd taken advantage of the opera house in nearby Dusseldorf - which, as centre of the German rag-trade, had a wide range of shops; we'd become regulars at the fabulous Saturday street markets in Roermond (great fresh produce and delicious Dutch charcuterie) and after a busy Christmas at home, joined by both children and some old friends, had taken off to Amsterdam for the New Year, celebrating the evening in a jolly Italian restaurant. About mid-January, with life returned to normal we decided to ignore the snow and drive down to the South, staying a night or two in Munich (Germany's Cheltenham?)and Heidleburg, taking in 'Mad Ludwig's' extraordinary Chitty-Chitty-Bang-Bang castles along the way. Once back at home, with enough to keep us happy socially, we pithered along until once more, it was decision time on the posting front.

But - surprises all round. G. was offered, and decided to accept, a job of Area Secretary, London. This meant his retiring from the Army two years early and based at - no prizes for guessing - The Regimental

Headquarters at the Tower. Well... Asked to 'Keep the regiment in the public eye' he promptly declared a ban on (his) commuting and announced that the London house-hunt would start a.s.a.p.

With just two months remaining of our final tour, the majority of weekends were spent driving frantically between Rheindahlen/Zeebrugge/Dover/London - leaving and arriving everywhere at what may reasonably be considered 'Unsocial hours'. Dom, as our London resident, had accepted the task of viewing and weeding out the 'possibles' selected from our estate agents lists (taken from U.K. newspapers) and as usual, she did her best: not easy as our budget was tightly squeezed, with little room for negotiation. The six-weeks retirement 'Bricks and mortar' course was next on the agenda and, happy to rough-it for the short time, we moved into a sub-standard quarter in Caterham. Two weeks later, G. went off to negotiate the vagaries of simple D.I.Y and play 'How to spot the cowboys'. Luckily, the move back had been hiccup free. We'd returned home in convoy on a sunny August day: best described as a journey of interesting moments, but follow my leader I did and we arrived safely at Foxton Close, Caterham. Settling in was simple. We'd be almost camping, but comfortably so and after two weeks - which had happily included both Simon and Dom. - the 25 or so boxes were delivered and stacked neatly in the dining-room, around the table, leaving sufficient space for eight sitters.. No one minded our designer 'Berlin Wall' and visiting friends often generously suggested Takeaways'. One day, en route somewhere, we even managed a swift gallop around a Boot Sale and eight pounds later, were happily stashing six pine kitchen chairs - three a startling orange and three an equally startling emerald-green - into the rear of the 'wagon'. Bring on the Nitromorse.

G's course ended and he returned, proudly clasping his carpentry apprentice piece - a small, pine stool, beautifully jointed, planed, waxed and finished. It was good to have him back although the time had scarcely dragged. Outside, in his absence - bikini-clad and soaked in tanning-oil against the broiling August sun - I'd stripped and waxed the chairs, toiling long and hard at the stubborn remains of green and orange gloss paint, missed by the pungent solvent.

That, plus (very) limited spurts of housework, along with regular trips to a thriving local launderette had become something of a novelty. I even made blackberry pies; the fruit lush and prematurely ripened, leisurely gathered from the mass of brambles barely visible at the bottom of the long rectangle of yellowing grass; the lawn of yesteryear.

We'd already drawn a circle around acceptable 'buy-here areas' and complete with our sheaves of 'possibles', including the fast re-developing Docklands, began with Dom's bundle. Gradually we weeded: recalling our little house in Brighton, three years earlier, and the artistic license of Estate Agents whose 'Details' often bore little more than a passing resemblance to reality. But one mad morning, due to seriously tempting photographs from an agent in Edmonton (a name previously only spotted on a London bus) G. drove us deep into the hinterland of - I believe it was E9 - entirely new territory and certainly miles from the 'circle'...But what a find. 'Lambs Cottage', in Church St., once the home of the Essayist Charles Lamb and his sister, Mary, was a gem: a detached 17th century, perfectly preserved house, complete with large garden and 'Wash-house' enclosed by the original railings. We loved it, but luckily, being already under offer, it was way too far from the Tower.

Finally, after the first hundred or so viewings – new; old; flats; houses; warehouses in Wapping - even a gorgeous houseboat, a beautifully converted Dutch barge on Chelsea Wharf - we settled on an early Victorian (1845) end-of-terrace in S. London, on the edge of an attractive square, complete with gardens. Home to a well-known ballerina and her husband, an Academic and ballet critic of the Sunday Telegraph, it had not only the required space but also a small walled garden, parts of which were attractively paved in well-preserved York stone. We'd have three stories, plus an extension bedroom and bathroom, three other bedrooms, a first-floor sitting-room and downstairs, a kitchen, utility, study and dining-room - complete with french-windows. A ground floor cloaks. and perhaps a small bathroom at the top would have been ideal but those could come later..But a voice whispered 'No. No. Wrong vibes.' And then our vendor - whose workplace turned out to be on Tower Hill - said to G. 'I can be there within fifteen minutes of leaving here and I don't want to move. It's my wife who's unhappy'. G's beaming smile would have melted the strongest steel.. The property might have been roofless and windowless..No matter: the Beloved would have been first in the queue...Only fifteen minutes travelling ...Now what?

As predicted, three weeks later, after much arguing, soul-searching and compromise, our offer was accepted, one reason being that the roof had only recently (the previous year) been renewed.

And so - with mixed feelings, after twenty-four years as 'Wife of' I scoured our last army home and G. handed it over. But with the inventory minus a mower, he'd actually said 'Leave the lawn...'

Two Good Starters.
1). Tomato, Aubergine and Pesto Salad serves 4.

First make pesto as follows: 50 grm.pine nuts - browned lightly in a dry frying pan. Large bunch Basil, 2 garlic cloves, crushed: 50grm Parmesan, 100mls good olive oil. Retain a few leaves basil for decoration then put everything except oil into blender and blend together. With motor still running, dribble in olive oil until you have a smooth sauce. Pour into jug .

Take 2 med.sized aubergines - peeled and cut lengthways into 1 cm. thickness then cut strips in half lengthways. Sprinkle with salt and place in sieve or colander to drain for 40 mins. Then rinse under tap and dry with kit. Paper. Place in baking dish and brush liberally with oil. Bake at top of 180c oven until golden Remove and put aside to cool.

Skin 3 red & ripe beef tomatoes by 'nicking' sides with a sharp knife. Plunge into boiling water for 30 or so seconds then remove and peel off skin. Core and slice neatly.

Arrange tomatoes and aubergines on large plate. Dribble over as much of the pesto as liked : remainder will keep up to a week in 'fridge. Decorate and serve with crusty bread.

2). Crab Gratin, with Brown Toast (serves 6.)

500grms. fresh mixed crab meat – or frozen (if so drain well).

50 grms. unsalted butter.

14fl/oz double cream.1 med onion - finely chopped and fried gently in the butter: Pour cream in over cooked onion and simmer gently until quantity reduced by half. Add 2 tabsp. med. sherry, spoon of Tabasco, if liked, season with salt and pepper. Place crab meat into fireproof gratin dish; smooth all over and pour over hot, cream and onion sauce. Sprinkle with 2 tabsp. grated Parmesan cheese. Place in hot preheated oven & brown evenly. Sprinkle with finely chopped parsley. Serve with brown toast.

Chapter Twenty Three

WITH US, MOTHER PLUS FRIEND and children plus friends, we'd be ten for Christmas. It might have been more but due to limitations (builders, plumbers, plasterer and unfinished kitchen) we stopped there.

Our jolly boys, the builders, moved in to No. 2 shortly after we'd stacked the final suitcase; and promptly took over the kitchen. We subsequently operated from the extension bedroom, which for reasons unknown housed a stainless-steel sink and draining-board. The previous owner, in reply to my puzzled 'Oh. A sink. And draining-board?' had simply replied 'I always feel it's rather useful to have a sink in a bedroom, don't you ?..'And at that time it suited us well as with a small kitchen table, the chairs and the elderly gas cooker 'left' in the original kitchen and soon re-sited, we were able to muddle along until downstairs was workable.

Cowpens Sth Carolina with re-enactment society and Trevor Gatty

November, and with energy and staying power in short supply, having promised ourselves to 'Make up for it next year,' our 25th wedding anniversary was celebrated quietly, No party - just a meal for two and a trip to the theatre : the words 'Harvest Supper' strike a limited chord ...obviously not very memorable. But what a hurdle. Christmas '81 promised to be white, the first spread of pristine, snowy loveliness appearing overnight, sometime in late November. Yesterday's grassy rectangle, as yet unmarked bar a few bird tracks, now sparkled brilliantly in the rays of bright morning sun streaming through the branches of the tall Plane trees, apparently one of the few arboreal specimens sufficiently hardy to survive the pollutants of the Industrial Revolution. In a rare moment of inactivity, I stood gazing through our grimy study window, speculating the future.

Admiration for the Christmas-card vision however, rapidly disappeared as, despite the delights of a super-efficient central heating system, the increasing snowfalls led to more and more inconvenience. The builders were - well builders - and as is their wont, liable to vanish for hours 'For supplies' leaving, if I was lucky, one lone worker (always 'I' as G, relishing his new job, disappeared promptly at 8:30am to his palatial office at the Tower - what I wouldn't have given, then, for an office). But by week 3, desperate for a workable kitchen for Christmas, my ultimatum finally sank in. 'No worker leaves this house accompanied or all teas, coffees, bacon butties, or Friday bottle of vino will cease .OK?...' In reality they were good boys and fun, but the kitchen and downstairs loo had to be operational by Christmas and the present arrangement, useful though it was at the time, replaced.

With various rooms re-carpeted, our remaining boxes and furniture appeared on 18th December at 7pm, delivered by two large vans from the Brighton repository, both vehicles having broken down en route, along with one of the van heaters. The shivering, but stoic crew, thawed out with hot soup, had gratefully accepted our offers of a hand with the unloading and two hours later were back on the road. They'd done a great job, never once complaining when G. returned several items 'For the next house auction' with a puzzled, 'Why on earth did we store this?' Amongst the returns were four lawn mowers...Four mowers. To this day, one of life's little mysteries.

'Why on earth did we store this?' Amongst the returns were four lawn mowers...Four mowers. To this day, one of life's little mysteries

With the certainty increasing by the hour, that our lives were fast approaching their end, No.2 gradually took on one of its own, lending itself to the red bows and mass of greenery I'd thrown up everywhere. By 22 December, G's birthday, having dressed the tree, we wandered off to celebrate in a friendly local restaurant, joined by Dom and Charlotte, now working in London and Simon, further afield in Brighton where he beavered for a publisher. The festivities loomed and in less than forty-eight hours there would be ten of us... Short of turning into the Christmas fairy, I'd no idea how - or indeed if - it would all gel. But with chimneys swept and the thermostats lowered, we lit our first real fire, switched on the tree lights and after a king-sized fish-pie in the as-yet-undecorated-but-heaped-with-candles dining-room, managed to make the Tower by 11:30 for the first of many moving and soothing Christmas Eve midnight services.

Despite still needing tiles and extra units, the kitchen worked well and whilst much of the time had passed in a haze (owing less to alcohol than the diminution of brain cells; by then. G and I probably shared a maximum of three) on Twelfth Night - or rather morning - the crispy, denuded tree left the sitting-room as it had entered - on the end on a rope through a window. Delighted to be clear of festive clutter, I recall slumping in a chair with a mug of hot something, already starting the next list. From above, the sounds of brisk hammering meant that our jolly boys had begun work on the framework necessary to accommodate the Japanese soaking tub, ordered from an ad. in one of the Sundays: almost square and about a metre in depth, it would be just the thing for our new, oddly-shaped but functional, second bathroom.

Soon, the decorating was completed. Having lived mainly with assorted shades of green and magnolia for close on twenty-five years, we settled on Terracotta for halls, landings and G's study, and for the dining-room, a gorgeous Osborne and Little wallpaper - spotted one evening from the car, in the well-lit but uncurtained sitting-room of a small Chelsea house. We had to have it. Yelling 'Please stop a sec. must find that wallpaper' I'd rushed out and rung the front doorbell to be greeted by a bronzed, blonde god.. 'Antonia, how lovely to see you. Do come in, I'm on the phone to Spain. Following - bemused but curious - through the elegant hallway - complete with large, free-flying brilliantly-feathered parrot - I perched, as directed, on a sofa, whilst facing me, Mr.Loveliness completed his call before saying 'You're not Antonia? What can I do for you?

'I don't know how you have the cheek' said G, but it was the only way. No offence had been taken, indeed, I'd even turned down the amused offer of a drink - and two weeks later, having tracked down the paper and hung it, reasoned that the cash saved on the services of a professional decorator more than well-covered the cost of the goods.

In the buzz of London life, that first civilian year melted. We were lucky to meet up regularly with Simon and Dom., Charlotte too, who, her commuting time shortened, had moved in nearby to house-share with friends. Simon, now an In-House-Editor was still beavering in Brighton, and Dom. - also sharing, in Wimbledon - worked for the designer of 'Rubik's Cube,' an '80's novelty puzzle which probably made her employer a small - or perhaps even large - fortune. G., exercising his usual public spirit, had joined the local residents' association and at work, concentrated on P.R. for the regiment. Consequently, as invitations snowballed, often including us both, revamping my wardrobe became vital; restricted to borrowing from Dom. and 'Sales'. Thanks to G's expanding list of contacts, we enjoyed generous hospitality at Henley and Wimbledon as well as several memorable evenings at Covent Garden and Glyndeborne. There were cocktail parties, Livery dinners, Regimental events at the Tower and catching up with family and old friends as together, we happily swapped weekends: theirs in the smoke for ours out of it.

Between May and August when London fizzed, the house came into its own with just about every visitor commenting on 'The lovely atmosphere'. However, from an odd happening, not long after Christmas, we decided, as a result of the following, that what it really liked was a good party. One Saturday, around dusk, we'd returned home and on opening the front door were startled to hear loud '20's-type music and, undeniably, the noisy buzz of a party...'Ah.. Radio on somewhere' I'd said and at that very second - as if a tap had been turned off, or a button pressed - there was total silence. On checking, we found our four small radios and one elderly TV were all firmly 'off.' We'd both heard the same things at the same time...Even G 'King sceptic'- has yet to produce a rational explanation; and neither has anyone else.

Meanwhile, the chest problems continued, as did my relationship

- both as an 'In' and an Outpatient - with the exceptional Royal Brompton Hospital. Not once in over thirty years of care has the skill, care, kindness and patience of the staff failed. That, along with the help of our brilliant physiotherapist friend and neighbour, Susan Pink, meant that most of the time, I remained vertical.

Sometime in mid-November we had a call from 'The Good Book Guide. 'Would you be interested in joining our team to help with the Christmas rush?' The offer from the 'Guide' - then situated in a couple of Battersea warehouses (recently discovered to be still thriving as a company but re-housed in Blackpool) being less than a ten-minute drive from home, was worth consideration. Whilst the word 'Employment' was scarcely top priority at the time - extra cash at Christmas is always useful. Deciding to accept, I popped in for 'A chat and a tour' and subsequently, was employed 'For Christmas'.

Sauce for Pasta Salad

As so many pasta and rice salads seem to taste of very little, this simple sauce cheers them up no end. Mix together and pour onto hot pasta or cold, cooked, long-grain rice.

1 med. onion finely chopped, 1 tabsp, chopped coriander, 150fl.oz, French dressing, 2 crushed cloves garlic,1 tabsp,mayonnaise, 1 tabsp. tomato puree, 2 dessp. soft brown sugar.

Chapter Twenty Four

OUR CONTACT WITH THE GUIDE, founded some four or five years earlier by Peter Braithwaite and Bing Taylor, an American, had begun in '78, from Brunei, when G, having taken over the budget for the Berakas Camp library, had recruited me to help. Aware of my previous role, the 'Guide' job description had read 'Book Picker. Selecting books for customers' orders'. This was subsequently (and foolishly) translated by me to G, as 'Probably perusing book lists to suggest and choose titles for the undecided customer in need of advice.' - to which he'd replied   'Probably'.. Oh dear. Who did I think I was?..When unexpectedly, the work turned out to be considerably more physical than mental, I realised that it was my brawn they were after; forget the cerebral. As the piles of bulging sacks increased, we humble pickers were   joined by just about every other member of available staff, including Peter and Bing, our combined energies devoted - initially - to the overseas posting deadlines. This had to be the team effort of the century.

The tightly-packed bookshelves stretched endlessly along the warehouse acreage, while to the strains of non-stop Radio 2 (Musical Youth's catchy No.1 'Pass de Duchy from de Left-hand Side' invaded my slumbers for weeks) we 'pickers' trotted silently but swiftly up, down and along, forms tightly clutched, seeking our prey ('in my case white-faced' might be added, due to my total inability to grasp how the picking system actually worked). Then, with each completed stack checked, and moved on to the packers - a chirpy group of youths whose triceps expanded almost visibly as the the heavy cartons were tossed between them as if weightless - we'd grab another form. As a lifelong stranger to the word 'logic,' particularly when applied to the phrase 'Book-picking', I'd maybe have been better let loose on something totally physical. Wrapping or stacking; even sticking on labels.

January seemed about the right time to move. The majority of the other pickers had been easy enough workmates - a little earnest but pleasant - who'd soon had the system sussed, leaving maybe just three of us still baffled after the first week. However, a swift chat with Alan, my immediate boss turned out to be full of surprises as, after profuse thanks for 'All your hard work' it was 'We'd like you to stay on to help sort out for a while and perhaps you'd consider covering a stall at a forthcoming Book Fair, in the city..'Well. The Fair went well and was interesting, but in mid -April, having promised to arrange the wedding flowers of a dear friend, I waved the Guide farewell.

The wedding took place in June, in the splendid Chapel of St.Peter ad Vincula, in the Tower and, after years of helping decorate various messes and venues for parties and receptions (thanks to the odd Floral Art course and learning along the way) the terror of the overloaded pedestal featured less and less. Late May and June probably produce the finest of English blooms and from a selection of Peonies, Sweet-peas, Larkspur and early Antirrhinums etc. we chose a delicate colour-scheme of pale-pink, white and cream, On the day, the chapel and Reception area - once the Officers' Mess - attracted many compliments, though nowhere near as many as the gorgeous bride.

Towards the end of the reception, the caterer had asked 'Any idea who did these lovely flowers? After a brief chat, not without a certain diffidence I'd agreed to her passing on my name, trusting as usual, to providence. However, whilst considered competent on both the planning and decorating fronts, it's doubtful that either husband or dearest friend might have been heard to refer to 'Bev's Great Head for Business...' But with the new, bustling Nine Elms Flower Market just a short drive from home, it seemed that providence - whatever or whoever it is - already had a toe in the door.

A week later, at lunch with a friend, the third guest (Providence?) turned out to be an interesting ex-florist whose recently opened teaching studio steered the students - mainly wives of diplomats - through the gentle maze of 'Arranging Flowers for the Home'. After swapping anecdotes, I asked hesitantly for advice, and delightedly took notes on vital tips, backed up by years of experience. The 'Do's, Dont's, Buying and Costing' ended with 'And unless you're a really fast worker and good at bouquets... No? Just farm them out. Otherwise you can be up all night' (Oh yes.). And so, after a comparatively small outlay for kit, the bookings - also initially small - began to pop up.

Dependent on just word of mouth and a few business cards, bookings gradually increased. G. - any weekday between 4:30 and 8am. - already pristine and suited for the office - could be found acting as chauffeur and loader-in-chief, skilfully manoeuvering one of the unwieldy trollies between the various stalls as I 'shopped'. Cockney market folk are full of chat, exchanging insults with wit and humour and although the Summer mornings were often a pleasure, those pre-dawn starts of Winter did little for my equilibrium - despite a brief stop for coffee and a bacon roll. G. - after years of unsocial early starts in strange circumstances, never complained, cheerfully (usually) dropping me home well before eight, after which, having helped unload, he'd take off into the heaving mass of city-bound traffic. How soothing his calm, spacious office must have felt after our frantic sessions of 'beat the clock.'

At home, after a couple of hours stripping, snipping and sorting, with everything finally 'bucketed' - the most delicate blooms under our dining-table clear of any sunlight - the following day's containers would be stacked, ready for fitting with Oasis or /and wire. Soon, there were inquiries and orders for weddings, dinners, receptions, just about every kind of themed party – and the odd funeral. Also, time was set aside for planning and costing: but as the workload increased, so did my visits to the Brompton.

Madeira Sauce (for 6)

Serve with poached chicken breasts.To I med. onion, finely chopped and sauteed in a little butter add 125 grm sliced, button mushrooms, add a little more butter and cook gently: season. Blend in machine until pureed. Add 200ml.chicken stock or tinned consomme and 200mls of Greek yoghourt and crème fraiche, mixed. Heat 4 tabsp. Madeira wine and bring to boil. Remove from heat and stir into sauce.

Chapter Twenty Five

SOMETIME IN LATE SPRING, G. received a totally unexpected offer from a retired member of the regiment, one Trevor Gatty, then H. M Consul General in Atlanta,Georgia: 'How would you care to visit us - sometime shortly, all expenses paid - to join a seminar and watch a re-enactment of 18th century 'Battle of Cowpens' (part of the American War of Independence) in which the regiment had not only taken part, but had lost the battle; and its Colours. Delighted to be asked - though unfamiliar with the event in question - G. accepted instantly, following it up by hours of reading, until, as clued up as any participant and complete with bulging brief-case, he flew forth, alone. Whilst included in the offer, my services were already committed, to another wedding... The trip turned out a great success. Whilst enjoying a week of generous American hospitality and put up in some of the finest hotels,

85/86 July
Annual Square fete SW8

he'd been interviewed on both TV and radio and wined, dined and flown all over the State, returning home full of stories and modestly delighted to have 'I think, got it right'. (One story involved an introduction to two very elderly ladies, who, during a chat, raised a smile by referring to the American Revolution as 'That late little unpleasantness..' before gently inquiring 'And Colonel, how is your dear Queen'. His reply of 'Fine, last time I saw her' failed to mention that it had been some years previously when she'd pinned a medal on his chest). Luckily, a year or so later, when Trevor's daughter was married in St Paul's, her right as close kin of a member of The Order of the British Empire, we were able to return just a little of the U.S. hospitality with a lunch party at home.

My charming Consultant, the esteemed Dr.Geddes (now Professor and retired), kept a close and constant eye on my welfare, and soon, I'd been tested for just about every lung disease, complaint, problem, condition - whatever - known to the medical world. Despite the lack of a clear pattern, the words 'Cystic Fibrosis' began to feature regularly, but again, nothing was confirmed; although one such 'procedure' came up with 'Bronchiectasis' - just before the collapse of both the table supporting me and a piece of electrical equipment (problems with 'electrics': again).

As entries in the order-book swelled, a growing suspicion that in some way the flowers, foliage and perhaps other things might be contributing to my increasing health problems, led to a chat with our son. Already himself diagnosed with allergies and sensitivities to several foods and chemicals, Simon suggested I seek the advice of an Allergist.

But first, another wedding in what was probably the stickiest August for decades. This time for Nicky Martin, the clever creator and producer of the instantly successful Eurovision Song Contest Winners 'Bucks Fizz.' Gilly-Rowland-Clarke, caterer for the Regimental H.Q. having been booked to produce the food, had kindly put me forward as 'Flower-lady'... Quite a challenge but, after much consultation with the wonderfully cool bride-to-be, friend Liz was immediately recruited and together, we made lists before assembling the various accoutrements and trawling the market for the explosion of blooms and foliage required for the production line of Friday's nuptials.

Eight sharp on Thursday morning and already steaming, we set to, beginning with the ancient village church: cool and sheltered, before moving to the house: its low, beamed ceilings and latticed windows filtering out the worst of the sun. Generously fed and watered with a constant flow of juice, coffee and sandwiches, the afternoon flew as we filled three beautiful brick Inglenooks and several dark corners with large, country arrangements, leaving the walkway-pedestals and marquee-baskets for the evening. The table centres (completed and covered with tissue) would be placed the following morning when I'd finished Nicky's requested 'Very informal' bouquet of pale-pink roses, pink honeysuckle and Ivy and then - D-Day...Friday saw us dashing around, spraying, and checking for 'droopers". But Providence - that word again - behaved beautifully and I recall offering up a few hasty words of thanks. Unfortunately - with weekend guests due at six that evening, we'd turned down Nicky's generous wedding invitation and headed for home. Little did we know then that we and Cheryl Baker, one of the 'Bucks Fizz' two girl singers, would, a few years later, be brought together, by - of all things - the skills of a Neurosurgeon.

A week or so later, having driven down to the South of France, we lay supine ('Ageing our skin'-Mother's phrase) on the terrace of a friend's beachside apartment. Two whole weeks, with little activity beyond lifting the odd paperback from our trashy pile; meals restricted to seeking out obedient waiters with tempting menus. Having navigated us from South London to almost the French-Spanish border, my input on the catering front would be strictly limited to breaking bread and brewing coffee. But best of all, before leaving, we'd managed to detach 'Jose' the lingering lodger.

Our 'stray' - a 31 years old South American language student, had been acquired by chance when an acquaintance had mistakenly over-booked her intake of P.G. students. Agreeing to help with 'A couple of weeks B&B' and done our stuff on the 'Welcome to England ' front, we despaired a month later when, having deciding - 'post-inspection' - that he far preferred our accommodation to hers, he refused to leave, saying 'I not go. I not want go. I like here. Is good...I stay (despite my dignified pleas of 'But this is not what we do. Our agreement was for two weeks only'). Added to which, as a partner in the family construction business - apparently almost Brazil's 'McAlpine' - his fully-staffed luxurious pad, pool and the on-tap use of the company jet (we'd seen the pictures) dwarfed anything on offer at our end.

But - he'd also turned out to be a demanding tightwad 'London very expense' making early-morning raids on the fridge to avoid buying lunch..Next came 'Launderette too expense. I use your machine. You do for me.Yes.' ('No No No. 'Please, we'd like you to leave. We need the space')...No longer solo, he'd soon acquired friends, a girlfriend and a massive Harley bike; and his income would no doubt have covered rooms at the Ritz. Grrr. It took a while; but we persevered and eventually he roared off into the night 'To visit friends ...Switzerland'. Oh happy day. The phrase 'staying power' had taken on a whole new meaning.

Meanwhile, life had continued apace as games of what might be called 'Family Chess' were played. In various parts of the country, moves saw partners and jobs swapped for someone, or something better leading to the purchase of a flat here, a house there and for Simon, about to start his own publishing company and Charlotte - a new life, together with their two recently acquired 'mutts': Ben and Bob; brown, affectionate and the closest of friends.

Whilst negotiating for a flat in Herne-Hill, sufficiently spacious to accommodate not only the two of them but also a decent-sized office, they, along with the immaculately behaved '57s' moved in with us for a while. We loved having them and were full of admiration for S's sheer business nerve,

Pre-'Jose', we'd also had our first (of three) burglaries, and how very neat and tidy it was too. Totally professional; the only signs of disturbance being each drawer of each chest in each bedroom remaining open - resembling neat flights of steps - and the carrier-bags of cutlery hastily dumped by the chiffonier when I'd had the temerity to return home. With the cutlery intact, along with an inherited silver tea-service, we took stock. My few pieces of jewelery had gone but foolishly, a diamond and enamel regimental brooch - old and valuable - had been ignored. However they, or someone, got it six months later on a return trip.

Now in their second year in London and based in Chelsea, our friends from Somerset days, Shelagh, a vibrant,Welsh red-head and Paul Biddell - in total contrast, grey-haired and quiet, were housed in an elegant, detached Wren house in the grounds of the Royal Hospital. Both retired from General Practice, Paul was now 'Physician to the Royal Hospital,' whilst Shelagh practised part-time, elsewhere. A truly generous couple and never short of house-guests, we were regularly part of their 'Founders Day' celebrations, one of which was attended by a very young Princess Diana. They also threw 'Pre-Flower Show' suppers, held each June, the evening before the Show opened, when, after a delicious meal, we'd all troop off for a sneak preview around the stunning displays. It certainly beat joining the early-morning queue.

Social life that Summer, as usual often allied to the Tower, included lunch at the Mansion House and several Livery dinners, as well as a few less-formal happenings. Then, well in advance and totally unexpected, came an invitation to one of the annual Royal garden parties, in July. After the usual half-hour fashion parade of 'What do you think, This? This? or This?' 'The Day' - having begun with drizzle - finally gave in, producing a brilliant English Summer's afternoon. Suitably clad, we joined the cast of a thousand hats and patiently shuffled our way, in typically British fashion, toward our 'Gate' - G. clutching the stiff, white card. As imagined, everything worked as if orchestrated; not a hitch and within seconds of arriving we'd spotted one old friend conducting the excellent Military Band after which, it seemed that every few steps produced two or three others - no doubt also wondering exactly why they'd been amongst that day's 'chosen'.Tea consisted of substantial but elegant sandwiches, scones and pastries and then a little wander before our 'Royal few words', accompanied by H.M's full-beam transforming smile (seem to remember, somewhere along the way chatting to peachy-complexioned actress, Wendy Craig). After a dawdle around the gardens - sighing over the splendid borders - we stopped by the lake, its surface almost obscured by the mass of bright Flamingos, their pink plumage reputedly preserved with a diet of prawns. Then, thoughts of home, hoping to find a cab before the mass exodus. But it would be a good tale for the grandchildren.

At the end of the year, our ex.neighbours from Brunei, Ann and Robin Matthews, suggested we join them 'How about Feb' for a couple of weeks holiday in the Canaries: Lanzarote? We balked, never having previously been away with anyone except the children. The phrase 'You never know people until you live with them' rang in my ears...But - after all the protestations of 'Ist time for us' and 'We may all end up hating each other', plus the awful business of 'finances' - as old hands at holidays-with-friends they seemed to have it sussed. Surprisingly, it worked. 'I-always-get-the-best-deal-Robin' our self-appointed arranger-in-chief, had booked us into a comfortable, 2bed/2bath-close-to-beach villa, and out-of-season Lanzarote proved sufficiently hot enough to enjoy without sapping our few remaining post-Christmas scraps of energy. We shopped together, shared chores - apart from breakfast, which Robin enjoyed producing - and ate out more than in. The cash problem was sorted by sticking to a 'housekeeping purse', as in when our original contributions - covering meals,drinks,papers, ice-creams and all consumable shopping - ran out, the purse was replenished with a set amount from each couple In fact, with surprisingly little to argue about, we discussed the possibility of returning.

Once home, the crop of orders for weddings and parties rolled in as irritatingly, did the health problems. However, drifting along on 'slow' and the invaluable help of Dr. G. - known at home as 'Dr. Loveliness - things were held together with the odd two or three-day guilt-ridden 're-charge' in bed and the physio. skills of friend Susan (that rare being a 'pearl beyond price'). Since my very first 'stay' in the Brompton, G. had helped out on the chest percussion - as it was then called (things having since moved on a bit) and I also managed it myself on a (mostly) daily basis. But still, the word 'Allergist' needed investigation. But: there always seemed to be something far more pressing to deal with.

Such as that year's biggest feature. One morning, back in harness, and half way through a large arrangement for a forthcoming party at the Tower, I looked up to see a breathless G. rushing toward me, his face one huge smile. '|...Just had a phone call from Simon...Are you working next Thursday?

It was a small celebration, the nuptials of Simon and Charlotte, as 'We really didn't want a fuss' (a familiar phrase) and despite being parents of the groom we considered ourselves fortunate to have been included in the small gathering (though not quite as small as our own). Later, in the delightful gardens behind Brixton Registry Office, the warm May sunshine shone brightly on the happy pair - a beaming Charlotte, looking lovely in a cyclamen white-spotted dress and an equally beaming Simon in a grey suit – relaxing together as someone snapped away 'Just one or two..' Almost in their tenth year together 'the event' was scarcely a surprise, only the apparent swiftness of the decision...But what do parents know? Although the word 'babies' had cropped up once or twice recently and they were obviously keen. But we'd have to wait a while.

One intermittent - but increasingly expensive annoyance in our lives - was the roof. Whilst builders may groan at the phrase 'valley-roof' few seem capable of dealing with the problems such fixtures are inclined to produce. No 2. - apart from its close proximity to the Tower - had come with an almost new (three years old) roof, covered - pause for hollow laughter - by a 20 year guarantee. Watertight? (sorry for the pun). Not a bit of it. When our 'within-2months-of-moving-in' bedroom leak flourished, a call to the boss of the outfit responsible for both roof and guarantee told us gleefully that 'We didn't guarantee you, we guaranteed the previous owner. You haven't a leg to stand on. Try it '. Oh dear. 'Sad, but true' said our solicitor, adding a wry 'Not many people know that...' Only when we threatened to parade - plus family - outside the shop premises with placards, did he send a so-called repair team. Two years later, after an anxious Christmas morning spent 'aloft' in a vicious gale, struggling to cover our now larger, problem, with a groundsheet and bricks, did G. decide we were probably in for a long run of cowboys: but most probably a new roof.

And so it came to pass. Regular patchwork - often featuring Irish Tommy, comical and irrepressible but reliable in as much as he always turned up, and TWO new roofs. The first, apparently totally lacking that essential ingredient - lead - had unsurprisingly given up completely in its second year; just about the time its crook of a creator went bust. But at last, thanks to the full renovation and 'development' job taking place next-door, we not only used the excellent and realistically priced services of their ace-roofer, but were also given free access to their scaffolding. Problem solved.

Although our mornings often began with a quick resume of 'How many for breakfast'? (being the popular London-friends with a couple of spare bedrooms) G's job produced enough unusual events and introductions to last three lifetimes. One such happening was a birthday party at the Tower for Lord (then Mr.) Michael Spicer M.P., a longtime friend of the regiment who later, kindly gave us lunch in 'The House, followed by a fascinating tour.

Well before the party, G. received his copy of the guest list, which impressively included several of the Great and the Good (although we were actually neither). Thanks to Ann, Lady Spicer, we were introduced to just about everyone there, but about half-way through whilst G.'floated', I was having an interesting time with the 'Get on your bike to find work' Norman Tebbitt and his delightfully approachable wife, Margaret (now Lord and Lady Tebbitt). Lord T. has to be one of not only the sharpest, but also the funniest men ever - certainly the funniest in Parliament - possessing the driest of bone-dry wits. Just fifteen or so minutes with them both left an unforgettable impression of warmth, keen intellect, good sense and fun. I've long regretted - due to a combination of 'the flowers' and health problems - being unable to take up Lady Tebbit's suggestion that we meet up again if my work included 'Something near the Barbican', particularly when the following year she was left wheelchair-bound as a result of the cowardly Brighton bombing.

Writing of incredibly brave woman brings to mind another: Odette Hallowes, one of my earliest heroines and Guest of Honour at another Tower lunch for those awarded the Victoria Cross. In W.W.2. 'Odette,' as she was known, survived cruel torture as a prisoner of the Gestapo and as an impressionable eleven-year-old, I remembered sitting with a friend in a Saturday afternoon cinema, enthralled by Anna Neagle's mesmerising performance in the film 'Odette' (wondering if we dare stay and see it round a second time..). So many years later, our meeting with this indomitable, chatty Frenchwoman, then in her amazingly vibrant early eighties, remains. "They really don't make 'em like that anymore". Then, just a couple of years or so later, another odd coincidence; once again due to our involvement with Anthony Strong, a Neurosurgeon, when for a while, we became part of the life of Odette's lovely grand-daughter. Maddy.

And so, after a frantic couple of months, I visited Dr. G. who kindly sanctioned the suggestion that I consult an Allergist. The very last thing intended was for him to think I might be dissatisfied in some way with his years of T.L.C. but he simply listened to my fears, saying little and as a highly-skilled, scientifically-trained specialist in his field, he received my strictly non-scientific ideas in a remarkably forward-thinking and accepting manner, adding only that if I went ahead, he be kept totally abreast of all diagnosis and treatments.

Grateful for his remarkable breadth of vision, not to mention, patience, I contacted a friend - and former patient - of Dr.Jean Munroe, a Consultant in Environmental Medicine, based in Hertfordshire.

The initial visit to Hemel Hempstead led to two weeks of tests covering everything from dairy-foods to chemicals and a vast selection of petro-chemical products. And the verdict? 'Multiple allergies and sensitivities to chemicals used on commercially-produced flowers and plants,' plus allergies and intolerances to a multiple of foods and common chemicals found in many household cleansers, particularly Chlorine (which at least explained years of nausea and headaches after swimming, and times when my brain appeared to have shut down completely). In fact, the entire diagnoses accounted for my often manic pace and spurts of frantic energy followed by total lethargy, bloating and 24hrs.of flu-like symptoms after using anything containing strong chemicals - particularly paint and strippers. Having reached 57 on the list of 'No.No's' I stopped counting. From now I'd need to avoid gluten, maize; dairy produce (goats and cows) alcohol and chocolate... followed by a ban on paint, varnish, turps. wood/tobacco/bonfire smoke; perfumed bath products and many cosmetics. All rather inconvenient. In fantasy mode for a moment, I pictured supermarket aisles clearing rapidly as I drifted round with a large bell shouting 'Unclean': shopping completed in a flash!..But my little business would have to go. And from Simon, my allergy mentor - 'I thought it was worth a shot..After all, where else would I have got my problems but from you?

The Original (I'm assured...) Caesar Salad – Serves 4

Place 2 egg-yolks in a bowl and mix in 2 finely-chopped hard-boiled eggs, 6 drained and chopped anchovy fillets, 2 crushed cloves garlic, 50grm.grated Parmesan and juice of one lemon. Gradually mix in 200mls.grapeseed oil. Flavour generously with Worcester sauce and Tabasco, then add sherry vinegar to taste.. Separate, wash and dry leavers of a cos lettuce. Pour over dressing and finish with croutons and a shave of Parmesan. Really good.

Chapter Twenty Six

HAVING CONSULTED DR. MONRO, I began treatment - an organic, severely restricted diet and daily self-administered, desensitising injections of 'Antigens', a specially produced compound containing minute quantities of my particular irritants. Results would be tested regularly and the Antigen doses revised as necessary. All time-consuming and eye-wateringly pricey (since then treatment no longer includes desensitising by injection). But so desperate was I to try and reduce the nausea and bloating, that it was followed to the letter. Sunday mornings saw us transported to a world of label-studying; ambling around Spitalfields market - then a haven of assorted organic produce (toothpaste to tangerines) - where, with three greengrocers, a large grocer and two butchers (one of which was later checked, prosecuted and banned forever from the market for selling non-organic meat) my weekly shopping bill - shamefully - would have fed the average family of four. Dr. G. however was unhappy at my weight loss: the diet, lacking much in the way of calories and other fattening goodies - whilst perfect for slimmers - saw me shrinking fast and consequently, with that almost-Christmas rush looming, another infection took hold. Back to Foulis Ward for another two weeks sojourn and a few waves of the Brompton magic-wands.

Being 'inside' meant that between treatments and writing Christmas cards, there was time to marshal a few thoughts. With business sadly abandoned, apart from the dull and daunting diet, life would change more than somewhat, but at least - without the frantic dawn dashes to Nine Elms and the physical effort of keeping it all together, things had to be easier - and at least I was spared having to sell off the kit. Our car - complete with a bulging boot of pedestals, new boxes of Oasis, and a selection of 'accoutrements' - had been stolen just two weeks previously, and whilst rescued shortly afterwards, the cupboard was not, unexpectedly, bare. G, then a Magistrate, said our 'Hardly-special Ford ' having been dumped, on Acton Broadway, probably owed its swift recovery to a copy of 'The Magistrates Handbook' laying open on the front seat.

Undoubtedly, Dr. Monroe's treatment and diet, plus my lack of exposure to chemically- plastered blooms, saw some symptoms vanish and others lessen. Small wonder that over the years, my increasing lack of tolerance to substances used in cleaning materials and cosmetics etc. had, apparently, also been assisting my sputum production by 'feeding' one or other - maybe all - the bugs I seemed to attract so frequently on my rather 'damp' lungs. As time went on, the health continued to see-saw in its usual fashion, varying when exposed to irritants and the odd lapse in diet (commonly known as gluttony) also, by that time I was keeping a diary in an effort to find some kind of pattern.

June 85 Oxford
S after receiving BA&MA with G&B

However, the wretched Pseudomonas bug so familiar to Cystic Fibrosis sufferers, still popped up regularly, whilst any new tests labeling me positively 'C. F.' remained stubbornly 'Inconclusive'. But where would I be without the cosy 'Brompton Blanket.'

Right. At the risk of my musings becoming this month's 'Anatomy of an Illness' I shall resist further detail. Indeed, were it not for proceeds of any sales (that's assuming there may just be one or two)

being donated to charity, my affliction would have remained my business but as everyone likes to know exactly what they're paying for, it seems only right to include a few facts concerning one of the country's finest hospitals and its special efforts to improve the lives of the many patients fortunate enough to be treated there. (The faint-hearted have full permission to skip anything upsetting).

So, onwards. G. - full of surprises - announced one evening 'How about a trip to Italy?..Henry (Duckett - a friend and exceptionally kind ex-Royal Fusilier who had donated generously to the Soldiers' Sports Fund) has suggested we spend a few days with he and Mickey ' (his wife). They lived within a half-hours' drive from Venice so who could resist.

Trotting around Venice with Henry and Mickey was indeed a memorable experience as Henry, once a successful businessman, and widower, prior to marrying Mickey, knew just about everyone. Soon, it became impossible to walk more than five yards before affectionate shouts of 'En-ery.En-ery' punctuated the comparative quiet of the afternoon (the real 'season' having not yet begun) followed by a lively barrage of Italian chat, hand-waving and much back-slapping. Later, whilst in a water-bus, chugging leisurely through the oily waters of the Grand Canal past one of several still splendid-looking Venetian Palazzos', we were amazed to have Henry point out one of the loveliest and earliest examples, going on to explain how for twenty years, he and Maria, his first wife, had lived there when she'd inherited on the death of her father. Impressed? Certainly. We looked forward to hearing more.

Later that evening, G and I studied a thick, impressive catalogue, printed when - following the death of Maria - the Palazzo had been put up for sale. Glossy photos of the contents featured some beautiful furniture and several paintings, some - by famous artists - dating back to the 14th century. 'Why did they all have to go' we asked naively, to which Henry replied philosophically: 'In a phrase: 'Death Duties'. They had the lot. But (with a certain relish) it was all good while it lasted'.

With us no longer, but then in his mid-70's, Henry was a striking-looking man whose hooded black eyes missed nothing. His fascinating life - solid with anecdotes - would have made a highly entertaining film of its own, much of it, post-war, having been spent amongst the rich and famous: and a few infamous. Friend of Dior, Picasso,

Chagall and several Hollywood names, he was something of a chancer, as well as bossy and forceful: but also unfailingly interesting. As one of the smoothest operators behind the wheel of a car he was, perhaps, a loss to the world of motor-racing, negotiating the tightest of hairpin bends, often at night on dark, vertiginous mountain roads (having enjoyed an exceptionally well-fuelled dinner) with the panache of a man in his 20's. On a further visit some years later, we were driven down to Florence on what felt like a jet-stream; this time by another expert driver, Mickey, Henry's bright, attractive and immaculately groomed young wife (later dubbed 'Fittipaldi'- a Grand-Prix winner from way back - by our son.). A quick look at the map on arrival and the distance covered in what had to be the tightest possible time, endorsed our assumption of having occasionally approached the speed limit - if indeed such a thing existed - from the opposite end.

Our ' hosts with the most', made sure we visited all the local places of interest. One day Lake Como, another Verona, stopping for lunches at isolated country restaurants whose excellent food was among the best ever (oh: the restrictions of the diet).Venice was saved for last but weatherwise, being something of a grey day, the lack of sunlight endowed me with a certain melancholia, adversely affecting my overall impression of Italy's 'jewel'. After coffee in the Square, we made for the famous Bridge of Sighs, later wandering off to watch the glass-blowers at work, marvelling at their skill, artistry - and lungs! On then to Henry's favourite restaurant where with lunch already booked, he was once more greeted with much affection and chat. As we studied the menu, Mickey - herself an excellent cook - cemented our choices. So much deliciousnes...Later, it was time to take in some of the many churches where, as the others pointed out one splendid artifact after another, I, still full of gloom, feigned enthusiasm, unable to wholeheartedly share their pleasure. That evening, after drinks at the Danielli Hotel, we drove back to the house, where still feeling something of a Philistine, I decided that the time of year, combined with my inability to ignore the darker side of the city's history, had somehow overtaken my natural appreciation of the old, rare and beautiful. G, had enjoyed everything but admitted to being in no great hurry to visit another church 'Just yet'.We agreed that Venice, a truly breathtaking, unique place, qualifies as 'something of a rich-diet'; but as with all good food, there's always space for a little more.

Singing to the Goldfish

Our next year of urban life seemed to consist of even more comings and goings with some friends - homeless after selling earlier than anticipated - staying for a couple of months before moving back to Oz. Their room however, was soon occupied by friend Liz, house-hunting in East London prior to starting a three-year course in Antiques Restoration at the City University. Whilst No.2 seldom housed just us, the bonus was that when full of people, our bed and bath, splendidly isolated on the top floor, meant guests had their own space.

And then it was June and time for the annual Summer Fete, held as usual in the Square Gardens, the various stalls and home-made produce giving our (very) urban area something of a village atmosphere: not exactly 'Camberwick Green' but for such a diverse community, a good sense of togetherness. Over the past thirty or forty years, much of London seems to have evolved into a series of 'villages' each with its own ethnic mix. Ours, home to many Portuguese families, had, after a while, become known as 'Little Lisbon,' with many of the local shops and cafes bringing a much-needed touch of the sun to the South Lambeth Road.

Before thoughts of Christmas took over the top half of my brain, we decided to take the car for a few days to Berlin, staying in the apartment that Trixie - now married to Essam, an Egyptian, impressively titled - Consultant in Nuclear Medicine - had retained. We shopped - watched 'A Chorus Line' in German - went to the opera and generally caught up with friends, some of whom kindly treated us to our first 'meal' of 'Nouvelle Cuisine (remember that? Fab. food for fairies). But the trip was particularly memorable as whilst travelling back overnight on a Hamburg/ Harwich ferry, at about 1am I found myself on the cabin floor - as opposed to the top bunk. Amidst much shouting and general hubbub, G. having surfaced for a second - totally ignoring my 'I'm sure we've hit something ' - simply opened one eye, muttered 'What are you doing there? Go back to bed...' and promptly fell asleep.' Lacking instructions to either 'Man the Lifeboats' or 'Abandon Ship' or whatever the accepted course of action suits such a situation - I returned aloft. Next morning, we listened as two fellow travellers debated 'Our arrival time in Hamburg'... My gentle interruption of 'Hamburg? But we're due in Harwich at eight surely?' to which the reply was an astonished 'And where were you last night?

Take a look at the front of the ship.' Ah, so. We'd hit a large barge ... enthusiastically, judging by the damage (photo now in a scrap-book) and the shipping company, having declined 'English repairs' was indeed returning to Hamburg. Passengers, on the other hand, were given D.M.100 'For either petrol or transport' and instructed to make their way to the Danish port of Ebsjberg, some 100 ks. or so from Hamburg 'Where you will board a later ferry and be looked after' (scarcely at all as it happened but compensation came there none...)

Simon and Dom had been on the move again. Dom, now in a different job, had swapped her tiny Wimbledon cottage for a terraced house nearer the tube; whilst Simon and Charlotte, having sold their flat in Herne Hill, were also in a terraced house, in Nunhead, where Simon's business 'Black Spring Press' was flourishing. And the real, great excitement of the year was the surprise announcement of Charlotte's pregnancy. In Feb. '88 we were to become grandparents.

Tenderloin of Pork with Apples and Calvados (serves 4)
500grm pork tenderloin trimmed and sliced downwards into 6 pieces. Batten until thin.

100grm unsalted butter

250mls double cream

3 tabsp. Calvados

3 large Golden Delicious apples – peeled, cored, quartered and thickly sliced, extra butter for cooking. Fry over low heat until soft: reserve.

Season pork slices and flour lightly. Melt butter and saute pork over fairly high heat -2 mins each side. Pour over Calvados or Brandy and flambe. Pour over cream. Reduce heat and leave for 5/10 mins. Lift out pork onto hot serving dish – spoon sauce over and garnish with apple slices.

Super-Refreshing Fruit Salad.
I ripe melon – cut into bite-sized squares or if you have a tool, small balls + 250grms seedless grapes, washed and halved + 5 ripe kiwi fruit - peeled and cut into small pieces + 6 pieces stem ginger, thinly sliced. Mix together in glass bowl.

Make sugar syrup as follows. Pour 200mls boiling water over 3 tabsp. caster sugar. Stir until dissolved then bring to boil(without stirring) boil for one minute. Cool and pour over fruit. Leave in 'fridge and decorate with mint leaves.

Chapter Twenty Seven

DUE TO A 'NASTY-INFECTION-PRE-HOLIDAY-SPELL' in Foulis Ward, feeling grim and cross with myself, Christmas with spent quietly with the children and Charlotte. By 5th Jan, however, was delighted to put up our old friend Ashley - now a Consultant - for supper and a chatty evening and recall remarking to G. as he and A. got to the car the next morning - one tall and slim, one shorter and not-so, that 'A little diet might be a good idea'... Seconds later, as they drove off, he shouted 'I'll ring you later, about lunch. Adelaide and Bertie are due at 12:30'.

After clearing the table and skimming through our daily 'comic' - I reluctantly heaved myself up to the sitting-room and stood for a moment, deciding that the Twelfth Night crispy tree and yuletide greenery could wait until that evening (odd how each detail of that morning remains particularly vivid). Later. stuck in traffic at Tower Bridge, it occurred to me that G. hadn't rung; but no matter: there was plenty of time.

Having found his office empty, I traced him to the Regimental flat, complaining of 'A really bad headache' (recalling it to be his 4th in the past two weeks). His explanation of 'A big explosion in my head' was indeed alarming, followed by 'Mrs. Bennett gave me some Nurofen and has called an ambulance'. Next came 'I think I've had a brain haemorrhage'...so incongruous from someone not only unable to read a thermometer but also totally lacking so much as a syllable of medical knowledge.

Feeling suddenly sick and shaky I prayed he was wrong, but his description had sounded horribly fitting. (Whilst not exactly on the recommended list of treatments for Brain Haemorrhages, if in doubt, take Nurofen...).

Our swift ambulance trip to Guys Hospital had resulted in an examination, followed by a seizure, after which a scan revealed G. had indeed suffered a severe Subarachnoid Haemorrhage 'Often' I was told, 'Fatal'. Wretched at not having insisted he visit our G.P. earlier, I sat awaiting our children - summoned on the advice of the doctor. Provided with a full police escort we were taken to the then

Neurosurgical Unit of Guys, also part of the Maudsley Hospital, in Camberwell, where, after an examination, a semi-conscious G. was settled into what would turn out to be be 'home' for us all for some weeks to come.

G's aforementioned Neurosurgeon, Mr then - now Professor - Anthony Strong turned out to be the most skilful, unflappable, kind and patient of men, explaining gently to us that as the next 24hrs.were particularly vital, we were welcome to stay at G's bedside, stressing that we hold his hands and speak quietly, but regularly, to him. That first night we remained by his bed, dozing fitfully, and at around 8am he came-to, appearing perfectly normal - for just fifteen or so minutes - when, with Mr. S. alerted, he suddenly dropped into a state of semi-consciousness. Fearing the worst, we moved off into the corridor to wait whilst he was prepared for what we feared might end up as a 'long-stay'.

On day three, having driven the short distance home for a quick bath and change of clothes, clad in just a towel, I'd answered a ring at the door to an unknown lady who turned out to be Helen, a Deacon at St. Stephens, our local church, who explained that she'd heard of G's illness... We rushed up to the bedroom together and as I dressed, she asked that if we had no objection, she'd like to pray by George's bed for a while. Once back in Camberwell, the children and I left Angel-Helen on her knees, the bed curtains tightly drawn.

Emerging a while later she hugged me, saying 'Try not to worry. He'll be alright you know'. Such faith is rare but her smiling face held a message of such impossible-to-ignore hope that we felt sustained.

Those first few nights we'd taken shifts to nap on the wooden bench in the chilly corridor, our days spent around G's bed where every hour he'd be addressed loudly by a nurse who, after firmly grasping his hands began with 'George, squeeze my hands'. This was followed by a set of questions: 'Where are you? Your name is? Address ? Birthday? Occupation? Name of the Prime Minister? Etc. undertaken in the hope of noting any possible brain-damage and/or signs of deterioration.

After a week or so, when he stopped answering every single query, I suggested that he was simply tired of being questioned and whilst aware of their efforts to help, his attitude was probably due more to a lack of interest, rather than deterioration. Some days he'd co-operate but not always.

And so followed the next weeks - except that having become 'The family that sleeps in the corridor' we'd accepted the kind and totally unexpected offer of a twin-bedded room in a closed area of the building, subsequently working what is often referred to as 'The hot-bed system': the children taking it in turns to sleep through the night but insisting I, not long returned from my own little stay in hospital, go off before eleven, appearing again around 6am to relieve either Simon or Dom. from night duty.

Charlotte, due to produce in less than eight weeks, visited daily, bringing in little treats and the odd takeaway meal, staying to chat whilst Simon dashed home to check on his business. Soon, our ever-practical daughter-in-law provided Dom and I with wool and needles, suggesting we knit squares for a baby blanket 'Better we all do something productive.' How could I ever have coped without the invaluable support of them all, Simon, Dom and Charlotte, each wonderful, propping me up and often bringing humour into the grimmest of days.

Permitted the use of the hospital facilities, which included the staff canteen, we were never made to feel 'in the way' and treated by the exceptional, desperately hard-working staff with the greatest courtesy. After mentioning that G's Health Insurance would have freed his bed for another patient, I was told that 'We want him where we can see him and haven't the staff to deal with a private room.' Feeling useless and restless, my suggestion that I take over G's daily shave and assist with his bed-bath, was accepted gracefully and our flat-out patient made not a movement throughout, snoozing peacefully through all (gentle) assaults on his supine person. Whenever, for whatever reason, his bed was moved from the ward, I'd rush off to the kitchen and - lying through my teeth - beg one of the uncomplaining staff there for a mop and bucket of hot soapy water 'To clean up the mug of coffee I've just spilled..' The standard of hospital hygiene was actually good, but the empty space presented an opportunity to just 'Give it another quick 'go'...

As a family, I suspect that in the eight weeks spent in the hospital. we learned more about people, love, patience, devotion, courage, faith, frustration - and ourselves - than either before or since. I understand that any form of brain injury can produce a state of coma which means that waiting becomes a fact of life. Soon, families and friends accept that as regular hospital visitors they will spend hours just sitting around, often with other 'waiters'; in time chatting together at length, discussing in detail how the illness, accident or injury happened or began, plus their opinions of the staff, the food and the facilities - everyone pooling their hopes and fears - desperate to find the tiniest grain of comfort somewhere along the way. By the time George had surgery, an entire five weeks after he'd first been admitted, we knew the case histories of almost every patient in the large ward.

Whilst every story touched us deeply, the saddest of all were those involving a child. At odd times, during doctors' rounds or medication dispensing, we'd sat chatting in the corridor with a young Scottish woman who - having produced wool and needles of her own - was helping knit squares for what was now referred to as our 'Maudsley Blanket'. One day, quietly, and without either seeking or expecting sympathy, she explained matter of factly how the previous morning she'd heard the results of tests which had decided the fate of her beautiful, six-year old daughter: 'they were so nice, and I felt so sorry for Mr. - having to tell me that there was just no operation or drug that could help her... the tumour is so close to her spine, surgery could easily paralyze her and he's unwilling to risk destroying what then still may turn out to be only a very short life. We'll be taking her home tomorrow …' There was courage in each bed and on every chair and the feeling of quiet desperation combined with hope, almost palpable. One patient, a young man, perhaps in his early 30's, admitted a month previously, had yet to be identified; consequently, he'd received no visitors having been found in the street, almost dead from severe head injuries.

But once or twice, a lighter moment or two appears from nowhere, even if it is at another's expense - although in this case, the chap involved really would have seen the funny side. One morning, whilst Dom smoked a post-breakfast cigarette in our usual half-hour slot along the corridor, we spotted a familiar figure weaving his way slowly toward us, resembling what can only be described as a 'Bionic Medusa'; but instead of snakes, from each of twelve or so points of his head sprung a long thin electronic lead, each swaying gently as the coloured plug at its end threatened to take off in a different direction. Mesmerised, but aware that the first to giggle would set us all off, Dom managed to say 'Joe' - not his real name - 'You've unplugged yourself' (from a machine designed to pinpoint the site of his epilepsy)... Then 'Do they know you've gone'? The reply of 'Oh yeah, but I'm desperate for a fag...they said I could have one; honest'. But I've run out'... left us sceptical, but after several attempts to discourage him, Dom finally handed over just one. And just one puff was all it took. Immediately 'Joe' dropped as if stunned - luckily- right by the feet of a passing nurse. 'Don't worry' he said, seeing our dismay - 'he'll be ok. But he's supposed to be off fags.' We heard later he'd soon recovered but the vision he'd presented that morning will I feel sure, be with us all forever.

Due to G's see-saw state of health lacking stability, surgery was delayed with Mr. Strong telling us 'I've never before waited so long.' But suddenly, after four weeks, on arriving early one morning in the ward, Simon and one of the duty nurses announced to me 'He's awake. We're waiting for Mr.Strong'. Appearing as if from nowhere, Mr. S. after examining G. pronounced him 'Remarkably well, if confused".

Yes, there was confusion, sometimes providing an unintentionally amusing, if bitter-sweet, moment and at that time, he seldom objected to a 'Don't think that's quite right, love'. I recall how after his first bath, when lowered into the water wearing a harness had obviously reminded him of a long-ago parachute course, he'd told us afterwards, including my visiting mother, that he'd 'Spent the morning parachuting'. Another day, having gravely invited Charlotte's very attractive mother to 'Share my bed' her game reply of 'I will if you will' left him beaming - but at the same time protesting 'Yes. I know' at my 'Actually love, that's Sheila, not me.. (Years later, asked if he'd ever nurtured 'A secret passion for friend Sheila W.' he'd replied abstractedly 'No. What made you think I had?)'.

The next week was one of constant surveillance and coercion at meal-times. Food had to be kept simple as, for anyone laying flat, chewing is a problem and on that very first day of consciousness, after just two mouthfuls of hospital Cottage Pie, without a trace of irony he'd asked plaintively 'Why are you feeding me dog-food? Thereafter, each morning included a trip to a nearby supermarket for a selection of foods easily blended into my best creamy mash, plus an assortment of his favourite puds. After four weeks of fluids, the 'little diet' I'd suggested on the morning of his admittance now needed reversing and thanks to the patient kitchen staff, my daily meal production sessions were carried out without complaint at my 'using their space' (which I was always careful to leave 'sparkling.').

'The five and a half hours surgery had been successful and G's swift - less than an hour - awakening and subsequent acceptance of his situation was a great relief for us all: for just ten or so minutes. Mid-sentence he'd suddenly lost consciousness, and with Hydrocephalus (Water-on-the-Brain) suspected, we left the ward. Tests indicated another trip to theatre, for the insertion of a 'shunt', necessary to divert the fluid from the head to be passed naturally. Sick at heart, but, for the children's sake, saying little, I wondered 'What next?'.

Two weeks later, we took him home. Now back in situ and wondering how we could ever thank the hospital staff for everything they'd done, not only for G., but for us as a family, I also tried to imagine, selfishly, how I'd cope. The returning man was far removed from the one who had left so cheerfully on the morning of Twelfth Night, just eight weeks earlier.

Chapter Twenty Eight

WITHIN 48HRS WE'D RECEIVED NEWS from Simon that we were now grandparents to a baby girl - Georgia - named of course, after the grandfather who almost never was. Together, we set off for Westminster hospital, a tricky journey due to G's reluctance to accept his 'No driving for twelve months' rule (placed by law on all patients following brain-surgery, automatically negating their previous Insurance cover due to the possibility of an Epileptic 'episode' occurring).

Georgie, as she quickly became was (and is) of course, totally gorgeous: with everything in the right places, light-brown hair and big blue-eyes and for a few moments, before reluctantly passing her across to G., I sat just gazing, enjoying that special perfection of a new baby, before gently examining her perfect fairy hands and feet; a delicious little bundle. G. - looking pleased but slightly puzzled and probably aware of not feeling quite together - handed her back after a moment and announced he'd 'Like to go home now, please'. Our visit was short, but probably long enough for the new parents: the previous weeks had left their mark and they'd earned every second of breathing space before the beginning of what would soon be a very different life.

About to say our goodbyes, a remarkably switched-on nurse appeared and, having first checked our names and address, had me accompany her to another ward where an elderly ex-neighbour of ours, Evelyn, had been admitted earlier with a severe stroke. Apparently G. and I had been named somewhere 'To be contacted in the event of my death'. Poor Evelyn. Obviously close to her final moments, her gaunt figure lay silent, still and twisted from the effect of the illness. After a little prayer, I kissed her and wept silently. We'd known her for some years; helping her move to North London when a small flat became available. A delightful, genteel lady, a long-time widow and to her great sadness, also childless. What a strange coincidence that we should have arrived at that particular hospital on that very day to welcome the beginning of a new life and say farewell to an old.

The intervening days before G's. six-week check were among the most disjointed and unhappiest of our entire life together, and would continue for some time. Through no fault of his own, my poor husband now faced life with someone who had become not only his constant companion but also a 'Jailer' - a barrier to freedom and - the biggest sin of all 'Guardian of the car keys' and interrupter of his (highly inventive) stories' (after warnings by the medics that 'Patients are inclined to fill in memory gaps with fantasy but ignoring it will create a habit'- stop any confabulation). This once-reasonable person insisted too, that he bath and shave daily and, having read aloud news from a daily paper, later quizzed him on it all (suggested by the hospital occupational therapist to help improve a short-term memory).

The days more or less rolled into one with little to distinguish them, the saddest thing of all being that by 8:30 each morning, G. would be found in his study, stuffing the Telegraph into his briefcase before I had to tell him, again, that he wasn't yet quite fit enough for the office. This usually ended in a phone call to a member of the hospital team who slowly and patiently, would once again explain his situation to him - my own efforts having been met with total disbelief and anger. Unfortunately, just moments later, all details of the phone conversation had cruelly faded.

Our mornings varied little, often including a short walk across Clapham Common, and sometimes some shopping, but as a recent trip to Camberwell had resulted in his going AWOL for almost three hours (we've never discovered where) I had become increasingly twitchy, ever 'on duty' - anything but a relaxed companion, full of angst and severely short on humour, particularly as before leaving the hospital, I'd been warned that a further attack could well happen within the next three or four months. Taking each day as it came, I would ask 'And what are you thinking of today' seldom receiving even an offhand 'nothing much' and whilst his physical health improved daily, he was mentally unreachable. But, it appeared, only to me. When close friends came for supper - never more than two at a time - his manner, whilst slightly odd and brash was never rude. The children were welcomed but in no way shunned. I was now the enemy and as such, made to feel guilty for his predicament. Then a youthful 61, he displayed the symptoms of an elderly teenager - truculent, stubborn, difficult and unapproachable - and as an exceptionally strong personality - in need of a far more robust 'carer ' who instead of wilting, tried either to jolly him out of it or read the riot act in an effort to improve his attitude. Recognising my inability to overcome our situation and fearing increasingly for our future together (as someone is reported to have replied when asked if she'd ever considered divorce "Divorce? never: murder? often...") the scenario was indeed far from rosy, accepting the reality that the reason for our current state of being had seemingly been laid squarely at my head. Daily, after lunch, and a deep four or five hour sleep, I'd wake him at six with a mug of tea, dreading the evening ahead. Lacking either energy - or enthusiasm - to patronise a local restaurant and only occasionally accepting invitations, we'd usually sup. alone, in total silence; after which, with a cigarette and a Scotch and water G. would stare at the tv. for a while - sadly, absorbing little - before returning to bed.

The children were, as always - wonderfully supportive, visiting often and phoning daily, although they obviously thought I was exaggerating our problems and it was easy to see why. Dom. sweetly gave up many of her Saturday afternoons to entertain G. whilst I zoomed off to friends in Surrey for a short break. Gorgeous Georgia was thriving well, and while at that time, G. wasn't always entirely sure where she fitted in, he's certainly made up for it since. Then, having passed his six-week check with aplomb and desperate to return to work, in order to show him that the building still stood secure, we drove to the Tower one morning, spending an hour or so, chatting and drinking coffee. Peering over the shoulder at a ledger being worked on by his 'temporary replacement', G. swiftly spotted an accounting mistake, which - proving correct - earned him a heartfelt, if amazed, word of thanks. Life, it seemed, was beginning to move on, if only a little. Although being civil to each other was becoming increasingly difficult.

My priority now was to try and hold on tight and to help G. move forward, back to work: his job at the Tower having been kept open by the kindest of gestures from General Sir Jeremy Reilly, once his commanding officer. Our times alone together lacked either warmth or chat and gradually, resentment set in (how dare I: after all he'd suffered). In a weak moment, I confided my guilt to an old friend, telling how the effort of maintaining a confident exterior was fast reducing me to an exasperated, self-loathing harridan; exhausted and fearful for the future. She, whilst sympathetic, did her best but later, I recalled a visit G. and I had once made to a stroke-affected ex-officer, when his obviously exasperated and weary wife's manner toward him had - after arriving home - given rise to some harsh and ignorant criticism from us both. Experience, it seems, is all.

Medically, G. had been the recipient of the most skilled and brilliant surgery from which he'd made a phenomenal recovery; and it was still early days. However, I found myself unable to stop speculating; reasoning, in the odd rational moment how that first trip to theatre may well have left him incapacitated; unable to either walk, talk or think. Then I'd really have something to complain about. And what of those who, on a day-to-day basis, are faced with a partner suffering Altzheimers or Dementia? These are indeed the true saints. But rational thought seldom interrupts exhaustion, particularly when faced with an almost-stranger; a familiar but distant and indifferent lookalike, who, while possibly in need of help, is simply too proud to ask. (This account of our situation at that time has been recorded here entirely with G's blessing - along with the advice of a good friend who, in a similar position before her husband's death last year and distressed at her own feelings, found my honesty far more helpful than 'Buckets of platitudes', adding 'You really must tell it as it was').

But throughout, I somehow remained aware of how very blessed we really were, constantly offering thanks for our loving family. Not forgetting Dr. G's magic pills which, keeping me vertical, left my space in 'Foulis' - for the time being - free for another less fortunate soul.

In an effort to find G. an interest, my suggestion of a Cookery course at nearby Morley College merely prompted an amazed 'Why on earth would I want to do that?' and days later, an hour's Golf instruction had ended similarly with a firm 'Sorry. Not for me..' Work had always been his priority and with this in mind, less than four months after his surgery - much to the astonishment of everyone involved in his treatment - he was back in harness : initially part-time, but happier.

Picked up by car at 8:30, he'd be returned at 1:00, and after coffee and a sandwich, retire for what soon became known as 'The big Sleep'. His loyal Chief Clerk at the time - Mr.Gibson - was a kind, hard-working, man who gently helped steer him through those first tricky months, ensuring that all important dates were duly recorded in a larger version of the notebook carried by G. from his early working days.

But before that, we'd spent an easy week in Somerset at the kind invitation of the Biddells who, as medics, simply shrugged off any untoward moment with a joke. What luck to have such good friends and no one could have been more grateful than I for their immediate acceptance of our situation. Not long afterwards, invited to join four others for a week in Sitges, we welcomed the chance of another week's break accompanied - grateful for the extra 'diluted' time.

One afternoon, shortly before G. returned to the Tower full-time, I recognised the need to get a grip and to stop concentrating on my own misery. Occasionally, having met Simon for lunch, I'd return home, reflecting ruefully how the phrase 'Sparkling Companion' could never have applied to my less-than-strenuous efforts to disguise our true situation, only too aware that both children must have begun to dread spending time with their dreary mother, who after all, might from somewhere have exhibited more patience when dealing with their damaged father. Maybe a good talking-to was the answer, but whatever the remedy, speed was essential before I succumbed totally to misery and alienated everyone.

A while later, with G. back at work full-time, still banned from driving he'd be delivered home; obviously tired, but just a little more forthcoming and approachable. Any small improvement meant a stepping-stone towards independence for us both, but whilst his world was slowly making sense; lacking stimulation, my own remained static - accompanied by an unhealthy inclination to dwell increasingly upon the future.

French Onion Tart (6 slices)

Line med. sized flan tin with rich shortcrust pastry – about 275grms. (All-butter pastry now obtainable from 'best' supermarket) or make with 50grm lard 55grm butter, 1 egg yolk, 240grm. s.r flour, water to mix. Prick base lightly and line with baking paper filled with cooking beans. Bake for 15/20 mins in hot oven 200c (depending on ovens which seem to vary considerably).Remove beans and paper and leave to cool. Meanwhile:

Peel and thinly slice 2 large or 3/4 med. sized onions, Fry gently in 60grms butter but do not brown.Leave to cool

Beat 3 eggs and add about 350mls. double cream plus 6 tabsp. full-cream milk.

Evenly spread cooked onions over base of flan and season well.

Pour over cream and egg mixture, generously grate with nutmeg.

Place in oven 185c fan, unti top form to touch : about 25 minutes (keep an eye on it...)

Ratatouille.

First skin 1 and a half kilo. ripe tomatoes (Pour over boiling water, leave 3 mins, plunge into cold and skin - cut each into 4 and set aside)Add 200grms butter to 100mls good olive oil m Place in large heatproof casserole, melt and heat and add:

1)3 large onions thinly sliced and 10 crushed garlic cloves. 2)Stir in 1 large washed and cubed aubergine. 3)add 4 trimmed and cubed 4 mid-size courgettes. 4) 2 large ripe, red peppers -washed, de-seeded and thinly sliced. Simmer on med heat - stirring now and then & when softish, add tomatoes and 2 dess. sp. Sugar. Season well to taste. Cook together for 20 or so minutes.

Chapter Twenty Nine

IT WAS A COPY OF THE GUARDIAN THAT DID IT. Delivered one morning in place of our usual Telegraph, I'd idly skimmed through part of the Educational section and spotted an ad., to which, having first dug out a C.V. - I replied; more out of curiosity than real expectancy. Despite my lack of a degree, or even 'A' Levels (always pointless to be creative at such times, particularly as Americans are renown for checking) following a lengthy interview, I was amazed (and dazed!) some three weeks later to find myself on the staff of what was referred to as 'The London Programme' - a branch of America's Boston University - in charge of 'Student Affairs' (a title which fast became the butt of unlimited ribald remarks). The 'Programme' offered one 'Semester' ('Term' to us) of study in London for between 250-380 students (some already Graduates, some not) who, after their first five weeks of study were placed for the remainder of their stay in a Company Internship appropriate to their choice of future career.

Before accepting my new job, fearing any repercussion, I'd sought G's opinion, prepared only to 'join up' if offered his full approval. Remarkably sanguine, he'd - unpredictably - appeared totally in favour, offering a thoughtful 'I think it will do you good.', more like his old self. These odd patches of reasonableness were increasing but for very brief periods, often catching me out: particularly as he also seemed to have developed a talent for acting. Confusing? Very - bringing to mind the words 'A--e and Elbow'. But soon, a form of pattern emerged, with each 'difficult' period 'flattening-out' to an easier, pre.- illness time: the phrase 'The same but different' somehow summed it up. I understand that any form of brain-damage or disturbance - whether the result of accident, injury,disease, tumour or stroke - may result in strange and alarming symptoms - altering personalities in a second and producing dismay and disbelief in the onlooker, especially when experienced for the first time. But, in reality, any improvement had to be for the better.

And the children? What of their feelings regarding 'the job'? Disapproval? Maybe: but whilst direct accusations were never actually voiced, their silence, I felt, said it all. Feeling like a deserter - praying that neither G. nor I would regret what had essentially been my choice, also full of guilt at my selfishness, I immediately began to think of reasons to turn it down. Incredibly however, B.U.(Boston University) and I were to remain together for almost six years.

Based in Kensington, B.U. was an easy, thirty-five minute journey from Stockwell, our nearest tube, and On Day 1. I arrived in good time, having spent the entire trip wondering if I'd made the right decision. At least G. was safely at work and as both sets of car keys were stowed safely in my bag, there was no chance of his taking off again if he happened to be first home (in the early days, he'd twice liberated a set and whizzed off for an evening paper: my desperate 'You are not insured; please try to understand' on his return had meant another frantic call to the hospital).

What's the phrase 'Separated by a common language'? At times, certainly - but on the whole, working for B.U. made for a fascinating, memorable time - with more than a few highly amusing, as well as tricky, moments. Almost on arrival I was met by Jill, my boss, who, before introducing the other members of staff, pushed open the door to my office, revealing a light, good-sized room, complete with sofa and tissues - plus the largest safe I'd ever seen 'For student valuables, hard-to-get films for the Media class and extra cash...And there's only one key and you have to keep it'...Next, up on the first floor I was introduced to the other staff as they arrived, before being left left with Doug, a startlingly bright and cheerful ex-Cornell University Psychology Graduate, recently employed for a year as a 'General Assistant'. His words of 'Right, I'll now go and get you the Mac' left me puzzled, asking 'Er. What's a Mac?'(my knowledge of technology beyond the simple electric typewriter amounted to nil). His face said at all.'You know? The Mac? The computor'. Disbelieving, but finally aware that I hadn't the faintest notion as to what he meant, his slow, baffled reply has to this day remained etched firmly upon my memory 'You mean you don't know what a computor is'?

This was only 1988, but quite obviously I had immediately qualified as 'Queen of the Half -Witted' (even more so in '89 when the students were requesting directions to the 'nearest Internet cafe).' Whilst the first of a few surprises 'the Mac' was perhaps scariest of all, with part of the job involving the creation of an informative, interesting and chatty student newsletter - 20-24 pages, produced weekly on 'The Mac'. Once again 'Fear concentrates the mind' as super-technocrat, Doug, put me through my paces. The first edition, or rather, my first edition, featured, among other riveting pieces, a 'mini-biog'. ('You must include a one-page profile of yourself') the execution of which had probably involved more energy, bad language and angst, than expended upon the entire construction of the Empire State Building. But after actually getting the thing together, it needed to be printed: one for each student and one for each member of staff: (around 300 that first term). More technology. This time 'A very simple piece of equipment' - a photo-copier - presided over by Pauline, a young Australian girl, from Sydney, whose dry sense of humour often saved the day. Intimately acquainted with all office machinery, Pauline could scarcely believe my effect on 'her' photo-copier (anyone familiar with the Fonda-Parton film 'Nine-to-Five' will know what I mean) and before long - 'St. Pauline' would often volunteer her services. But as a complete change from the previous months, no set-up could have served its purpose better.

The students were - on the whole - a great bunch, mainly women, aged 19 – 27, although one Summer intake (always the easiest term with the happiest students) there were two grannies, both aged 52, who in their own words 'Had ourselves a ball'. In my entire time there, I'd little cause for real complaint, the students, by and large, being a pleasant, lot: chatty, often highly comical and grateful for any help. Having missed 'Arrivals Day' I was in time for 'Orientation', a daunting occasion when each member of staff gave a brief lecture on themselves, their job and where they fitted in... Skiing naked down Everest might have been an easier option.

With no two days alike the job was diverse, covering pastoral care which included supplying details of accessible Allergy, Drug, Eating, Abortion and Family-Planning clinics, plus up-to-date HIV information and the checking of appropriate 'jabs' and travel insurance for the wanderers. Students were housed together in various-sized flats around Kensington and Earls Court and as each term ended and damages were dealt with, lovely Karim - a knowledgeable, clever man, responsible for 'Much Maintenance' - and I, would shop for small items of crockery and furniture and often, linen - some of the men having remained in the same bed-linen from day one... There were also excursions and theatre trips to arrange (always the best deals for tickets and travel) and instructions for 'finding cheaper food ' accompanied by recipes from simple pasta sauces to the Thanksgiving Turkey. At weekends, cars would be hired by groups of four, each armed with their license, routes, maps and road rules, taking off happily for Scotland, undaunted by either our British driving customs or the planned mileage, often 'doing' Oxford, Stratford and the Cotswolds en route (incredibly I only ever recall one accident and that featured a stone wall somewhere in Northumberland: but no other vehicle!). Invariably there were problems with flatmates - 'I'm not living with 'her' or 'him' or 'them' - along, with a few issues of theft, but it could all have been so very much worse. Reported alcohol incidents were comparatively few (with maybe just a handful finding their way to me) and drug situations only really featured when students - 'highly-scented' after a weekend in Amsterdam - returned and after two minutes in the office were immediately dispatched to their flats with instructions to 'Shower, wash your hair and change your clothes'. Life had moved on just a little since our own young - now in their 20's - were teenagers; although, no doubt., they weren't exactly strangers to the odd puff or two. (My own very first - and last - experience came at the tender age of 56, when a disbelieving friend 'You mean you've never tried ANYthing?' produced a tiny amount of resin with instructions to 'Add it to your favourite fudge mixture': result, interesting fudge, accompanied by a solid 2 hrs. worshipping the porcelain...).

But I mustn't forget the listening. Complete with a sympathetic and totally shockproof ear, plus a full box of tissues, one filled in occasionally as a favourite aunt or best friend 'Back home' as problems were sifted through and sometimes even resolved. Experiencing life in a different country - maybe for the first time - is seldom easy, especially for the young.

Towards the end of the summer, I suggested to G. that, as a way of thanking the hospital staff for all the skill and TLC involved in helping him through his illness, combined with the kindness and understanding shown to us as a family, we organise a dinner in the H.Q. for everyone, followed by the historical 'Ceremony of the Keys': the ceremonial locking-up of the Tower gates which has taken place every evening, 9:30-10:00pm, for the past 6, 7, or 800 years (G. has always said 'Depending on whichever Yeoman Warder is on duty that particular evening)'. This would include every hospital staff member involved in G's welfare during his eight week stay, from cleaning staff to the team of doctors. I would cook and with the children to help serve, the only extras needed would be on the cleaning-up front. Happily he agreed, but confessed to being quite unable to recollect anyone in particular; apart from the Psychiatrist who had given him the 'All-clear' when returning for his first check-up.

Three weeks later, forty-seven of us - a full complement, bar one - sat down to dinner on a still, sunny August evening in the 'old' Officers' Mess in the Tower Headquarters. Our cold starter - a prawn and smoked-salmon mousse - was followed by a choice of poached trout (kindly donated by my sister and brother-in-law from their lakes) or chicken breasts in Madeira sauce, served with salads and new potatoes. After dessert, cheese and coffee, G's Surgeon, Anthony Strong, made a warm and amusing speech - as did G. who confessed to remembering 'Nothing, really, about my stay or my treatment and I'm sure you're all very nice people - but I have memory problems you know...' then, tongue-in-cheek 'In fact if my wife hadn't made me eat so much lettuce over the years, I'm sure I'd never have had a brain haemorrhage at all...' Everyone seemed to enjoy the occasion and G. agreed that having the ability to 'Do a small something' in such a memorable and historic setting for those who had contributed so positively to his recovery was something of a privilege, which in turn, he'd felt honoured to have shared.

G. was now back at Court and all the letters (about 90) 'wishing him better' on leaving hospital, had been answered - as they'd arrived, in batches. In the Spring of the following year we received a call from Mr.Strong asking if we'd be willing to help form a charity with Cheryl Baker, one of the two girls in the popular singing group 'Bucks Fizz'. The previous year, whilst touring in Newcastle - having found fame as winners of the Eurovision Song Contest - the group had been involved in a dramatic road accident involving a coach and taken to Newcastle General Hospital, where the most seriously injured of the four - Mike Nolan - was treated and subsequently operated on by Anthony Strong. Despite making a good recovery, Mike had sustained a certain amount of brain-damage which, while preventing him from driving, meant he'd also be unfit to work for some time. Then, as concerned fans do, cash was donated to something called 'The Mike Nolan Brain Damage Fund' which, although never formally registered as a charity, was saved in an account of that name and later, kindly transferred by Cheryl to what we agreed be named 'Headfirst' : formed to provide funds for research into the causes and treatment of brain damage sustained by injury or illness. In the hope of increasing capital, G. then drafted a begging letter, explaining the charity and its purpose, which was sent to not only various relatives and friends but also to friends of the regiment. We were delighted to find such a generous response to 'the call'.

We have remained small, with no premises apart from George's study, and have no paid employees. Also, our trustees claim no expenses. In the early days funds were raised - always with 'trouper' Cheryl's help and unflagging energy - with 'Balloon Days' (we then had our own, complete with the H.F. Logo designed by a member of our daughter and son-in-law's company) and several black-tie balls, the first of which was held in the lovely Surrey home of Diana and trustee, Ossie Jones. This was followed by one at Dulwich College and another at Pangbourne College, the latter instigated by the delightful Maddy, wife of a master there and also a grand-daughter of Odette Churchill GC. Next, Cheryl set up a great evening at the Imperial War Museum which included an excellent band and a memorably delicious four-course supper produced by the Gary Rhodes team (Gary is also another firm H.F. supporter). Some time ago, when invited by Cheryl to a ball held in a country hotel by one of the 'Ferrari Clubs' (from which a donation would be given to Headfirst) we found ourselves, across the following morning's 'Full English' being questioned by a rather inquisitive, long-time F. C. member as to 'Your connection with Ferrari'? ending with 'Do you have an old model, or is it one of the new ones'? Muffling my mirth, I gravely replied that he would find our latest model - my silver Astra - tucked in between a dashing Aston Martin and an elegant pale-blue Maserati, some half-way along the row of vehicles then facing us from the front window.

Our next move was to organise two or three Charity evenings at the Headquarters which, after a champagne reception in the Regimental Museum for 85 paying guests (the limit covered by insurance) dinner, cooked by me - was served promptly at 7:30.- caterers having been ruled out due to their prohibitive estimates. Using

G's 'hospital dinner' menu' as a guide, a couple of evenings at home took care of preparation and desserts plus a day's release from the office for transporting and setting-up (by this time Jill had been replaced by Professor Maurice Vile, one of the kindest, and most fair and accommodating bosses ever). As I was also hosting, with G., our quartet of experienced waitresses, long familiar with Tower events, helped out by checking the chicken and draining and dressing the potatoes. After dinner, guests were escorted down to Traitors Gate for the Ceremony of the Keys and as swiftly as possible, escorted back to the H.Q. for the raffles and the auctions. Nothing had been left to chance, nor could be as so much had to be fitted in before everyone began leaving the building at 11:30pm. Any remaining stragglers would be there for the night, no exceptions; although visitors often needed convincing, seeing it all as something of a joke.

The following October our big excitement came in the shape of a small person named Florence, to Simon and Charlotte. Another delightful bundle who arrived without fuss and immediately listed for another Pettifar Christening in the Tower Chapel Royal of St. Peter ad Vincula. Georgia, the first of our brood to be baptised there three years previously, was delighted to have a sibling, never once showing the tiniest shred of jealousy, proudly adopting the role of big sister. One weekend, when staying with us after a ballet class and still only three years old, she joyfully accepted our offer of a Christmas trip to 'Nutcracker' and in the event, spoke not a single word until the Interval when, solemnly she turned and said 'That was the very bestest thing I've ever seen in my whole life'...Afterwards, our annual 'Nutcracker' became something of a tradition, to the extent that G. and I reckoned that if seriously pushed, we might just double for the two leads.

Holidays with the Matthews had become more frequent, leaving an assortment of memories - the first being Robin's No 1 rule that 'Any hotel room could be bettered so never start unpacking until something more acceptable has been offered'. Our trips began with Lanzarote, twice; after which came N. Cyprus - in Asil Nadir's then new and luxurious Jasmine Court Hotel; Tenerife was followed by Turkey - where the hotel staff''s two-hour siesta took precedence over our vigorous use of the emergency bell in the lift... Barbados cropped up several times: our '10-day-post-Christmas-life-saver', with exercise limited mainly to page-turning whilst remaining in the horizontal. One

October break in Spain, spent in a friend's scrummy villa half-way up a mountain, near Malaga, cropped up regularly for many years, due to one of the resident cats, which, having demolished every last scrap of the delicious garlicky spit-roasted chicken to which Robin had much been looking forward - was treated to instant flying lessons and a few additions to its vocabulary.

In-between, we'd make time for twice yearly hops to Marbella: always best out of season, being neither too far, too crowded, nor too hot. Occasionally, G. and I took off 'a-deux'; once, for what turned out to be, a bizarre week on Gozo where, after a hectic 'talked-out' few months and in need of a dark, silent room, we were chatted-up on Day 2, in a local shop and somehow ended-up as the cabaret for some well-meaning, but obviously bored, ex-pats. Beginning with lunch in a rather sad hotel, complete with sagging wooden verandah and a derelict air, we heard ourselves agreeing to 'little trips' (necessarily so: the island measuring barely nine miles by five) But, life being full of surprises, a dinner-party invitation stating 'We never take no for an answer' hadn't actually included the word 'cooking'. Arriving on the other side of the island and ushered gently and slowly through the front door to join the other eight guests, it was immediately obvious that our refined, but monumentally-slaughtered hostess - had apparently limited her participation in the evening's event to the shopping... From somewhere came a lone voice. 'Bev. Can you cook'?

Throughout, as ever, lives on the Pettifar roundabout ticked on: a series of non-stop family happenings and dramas both near and far: weddings, divorces, births, house-moves, and the occasional funeral. G. still unpredictable, was slowly improving; S's publishing company, at which he worked diligently and successfully, received several favourable pieces of press and magazine coverage and the three of our four lovely girls, Charlotte -working hard for another publisher - Georgie and Florence, thrived. Dom, our first 'lovely' and now firmly established in Advertising, was very much together with Andrew Nicholson - an ex-colleague of whom we - and obviously she - highly approved (developments were awaited). Mother, diagnosed with mouth cancer and suffering stoically, appeared now and then for the odd few days when we'd hop around town, lunch at her old haunts, visit friends and take in a show or two. Celeste meanwhile, was a fully-fledged Senior Barrister's Clerk who, close for some time to Bruce

Savage - a hard-working Surrey poultry farmer - later married him at Guildford Register Office.

Our 3rd break-in had to be the worst. Having first assembled an arsenal of tools from the garden shed and cracked three powerful locks on the back-door, in they'd moved - our guests - in situ, judging from the amount of devastation, for the entire day. Having pocketed Elvira the cleaner's cash from a kitchen shelf and with my few remaining pieces of jewellery well hidden, there would have been limited interest in our one small, twenty-year-old (and 'remoteless') tv set. So with apparently nothing of value to steal, they found other means of entertainment and methodically, wrecked each of our ten rooms, jumping on photographs, stripping each bed of mattress and linen, scattering contents and clothing from cupboards and drawers, and emptying wardrobes. The ground floor came off worst with a large bowl of Bolognaise sauce from the fridge spread liberally over furniture, floors and walls, teamed with the remainder of the Christmas Rumtoft: a litre or so of purple soft fruits in its alcoholic juice ; brightened up the beige hall and stairs carpets no end. Next came the eggs, two dozen or so leaving G's study almost unrecognisable. Finally, the kitchen fire-extinguisher was called into action and sprayed over every available surface, transforming all into a nightmarish scene of Winter-wonderland. G. had returned home around 6pm and called Simon and Charlotte, who, bless them, when I turned up at 8pm after a hectic 'Arrivals Day' - had already worked wonders on the kitchen. After hugs and soothing words, Simon popped off to our nearest 'Indian', returning with a takeaway and some fizz. God bless the family

Chapter Thirty

G.'S RETIREMENT, FOR SO LONG IGNORED, suddenly became reality when one morning he announced. 'You know I'll be retiring at the end of this year? What would he do? At least his Court sessions would see

Bev with S&D's 25th wedding anniversary balloons - Nov 81

him through to his 70th birthday and maybe he could increase his sittings. Also, as Secretary of the now thriving Headfirst, he'd be able to comfortably fit-in H. F. business through the week, along with his two or three committees at the Tower, and free-up the weekends..And then? Last year he'd made swift recoveries from both Hepatitis and Shingles, thanks to swift action by George Preston, our great G. P. but suddenly, the passing of time had become a reality and needed some thought. My own health, whilst always a problem, could also do with a little mulling over..Seldom one to dwell and kept more or less vertical by the Brompton and physio-friend Susan - plus good behaviour on the diet front - though not always if fresh white bread, salty farmhouse butter and sharp home-made jam were on the menu (hardly Beluga and Bolly) it was becoming obvious that I tired more easily, had a problem retaining weight and sometimes, admitted to feeling truly grim.

In the event, a wonderful black-tie dinner was planned for G's retirement, and took place in the H.Q. Guests included two or three of his ex-Commanding Officers and several close military friends, plus, of course, the immediate family (Dom and I suitably turned-out in simple but bank-breaking creations: mine subsequently known as 'the arm and a leg'). After a delicious meal, excellently catered by Gilly and her team, several moving - as well as hilarious - speeches, were given before finishing with this 'Wife of' (all army wives are 'Wife-of') being 'presented and pinned' with a spoof 'Long Service and Good Conduct Medal', by G. That evening, we left for home with mixed feelings. A fun but rather emotional evening...'End of an era' really.

But for the immediate future, our social wheel continued to spin, occasionally putting us in the path of the famous. One such event, in the Travellers' Club, involved the warm and witty Carol Thatcher when, alone for a second between speeches, I spotted her moving toward me, with a beaming smile. Having complimented me on my dress ('the arm and a leg') she added 'My mother has something similar' after which I thanked her, saying cheekily 'Not once have I imagined myself mentioned in the same breath as The Blessed Margaret' at which she erupted with laughter. A lively companion, I thoroughly enjoyed meeting her and we chatted for a while before being joined by her father, the inestimable Dennis, later followed by G. Soon, as both Thatchers wandered off - their arms around each others' waists -

the wonderful bond between father and daughter was both moving and memorable and when the news of Dennis Thatcher's s death appeared in the press, Carol was the first person I thought of.

With G. now in the role of 'House-husband (never!) I was driven daily to and from the office (by this time he'd been on the road and 'safe' for almost three years). As a working day between terms might be spent in fifty different ways, from shopping for replacement household kit to turning out cupboards, 'dress' was more or less 'scruff-order'.

One such morning, a two-minute call from Dom offered two free Grand Tier tickets for that evenings' performance at Covent Garden - kindly donated by a client. Seldom obtainable and eye-wateringly pricey, her 'I'll get them biked round to you' was gratefully accepted, then 'Sorry - must dash. No info. except that you have to be there by 6:00.' Mmm? 'Wagner maybe? Not exactly G's favourite... Knowing that he'd be suitably dressed - his day featuring a formal lunch at H.Q, followed by meetings - left just me. With a critical eye I examined the day's ensemble - jeans, shirt, cowboy boots and long-cardigan: clean but hardly Grand Tier opera mode. The possibility of a quick shopping trip for dress and shoes faded as I waded through my list of 'priorities', until a glance at the clock saw me with just enough time for a swift 're-paint' and brush-through. G. - never late - arrived on the dot of 5:25pm. .

Such helpful guys, those responsible for parking, just around the corner from the opera house. With our car taken over, complete with keys, we ran back and flew inside, making for 'upstairs' - later than planned thanks to extra traffic. Our first sight on arriving was of Antonia Fraser and Harold Pinter; Jeremy Isaacs, plus entourage, and Cecil Parkinson en famille: all clutching glasses of what had to be fizz, each woman exquisitely turned out in full evening-dress, the men in black-tie. Realising I hadn't so much as glanced at the tickets before handing them over to G., with a sideways look I murmured 'A premiere, methinks. If you prefer to pretend you're not with me, I really don't mind', to which he replied 'I wouldn't worry. Not here. If anyone even notices, you'll be down as some eccentric heiress: probably American'. As the English seldom comment on oddities he was probably right. (and it was a premiere - to which I stupidly lost the programme - but Kiri T. was singing and the entire evening was just unforgettable).

London was still a good place to live; as well as exceptionally convenient and as natives, we enjoyed the local mix. At one time, between the street and the square, we had one rap-singer, one drug-dealer, one 85yr old sharp-eyed ex-policeman (whose determined efforts to find his stolen and much-beloved Morris Minor finally tracked it - still intact - to a nearby garage); several writers and journalists; a chatty, interesting chap who, for some years, schooled his ponies in the square gardens; plumbers, builders, dancers and musicians, one artist, the odd city trader, one Polish Count (!), one actress, one film director, a few folk 'In tv', three vicars, one 'Spook', two town planners, a member of the Murdoch empire, two caterers, one chest consultant and two doctors, a few members of the Bar, our Physio.friend Susan - three or four 'unknowns' - and two retired army-officers, of which G. was one.

And there were also the wanderers, some of whom appeared at the front door, fairly regularly, needing cash. One in particular I've thought of often, being neither regular nor begging for money, who drifted along early one warm Summer's evening as I deposited rubbish in one of the alleyway bins. A tall, rangy, bewildered-looking Irish woman, middle-aged and shoeless ('Oi last 'em') she was also obviously menstruating, but unprotected. Having deciphered her accent, it seemed she'd left a convent at around nine that morning with a friend, who later had 'Gone off wit' a man'. Colleen - not her real name - was now lost, having walked all day, making for a road I recognised, by chance, as being miles away, in North London. But first - if she agreed - a bath, or at least a wash (she chose the latter) plus some food and a change of clothes. After sandwiches and some strong coffee, I left her in the bathroom with a motley - due to her height and breadth - selection of clothing. From G. came a shirt, a pair of boxers and a pair of perfectly fitting casual shoes and as a good head shorter than Colleen and some four or five dress sizes smaller, my sole contribution to the ensemble was a long, Greek cotton skirt with an elasticated waist, an unworn holiday buy. With the shirt tied over the top of her skirt and her hair pinned up, she emerged a new woman. and whilst G. checked through the A-Z, we heard her story. Deserted by her husband and later, by her three children, she'd drifted; finally finding work and accommodation in a convent somewhere in the Irish

223

countryside: a familiar story but deeply sad nevertheless. At about 9pm, we got her back to Camden, to the relief of the nuns whose first question had been 'Is she sober? A regular visitor, she was well-known to them, staying in the convent for two weeks every year. After a while, we left her, animatedly holding court in a sitting-room. Since then, her name has cropped up often; always with a question mark.

After a hectic Autumn term, and increased student numbers leading to one of the busiest years ever, I began to consider leaving B.U. Half-way through my sixth year - feeling tired, jaded and decidedly below-par, the warning lights were on; also, after two or three bouts of sick-leave in the preceding twelve months, I needed to take stock. Hopes of a two-week magic resurrection in Marbella had instead ended in Foulis ward, for intravenous antibiotics and a few doses of Brompton TLC. It occurred to me then that my condition had been exacerbated by the term's high percentage of women students whose perfumes, hair-spray and deodorants, were increasingly affecting my chest.

It would be sad to wave farewell to Boston, but no longer feeling totally together, the decision was finally made. Prof Vile - dear Maurice (by then married to the lovely Nancy) had kindly suggested my taking a three month break, but to return after such an absence might result in an entirely different set of problems. It hadn't been easy, deciding to give up. Apart from the students, I'd miss several colleagues and a few of the visiting tutors and lecturers, although one or two, such as Rona - Psychology tutor and ego-booster 'Those students are just so lucky to have you, Bev' - we still see. Terry, who took the Politics class was always lively and amusing and as an ex-army wife, I'd enjoyed an office coffee or three with Merlyn Rees M.P., an ex-Minister for N. Ireland, under Labour. On a daily basis, there were Karim and Jonathan, jointly responsible for general maintenance and generally part of just about everything, bar the teaching - constantly in and out, needing maybe a signature, or cash for petrol, parts and repairs - their roles similar but different. Jon.(last heard of in Delhi) was the plumber, also a successful part-time model and actor whose great singing voice landed him roles in a few W.End musicals. Long-time friends, the two men often worked together, their combined skills keeping afloat not only the building in which we all worked but also the students' flats. Karim's ability to 'maintain the irreparable' kept our minds boggled and on the vehicle maintenance and purchase front, he had no equal.

Upstairs, on the first floor, dwelt The Internship Team': Tony, Andrew, Julie and Laura, who dealt with the student internships. Occasionally faced with the tricky business of fitting the odd square peg or two into the oddest of round holes, they coped admirably.

My replacement, whom I'd helped choose, was a tanned, thirty-year-old, bubbling and bouncing six-feet tall New Zealander, Sally, who appeared on the dot of nine, for an initial ten days 'Breaking-in and Training'. Single, bursting with energy and enthusiasm for the job, we were ecstatic at having discovered such a made-to-measure treasure and thought the students would find her not only fun, but also capable and helpful. Unfortunately, having assured us all that she'd be 'Just fine, thanks,' three days after 'Arrivals' she'd promptly disappeared; never to be seen, or, bar a brief note, heard of again.

Having rallied to poor Maurice's clarion of 'Bev, Sally's gone', replying to my 'Where?' with 'Who knows but she's not coming back ...'It's Orientation Day; would you consider coming in?' I whizzed back to Kensington and slipped back into the familiar: as it happened, for the next few weeks. After a fortnight of sifting, we'd settled on Pat as my replacement. Middle-aged, drama-trained and used to working in the hothouse world of theatre, she was also level-headed, humorous, unflappable and full of enthusiasm: and at least, having been helped through those first vital weeks, the trickiest part of the term - she'd have time to breathe. Content to be left and aware that those most in need of sensitive help were often either anorexic or homosexual, she'd made copious notes and taken our phone number. I left thinking 'And at least she knows her way around a 'Mac'. In the following months, we lunched together a few times and she seemed to have settled in, but then bailed-out shortly before the end of her first year: 'Not for me. Bev: I don't know how you got through it...But I hear we've been replaced by three men.' (I'd heard it too, from Rona). Ah well. By then, Maurice had also left, exchanging B.U. for a prestigious post closer to his home, near Canterbury.

Cherries Jubilee (quick and easy - serves 6)

2 Jars or tins of Morello Cherries in Juice. Open and drain, reserving 350mls. juice, plus a little to mix with level 2 dess-sp. arrowroot powder. Taste unmixed juice and add sugar to taste. Place in pan with 4 tabsp. brandy, or cherry brandy if you prefer and heat slowly. Add arrowroot mixture and stir until thickened and 'cooked'.

Serve hot with a good vanilla ice cream.

Brownies (about 20 pieces).

4 eggs - 200grm caster sugar - 150grms, sieved flour - 50grms chopped walnuts, plus - 150grms. Unsweetened good dark chocolate, 225grms. butter - place together in bowl over pan of gently simmering water with a t.sp.vanilla essence, not flavouring, stirring v. occasionally. Remove from pan when melted and leave to cool. Beat 2 of the eggs with 125 caster sugar until thick and fluffy then add 2 other eggs and remaining sugar and beat again until thick. Fold in flour and then nuts. Turn into buttered and floured, or lined, 9x13 bake in tin at 180c for 30-35mins. Cut into squares.

Chapter 31

G., DESPITE BEING RETIRED, spent little more time at home than when he worked, being constantly whistling back and fore to the H.Q. for meetings and lunches, or off to 'sit' in either Hampstead or Clerkenwell. How he'd miss the Magistracy when the dreaded 70th came. He was also Secretary of Headfirst, and luckily, interest was increasing. Meanwhile, he enjoyed it all and from his years at the Tower, had much to look back on. Moving one of our scrapbooks recently, a photo of him with Norma Major slipped out. Taken at a lunch in Downing St, it reminded us how many fascinating opportunities the twelve years of his job had presented him with: meetings with Her Majesty the Queen and other Royal personages along with several influential names throughout the city. Even at this stage, half-forgotten events still spring to mind, particularly when reading the reports and features regarding Margaret Thatcher's last days as Prime Minister, published since her recent death, one vividly recalls the strong current of envy and misogyny emanating from her Cabinet when, just days later, as guests at a small dinner-party attended by a Tory M P. his dismissive reply to the question 'Why was Maggie so cruelly and swiftly dispatched' had simply been 'Because she was bloody mad.' Shaming then and shaming now.

Despite us both now part of the great unemployed, the weeks galloped along. There were desserts to produce for various OAP lunches at St Stephens (now our church, although sadly, we'd never caught up with Helen, G's 'Angel' who had returned to New Zealand before he'd left hospital); meetings with friends for exhibitions and lunches, gardening, a painting class and for a while, a bible-study class held in the house of a friend: plus visits to Mother and Celeste in Sussex... then somehow, I found myself with requests for cakes - weddings, birthdays and Christenings, followed by orders for Christmas. In the winter months I scribbled - mainly short stories, still languishing somewhere in a drawer, spent time with the girls, cooked and entertained, and in-between, visited the Brompton.

1996 - and Dom and Drew turned up one weekend glowing with

news of a wedding: theirs. Fizz and flags, complete with hugs and salutations all round left us beaming with delight. They'd been together a while, were obviously happy and made a good team. Never ones to hang about they'd already - with their friends based mostly in and around London - settled on a venue for six weeks hence: a beautiful period country house, just over the Sussex border. That evening, the wedding wheels were already in motion as the largest cake-tin of the trio, its rich pungent mixture needing twelve to fourteen hours cooking, was slid into the oven, and earlier, Liz had been roped in on 'flower-duty', reminding me not to forget a protective mask. Shortly afterwards, we met up with Drew's family: easy, chatty normal people, full of humour, and got on well together. Next came the exciting dress and shoe hunt. White?cream? shell-pink?oyster? ribbed-silk or plain? decollete or coat-dress? long? three-quarter?..Dom. - having settled on opposite styles - finally plumped for the classic: a soft-white silk-taffeta coat-dress, closely-fitted, full length, simple and elegant in which she looked very beautiful and as mother-of-the-bride, I grizzled delicately (I hope...) The deep and even cake - its three tiers containing well over a litre of brandy and crowned with a small vase of snowdrops, stayed put (one wedding, attended on a sultry July day, had seen the top two tiers of an exquisitely-decorated tower sink gently together as the icing melted -along with the guests - in the suffocating marquee). There were no obvious drunks, no strippers and no hassle: all went as planned: free from angst and without a hitch. Oh happy day.

True to form, with not a second wasted, the next big event came towards the end of the Summer, in the shape of Bayley, a delicious bundle, just over seven pounds in weight with red-hair (now more a shade of mahogany: and almost 17 years later about to sit 'A' levels). Such excitement, the blessed gift of another grandchild. From the first mention of Dom's pregnancy, I'd envisaged she and Drew with three boys, forecasting (to G.) 'Bet it's another' when, two years on, our great Milo-in-the-middle was about to emerge (another 'initial' redhead - now dark-brown, like Dom). Pettifar Christenings at the Tower seemed to be coming round fairly regularly... 'Wonder if there'll be a No3' I speculated and sure enough. with Milo not yet two and a half, up popped Finn; now thirteen and more blonde than red.

That was also the year of our 40th Anniversary: scarcely believable.

Forty years.. G. only ever complained about his gout and his knees and I scarcely even felt forty. Preferring to keep things fairly quiet, we celebrated at home with the family, after which Simon and |Dom gave kind and loving speeches, closing with the totally unexpected and generous gift of an all-expenses-paid, four day trip to either New York or Boston'. We chose the latter as despite my years with B.U. neither of us had actually ever been there.

At the beginning of December, having flown in smoothly and comfortably with Virgin, we'd landed at Logan airport in the brilliant morning sunshine, all white and sparkly from a hefty fall of 'crisp and even'. That week, the city was apparently 'in Conference mode' and as such, hotels had been booked way ahead.'But I've found you what looks like a v. upmarket B/B in a gorgeous old house on the oldest and most attractive side of the city,' Dom had explained apologetically. No need whatsoever for the smallest misgivings: our accommodation might have come straight from the front of a Victorian Christmas card, set as it was overlooking the smooth, white Common. It was also warm, stuffed with antiques, cosy and at the same time, elegant - rather like our host: a single, middle-aged gent. v. much the Anglophile, who, on learning of G's associations with the Tower, quizzed us almost non-stop saying with increasing awe 'You mean you actually lived there. You really lived there'... (We wondered if he might suggest selling tickets to enable friends or passers-xby to watch us at breakfast - a notice explaining 'My guests, who once lived in the Tower of London').

Having set ourselves a programme, for the next three days we became total tourists. An easy city to explore, being small and walker-friendly, we first concentrated on the Christmas shopping, making for Quincy Market and various recommended 'bargain-basements', where the minimally-priced selection of designer goods left us open-mouthed. After lunch it was time for George St: a delightful upmarket area, close to where we were staying, full of small, individually-owned antique shops and boutiques which might have come straight from part of old Knightsbridge (somewhat short on bargains but an abundance of very splendid and varied goodies). The next day we took a train to the universities area to visit two well-stocked galleries before walking the tourist trail - a long, meandering, thick and clearly-marked red-line, taking in Boston's many historical happenings on the way. Finally at the end, we took a cab to the harbour area - cholesterol-corner - and greedily stuffed ourselves with plates of delicious fresh lobster, all swimming in hot butter. As the Americans would say 'Mm - Mmm...'

Waved off with many salaams and several 'Do come and see me agains' by our elegant host (he'd so love a night in the Tower flat) we were then sent off to the airport in a courtesy car. We'd had a great time, a great stay, enjoyed our shopping and had relished both the atmosphere and the easy accessibility of the city. But at home, Christmas waited. Luckily, with the freezer already full of the usual mass of prepared food, there was just the decorating and the wrapping remaining on 'the big-list'. But first, we needed to thank the children for their generosity which we felt, for both of them, had come at just about the toughest time of the year financially: but we so appreciated their great unselfishness and sacrifice.

1997, and after much head-scratching at the swift passing of time, we decided to celebrate G's 70th with a large 'Curry and fizz lunch' - at home, with somewhere around 70 guests. Not an inch of floor - or indeed - stair space, remained unoccupied but everyone seemed happy. G. - with no problems about hitting seventy - was more put-out at having to give up his Magistracy, remarking soulfully 'I suppose I'll just have to stick to signing peoples' passports now'. Alas, yes. We all felt for him but there was no way round it.

With both the street and the square changing fast, we found the familiar faces of yesterday replaced by others which soon became equally familiar. We still had friends in the area but slowly and subtly the atmosphere had altered and since 1981, house prices were soaring. Both sets of our original neighbours were long gone and for some years, on and off, skips had become almost an extension of the local landscape as internal walls were removed altogether or re-figured to suit the requirements of a new owner. The once-annual 'Square Fete' had petered out some years earlier and after three burglaries, we began to toy with the idea of moving. But where? As Londoners, it had to be either miles from, or still within striking distance of the city... Brighton? Fun, and fast becoming a firm favourite of the 'meeja' as Julie Burchill, Nick Cave and Zoe Ball began settling in, but as regular day-trippers we were finding it increasingly overcrowded and finally decided that once was enough. However, on the odd Saturday morning, we'd taken to whizzing down to Whitstable, in Kent, finding the still unspoiled small town charming and raffish enough to be interesting: also unhurried; unusual for an area so close to the metropolis.

For over two years we kept a firm eye on the Whitstable property market, having at least decided that our buying there would be dependent on finding a 'sea-view' - preferably old and within walking distance of the town. I'd predicted - correctly as it happens - years before we'd ever considered a move, that once the potential of such an attractive, unspoilt seaside spot was realised, the rush would be on and prices would fly. We viewed several 'possibles' but the only real des. res. was seriously overpriced and in need of a spell of both extensive and expensive structural surgery. Or we could re-figure our own house? As things were, a growing family ideally featured a larger kitchen. Our dining and utility rooms, plus kitchen, and a side extension would make a spacious open-plan kit-diner - but who needed months of builders? The permutations were endless but having finally decided to stay in London, we became 'professional viewers', our net constantly widening to cover Clapham, Wimbledon, Brixton (very vibrant, Brixton), Greenwich, Dulwich, parts of Chelsea, Docklands and Bermondsey - all day and every day, for months - ending up with enough material for a tv series. You name it, we'd seen it. New houses; old-houses; 'wings' of palatial mini-stately homes; on-plan and off-plan renovations and developments; pub, hospital, school and warehouse conversions where doors had been removed to create an illusion of space and the lights kept permanently 'on'; that left just the new-build terraced homes (kitchen on one floor, dining-room on another..Give that architect an award) and flats - asking price, plus £15,000 for an 'open' parking space: two white lines of our very own...

A new century... Wondering where we'd be at the same time the following year, our Millenium Night was celebrated with old friends, Regina and Peter, at a jolly party in Malvern (they were also considering a move but being highly organised, had already decided on Ledbury, just a few five miles away). After a delicious meal, it was fireworks and fizz in the garden with its splendid view of the seven hills, each silhouetted against the dazzling backdrop of the exploding night sky. Alone for a moment, I took a quick trip through the past, finally wishing for health, happiness, unity and safe passages for the family in 2001:and of course, world peace. What else is there?

Shortly afterwards, relaying our viewing sagas to Dom, she asked 'Why not have a look at Surrey'? It had honestly never occurred to either of us.

But first we needed to investigate a couple of ads - not exactly on the agenda but - ever the optimists - too good to miss. The following Saturday morning we headed for the Kent coast, in search of the 'Gem of a period home, in fun-filled, sunny Margate. Tenderly and sympathetically renovated..NOT to be missed' And what a gem. These builders really knew their stuff, producing a finish and attention to detail rarely seen. But alas. In a dreary cafe, over cups of unidentifiable liquid (G. swore he'd ordered coffee) we discussed the realities of this affordable dwelling, set in a once-gracious terrace that still bore traces of its stately beginnings - but after a lengthy drive around the locale, decided that the odds of our out- living any much-needed improvements planned for the tired and scruffy-looking streets, were more than slim. (Reading lately that Margate has recently become part of a booming re-development scheme, we wish it buckets of success).

Back on the same road, we bounced along expectantly toward the next 'maybe' and being a 'Wonderfully converted Martello Tower' was probably a waste of time (keen on the quirky, over the years we'd viewed a windmill, a water-mill, part of a Waterworks, a flat in an ex. Match factory and a Dutch barge: also a Water-tower in Suffolk).The Martello Tower turned out to be the most extraordinary of all; but, in its way, riveting. Wondering if the conversion had bankrupted the converters, we climbed up - and up, and yet up - round and round, from base to apex, stopping to view bed, sitting and bathrooms, finally reaching the spectacular state-of-the-art-kitchen-in-the-sky which we reckoned, may easily have covered the purchase of a fleet of Routemaster buses. Interesting, fascinating and amazing - but definitely not for us. And I never did get around to discovering how the shopping reached the kitchen.

By this time, No.2 had been on and off the market four times - due to our inability to find 'something suitable'... And were we difficult? Not really.... 3/4 Beds. Large sitting-room and decent-sized kitchen; study; 2/3 baths. cloakroom, dining-room and a small garden: all within walking distance of a shop, please. With a surveyor who came 'highly recommended' we spent thousands on 3 or 4 of them - but having finally made our choice, the house was on the 'net' 'pronto' and within days, had sold at the asking price. .

With various changes on the family front affecting where we might live, 'distance from the Brompton' hadn't been considered, so used were we to having it just 'over the bridge.' For some time, problems had been manageable, so I coasted along, popped the pills, did my exercises, steered clear of florists and large bouquets and generally - bar a certain amount of lurching between the odd bad days (another test for CF revealing nothing new) generally remained vertical. But, back to the search, this time in Surrey. Leaving London and our friends there would be a wrench, but Surrey was hardly Dorset and increasingly, G. fancied life 'out of the city'. Mother - now 84 - and my sister and husband, would be closer, in W. Sussex, we had friends in Surrey and Hampshire and while G and I loved the idea of living not too far from Dom and 'the crew' we made a rule that should we end up just a short drive away (actually just under 5mins.) visits will be 'by invitation only'. Vital for maintaining good relations.

There would probably be a few things we'd miss, apart from the city 'buzz': the inimitable London humour certainly; Holland Park opera in the Summer (where the peacocks sing along with the sopranos) and the Tower Midnight Service on Christmas Eve. Also, I hugged memories of great birthday evenings with George, Simon and Dom, who had generously provided fun meals, wonderful ballet and opera evenings at Covent Garden, plus dinner at the Garrick, Burt Bacharach at the Festival Hall and Jose Feliciano at Camden's Jazz cafe.

Moving time and the big de-clutter: over twenty-years worth... G. who for a while had been managing a nearby 'Mind' charity shop, became stock-booster-in-chief as suddenly, having discovered an ability to discard things which might be classed as neither useful nor beautiful, I became more and more ruthless. 'Apparently, profits have never been so good' said G, returning from yet another trip 'All from our old kit'.'

Once de-cluttered, there had been the anxietyof a highly intensive 'special engineering survey' (at the behest of the 'Expert in pre.1900 architecture' a relative who, we understood, would be helping out with the purchase price). Lasting from 8-30am to 5-30pm, we were finally pronounced 'sound in every way' and told by the surveyor) 'If they drop out, I'll buy this. I already own three houses in this area.'(obviously a lucrative business, surveying).

After what had become the usual crop of non-starters, with agents details bearing little relation to reality, we finally did all the things we'd said we never would...Bought a new-build, kept our two cars and moved to a quieter spot than planned. And eleven years later, we're still here; in a small development of four houses and these days, down to one car. We've found a friendly church and the view from our small 'pot garden' overlooks a large, lush National Trust field, home to a series of friendly ponies and, while only just 30 or so miles from London, this part of the Surrey countryside has remained remarkably rural; much farmed and complete with poultry, flocks of sheep and herds of Jerseys and Banded Galloways (re-named by me as 'Bandaged Galloways, the entire middle sections of their otherwise black bodies giving the impression of having been neatly 'dressed').

All in all, our choice was good (even better when a buyer can be found for our local village shop). No.3, is warm, comfortable and easy to run and with part of our family within easy reach, we've seen so much more of our grandchildren than anticipated, enjoying the privilege of watching them develop, catching up with their news as it happens and so far, always lucky enough to join up for Christmas and birthdays (with my 'big 70', celebrated with a delicious family and friends lunch and a trip to Verona - courtesy of Dom and Drew, for a wonderful three-day opera trip in the famous arena) the fact that I'd got there at all being down to the generosity of Dr. Diana Bilton, who, having replaced Prof. Geddes, at the Brompton, was kind enough to see me at v. short notice indeed.

So here we are: joined, just over three years ago, by good friends, late of Westminster and now happily installed in a nearby village. With others just further afield, simple parking, the amazing Yvonne Arnaud Theatre, cleaner air and so far - no burglars, we're just fine.

Fish Pie (serves 8 - if you're lucky..)

300grm. undyed smoked haddock + 800grms white fish, cod or haddock,+ 8 fresh scallops (with or without coral, your choice) + 225grms best shelled prawns (Maine or North Atlantic)+ 4 hard-boiled and finely chopped eggs + 150grm sliced, sauteed mushrooms+ 1 tabsp. Anchovy sauce+ mashed potatoes for 8 (about 8/9 med-sized)

1 med. onion finely chopped and sauteed in butter - do not brown.
2Tabsp. White wine.

300mls full-cream milk, 125grm butter, 2 level tabsp. plain flour,
75mls. double cream. Salt & pepper. Grated parmesan to finish off.

Extra milk & butter to mash potatoes.

Poach all fish, except prawns and scallops gently in milk. Cool and
flake into adequate heatproof dish. Cut each scallop into 4. Add wine
to cooking liquid and poach scallops gently ¾ mins. Remove and add
to fish. Strew with mushrooms and prawns.

Make sauce with butter, flour, onion and poaching liquid. Stir in
cream and anchovy sauce and season with pepper. Cover with mashed
potatoes when cool and finish with a grating of Parmesan.

Place in hot oven -180c fan -for 35/40mins.

Chapter 32

THIS, I PROMISE, IS THE LAST MEDICAL BULLETIN but, just over two years ago, after another spell in the Brompton and a few more tests, I was finally told. 'You are definitely suffering from Cystic Fibrosis and have been all your life'. Well... Being somewhere near the bottom of the scale, I count myself extremely fortunate. The diagnosis, a revelation to someone then aged 71 (the oldest ever, it appears, to be recognised as C.F.) had been elusive to pin down; one of my rogue gene formations only ever having cropped up once before, in a clinic in Tel Aviv'. 'So what's the Jewish connection? 'asked my skilled consultant: also kind, blonde, handsome and apparently some years older than he looks (about 19.) What indeed? So far, nothing, to our knowledge. But maybe we're all mongrels.

So, with luck and TLC on my side, we press on, thanking the powers that be for every day. The real sufferers, many of whom are young and thrusting, struggle daily to gain or retain normality in their lives whilst coping with the misery of an unpleasant, uncomfortable,often painful and thoroughly nasty condition; these are the brave ones: by comparison I simply do not exist. 'Tell it how it is' said someone who has become a dear friend and kind enough to use her previous experience to act as my 'reader', adding 'It's important you let people know how you feel about your illness and with any profits (please) going to charity, people with your problem will be reading this, many of them younger and often in a far worse state physically: you mustn't make light of it or attempt to gloss things over'. Maybe, but the truth is, we play the cards we're dealt in the best way we can. With scarcely a blush I curse, often and loudly, complete with a highly inventive vocabulary - mainly in frustration at my lack of breath on the stairs or when tripping over the oxygen lead. But never in the Brompton, where they all do their best. Each chest hospital in the country will doubtless have its quota of CF patients, but due to its fame, the Brompton treats people from every corner of the globe. Now in severe need of a total re-vamp, the hospital really needs your money - and that of anyone you know who happens to be searching for a cause on which to unload their unwanted cash AND/OR their organs. Please consider carrying a donor card. Can you think of anything worse than not being able to breathe? Without breath there is no life.

Eleven years have passed since the big move - years which have seen many changes within the family, as well as on the fringes. Mother sadly died just a few months after we moved here, weeks short of her 86th birthday. A lapsed Roman Catholic, she had expressed a desire 'Not to be planted in a formal cemetery' so we agreed the perfect spot would be on Celeste and Bruce's land, close to a stream where she often walked. Father Agius, a local priest, happily agreed to wear wellies and 'Say a few words at the graveside, followed by a short Service in the dairy'. With no access to the field bar foot, helicopter, or quad-bike, we chose the latter and Mother's small 'green' coffin, topped with a glowing spread of Spring flowers, was put on a trailer behind a quad-bike and transported down to the field - followed by many mourners, all sporting wellies. How she would so have loved the incongruity of it all. Five years and a day after Mother, my sister's beloved husband Bruce, also died. His Service, beautiful, moving and amusing, was held in an ancient 'full-to-bursting' local church: and we all wore shoes.

Our smashing 'grandgirls', Georgia, now aged 25, works and lives in Berlin, with Fried, her partner and Justus, their gorgeous son, blonde and almost two; while Florence, three years younger, sits in trepidation, in Nottingham, approaching her veterinary finals, due in a couple of months. Simon, our son, now unbelievably, a grandfather, works and lives in the lovely town of Hay-on-Wye, on the Welsh border. Dom and Drew's business, winner of many awards, continues (fingers and toes crossed) to thrive, and their boys Bayley, almost 17; Milo, almost 15 and Finn; just 13 are great fun; full of laughs and chat, as yet untroubled by the strain of having to make any firm decisions regarding their future. How blessed we are, although, as might be imagined, many friends who have popped up in these pages are sadly with us no longer.

This modest effort, but more particularly the machine on which it was created, has indeed led a charmed life, coming in for regular, lengthy and loud attacks of abuse, followed by threats of being hurled through the nearest window (not a chance; no strength). But - bailed out at intervals by kind friends and neighbours, especially the lovely Barry, plus 'The Professionals' Jade, Tom and Allan (who, am convinced, think I need locking up) it is now coming to an end. We so hope that some much-needed 'charitable' cash will result: not only for 'Headfirst' but also for the Brompton. It's a big hope, but one must be optimistic. And how dare I curse my machine: Shakespeare and Pepys did it all with a quill.

And the title; if you've got this far, you may well be wondering. Asked by a friend, first of all for 'Title?' immediately followed by 'Why' ? I explained that, having originally hit the production line in 2004 as 'Just an idea,' things moved along after chatting on the phone one day with young Finn, then aged just three. His reply to my 'So what have you been doing this morning' was 'I've been singing to the goldfish, Bee,' (my title) produced such a sweet, innocent vision, that within a few weeks, I began to scribble, just occasionally, at odd times, but more diligently once the CF diagnosis was confirmed. Reading through various chapters, musing as to whether or not, if presented with a choice, I'd do it all again, the conclusion reached was 'Probably; but next time, I'd ensure that through our frantic lifelong games of 'Beat the Clock', there would be more time set aside left for doing just that. 'Singing to the goldfish' what a lovely, gentle way of passing time.

Thank you for listening.

PS. I make no apologies for the butter and cream content used in some of the recipes: we all deserve the occasional treat.